Divided Nations

The Wilder House Series
in Politics, History,
and Culture

The Wilder House Series is published in association with the
Wilder House Board of Editors and the University of Chicago.

A complete list of titles appears at the end of this book.

DIVIDED NATIONS

*Class, Politics, and Nationalism
in the Basque Country
and Catalonia*

JUAN DÍEZ MEDRANO

Cornell University Press

Ithaca and London

This book is published with the aid of grants from the Program for
Cultural Cooperation between Spain's Ministry of Culture and United States
Universities and from the University of California, San Diego.

First published 1995 by Cornell University Press.

Printed in the United States of America

♾ The paper in this book meets the minimum requirements
of the American National Standard for Information Sciences—
Permanence of Paper for Printed Library Materials, ANSI Z39.48-1984.

Library of Congress Cataloging-in-Publication Data

Díez Medrano, Juan.
    Divided nations : class, politics, and nationalism in the Basque Country and
Catalonia / Juan Díez Medrano.
        p.   cm.—(Wilder House series in politics, history, and culture)
    Includes bibliographical references and index.
    ISBN 0–8014–3092–5
        1. Nationalism—Spain—País Vasco.   2. Nationalism—Spain—Catalonia.
3. País Vasco (Spain)—Politics and government.   4. Catalonia (Spain)—Politics and
government.   I. Title.   II. Series.
DP302.B53D54   1995
320.5'4'09466—dc20   94–47526

To Berit

Contents

viii   Contents

Tables

Preface

More than at any time in recent decades, our world is torn by nationalist and ethnic struggles. National groups within multinational states are seeking independence, states are trying to annex territories inhabited by minority peoples belonging to those states' dominant ethnic groups, and xenophobia is seemingly on the rise everywhere. As states begin to find themselves too small to compete in a global economy, their increasing cultural diversity, ironically, leads many of their citizens to think of them as too big.

Social scientists have been quick to react. Academic journals are filled with articles on identity, ethnic and linguistic conflict, and nationalism, and rare is the department that does not have its share of graduate students writing their dissertations on these topics. Yet when I began my research on Basque and Catalan nationalism in 1987 I did not for a moment imagine that nationalism would become such a major issue. Although the topic of nationalism had received some public attention in the late 1970s, coincident with the revival of peripheral nationalist movements in developed countries, interest had faded during the 1980s.

In the years that I have spent pursuing this project, the world has changed radically, and nationalist conflicts are now front-page news on a daily basis. Meanwhile, the theoretical contributions of the past four or five years have significantly advanced our understanding of the phenomenon of nationalism. It seems to me now, however, as it did then, that the academic community has tended to confound and conflate interrelated but analytically different dimensions of the phenomenon. These dimensions—for example, the emergence of the ideology of nationalism, the formation and degree of solidarity of national communities, the political mobilization of nationalist groups, the political objectives of nationalist movements, the success of

nationalist movements in achieving those objectives, and nationalist violence—are all distinct issues requiring separate explanations.

In this book, I address the *character* of nationalist movements. To understand why some nationalist conflicts become violent and why some nationalist movements are simply separatist or even autonomist, we need to move
beyond a general account of how national communities are formed, and
beyond explanations for the emergence of nationalism as a political phenomenon. After all, although most states are plurinational, and although in-
group favoritism is widespread and often blatant, the number of violent
nationalist conflicts that do erupt is relatively small and concentrated in relatively brief historical periods. And although there are many peripheral
nationalist movements around the world today, few of them seek independent statehood.

One way we can isolate the factors that lead to the eruption of nationalist
violence or the emergence of strong separatist movements is to compare
nationalist movements that are widely supported by the populations in question but that differ in the amount of violence they provoke and in the extent
to which they pursue the goal of independence. Alternatively, we might try
to analyze the trajectory of nationalist movements whose political goals have
varied over time and whose peaceful periods have alternated with periods of
violence. My historical comparison of the Basque and Catalan nationalist
movements follows both these approaches. Moreover, although my work
analyzes the role of socioeconomic structural factors, it diverges from previous treatments in emphasizing the role of political structures and processes
in these movements.

Completing this book has not been particularly easy, nor has it always
been pleasant. One lesson I have learned is that research cannot be a strictly
individual effort. Indeed, although I am ultimately responsible for the contents of this book, I would not have been able to complete it without the
help of countless others, all of them both patient and generous. Intellectu-
ally, I owe a great debt to my mentors, Jeffery Paige and William Sewell, Jr.,
and to Michael Hechter. But the list of those who have helped me through
this arduous pilgrimage is much longer. I am particularly grateful to Tim
McDaniel, Ákos Róna-Tas, Andy Scull, Gershon Shafir, Benjamín Tejerina,
Carlos Waisman, and León Zamosc for their moral and intellectual support.
I am also very grateful to those who have reviewed the manuscript, in particular Robert Fishman and David Laitin, and to Roger Haydon for having
faith in the book's potential.

Several institutions have also given me valuable assistance. I thank the U.S.-
Spanish Committee for Educational and Cultural Cooperation, the Rackham
School for Graduate Studies of the University of Michigan, the Centro de

Investigaciones Sociológicas, the Academic Senate of the University of California at San Diego, and the Fundación Juan March. Santiago de la Hoz, María Teresa Delgado, Sarolta Petro, and Adela Ros have helped me with the collection and codification of some of the information used in the book. Others have helped me make this book readable; Berit Dencker more than anybody, but also Doug Hartmann, Margaret Ovenden, Susan Turkel, and the editors at Cornell University Press.

Finally, I thank my parents and my wife for being with me from beginning to end, helping me to overcome all the obstacles I encountered along the way.

JUAN DÍEZ MEDRANO

La Jolla, California

Abbreviations

ADEC	Associació Democrática d'Estudiants de Catalunya; Democratic Association of Catalan Students
ANFD	Alliança Nacional dels Forces Democràtiques; National Alliance of Democratic Forces (Catalonia)
ANV	Acción Nacionalista Vasca; Basque Nationalist Action
AP	Alianza Popular; People's Alliance (Spain)
BRA	Bloc Republicà Autonomista; Autonomist Republican Bloc (Catalonia)
CADCI	Centre Autonomista de Dependents del Comerç i de l'Industria; Autonomist Center of the Commercial and Industrial Employees (Catalonia)
CC	Crist Catalunya?; no agreed-upon meaning
CCOO	Comisiones Obreras; Workers' Commissions (Spain)
CD	Coalición Democrática; Democratic Coalition (Spain)
CDC	Convergencia Democràtica de Catalunya; Democratic Convergence of Catalonia
CDS	Centro Democrático y Social; Democratic and Social Center (Spain)
CEDA	Confederación Española de Derechas Autónomas; Spanish Confederation of Autonomous Rightist Organizations
CiU	Convergencia i Unió; Convergence and Union
CNDC	Consell Nacional de la Democracia Catalana; National Council of Democratic Catalonia
CNT	Confederación Nacional de Trabajadores; National Confederation of Workers (Spain)
CNT-FAI	CNT-Federación Anarquista Ibérica; CNT-Iberian Anarchist Federation (Spain)

CP	Coalición Popular; People's Coalition (Spain)
CUDE	Confederación Universitaria Democrática Española; Democratic University Confederation of Spain
EA	Eusko Alkartasuna; Basque Union
EDC	Esquerra Democràtica de Catalunya; Democratic Left of Catalonia
EE	Euzkadiko Ezquerra; Basque Left
EGI	Euzko Gaztedi; Basque Youth
ERC	Esquerra Republicana de Catalunya; Republican Left of Catalonia
ETA	Euskadi Ta Azkatasuna; Basque Homeland and Freedom
ETA-Berri	New ETA
FAC	Front d' Alliberament Català; Catalan Liberation Front
FNC	Front Nacional de Catalunya; Catalan National Front
FNEC	Front Nacional d'Estudiants de Catalunya; National Front of Catalan Students
FOC	Front Obrer de Catalunya; Workers' Front of Catalonia
FUC	Front Universitari de Catalunya; Catalan University Front
HB	Herri Batasuna; Popular Unity
IU	Izquierda Unida; United Left (Spain)
KAS	Koordinadora Abertzale Socialista; Patriotic Socialist Coordinating Council (Basque Country)
MSC	Moviment Socialista de Catalunya; Catalan Socialist Movement
PCC	Partit Comunista Català; Catalan Communist Party
PCE	Partido Comunista Español; Spanish Communist Party
PCP	Partit Català Proletari; Catalan Proletarian Party
PNV (BNP)	Partido Nacionalista Vasco; Basque Nationalist Party
POUM	Partido Obrero de Unificación Marxista; Workers' Party for Marxist Unification (Spain)
PP	Partido Popular; People's Party (Spain)
PSAN	Partit Socialista d'Alliberament Nacional; National Liberation Socialist Party (Catalonia)
PSC	Partit Socialista de Catalunya; Catalan Socialist Party
PSOE	Partido Socialista Obrero Español; Spanish Socialist and Workers' Party
PSUC	Partit Socialista Unificat de Catalunya; Unified Socialist Party of Catalonia
SEU	Sindicato d'Estudiantes Universitarios; University Students' Union (Spain)
SODSC	Secretariat d'Orientació de la Democracia Social Catalana; Secretariat for the Orientation of Catalan Social Democracy
STV	Solidaridad de Trabajadores Vascos; Solidarity of Basque Workers
UCD	Unión del Centro Democrático; Union of the Democratic Center (Spain)

UCDCC	Unió del Centre i la Democràcia Cristiana de Catalunya; Union of the Center and the Christian Democracy of Catalonia
UDC	Unió Democràtica de Catalunya; Democratic Union of Catalonia
UFNR	Unió Federal Nacionalista Republicana; Nationalist and Republican Federal Union (Catalonia)
UGT	Unión General de Trabajadores; Workers' General Union (Spain)
USC	Unió Socialista de Catalunya; Catalan Socialist Union
USO	Unión Sindical Obrera; Workers' Union (Spain)

An Analytical Approach

Major differences in the programmatic character of Basque nation-alism and Catalan nationalism, differences that have endured for a century, have long intrigued social scientists and historians, but remain to be explained. That these differences were well entrenched decades before the Spanish Civil War is apparent from the following:

It is thus indisputable that the Basque people and society cannot, but with great difficulty, fulfill their destiny, nor can our race be saved, as long as we remain subjects of Spain. Bizkaya [the Basque province of Vizcaya], if depen-dent on Spain, cannot address God, cannot, in practice, be Catholic. [Sabino Arana, 1897]

From its constituting a nationality, Catalonia derives its right to form a sep-arate state, a Catalan state. [But from] the current political arrangements, from Catalonia's long-standing cohabitation with other peoples, derives a certain element of unity, of community, which these peoples ought to preserve and consolidate. [Valentí Almirall, 1886]

Decades after the Spanish Civil War these distinctions had persisted intact:

The Basque people . . . not only [are] entitled to take up arms to resist the destruction of the Basque nation undertaken by Spain and France, but also [have] the moral obligation to oppose the inhuman actions of the oppressive state. It is the duty of every son of Euskalherría [the Basque nation] to resist the destruction of the Basque nation, even if this resistance requires revolu-tion, terrorism, and war. [Federico Krutvig, 1979 [1963]]

> The solution to the Catalan politico-structural problem requires the development of a political regime that will allow Catalonia and its people to become stronger, which is what every man needs from the political institutions of his community. . . . The federal system is the one which, in principle, best suits Catalonia and the pluralistic structure of Spain. [Jordi Pujol, 1958]

The ideology of the founders of the Basque nationalist movement was thus both traditionalist and separatist. The spirit of the movement is captured in a celebrated speech (the Discurso de Larrazabal) given by Arana on June 3, 1893, four years before he founded the Basque Nationalist Party. In this speech, he bemoaned what he saw as the steady decline of the province of Vizcaya since the Middle Ages, when it became a part of Spain. According to Arana, the decline resulted from Vizcaya's oppressive and humiliating subordination to Spain, culminating in the suppression of its autonomous political institutions (the Fueros) during the nineteenth century. Throughout history, he urged, Spain had displayed a complete lack of sensitivity toward the Basque religious and moral spirit, its organization of political and economic life, and its language and race. In his view, then, the only road to the "salvation" of Vizcaya was political independence, and he pledged to dedicate his life to its pursuit. True to his word, Arana maintained a lifelong, nonviolent crusade against the Spanish state, a crusade that cost him years in prison as well as his health and personal fortune.

Ironically, Arana delivered his speech at a time when the Basque Country, especially Vizcaya, was by all objective standards one of the most economically dynamic regions in Spain, equaled in that respect only by Catalonia. But although the Basque Country had indeed become the center of Spanish capitalism, many social groups, such as the rentier class (those living on pensions or annuities), the petty bourgeoisie, and the peasantry, had been greatly harmed by the capitalist transformation. In the main, these were the social groups constituting the leadership and support base of the Basque Nationalist Party.

Over the years, the Basque Nationalist Party evolved in new directions, its demands tempered politically by the more pragmatic approach of the few, but economically prosperous, members of the local bourgeoisie who supported the nationalist cause. Nevertheless the Basque Nationalist Party, which in time prevailed over other Basque nationalist parties, retained a messianic, separatist, and anticapitalist program until the Spanish Civil War. A significant number of its militants and supporters continued to believe that achieving political independence was the only way to save Basque society from the disastrous consequences of secularization, capitalism, and racial contamination.

During the period in which Arana gave his Discurso de Larrazabal, Catalonia was experiencing an ethnic revival without parallel in its long history.

This burgeoning of cultural and political activity eventually culminated in the formation of the first Catalan nationalist party, the Lliga Regionalista. Unlike the founders of the Basque Nationalist Party, however, those of the Lliga belonged to the ascending bourgeoisie and intelligentsia. The Lliga's list of candidates in the general elections of 1901, for instance, was known as the "Roster of the Four Presidents," because it included the most illustrious representatives of the Catalan business and cultural communities. Supporting the Lliga's candidates were the bulk of the Catalan bourgeoisie and intelligentsia who, to quote Francesc Cambó, during the electoral campaign "rushed to the streets as they had not done in ages."[1]

Cambó, a charismatic figure and one of the founders of the Lliga Regionalista, notes in his memoirs that the chief reasons for nationalism's emergence and success in Catalonia were the Spanish state's loss of prestige once the last major Spanish colonies (Cuba and the Philippines) had achieved independence and the Catalans' pride in the rapid economic development of their region.[2] These motivations are perfectly reflected in the words of Mañé i Flaquer, one of the spiritual fathers of Catalan nationalism, who, commenting on the Spanish ruling parties' ineptitude and on the recent formation of the Lliga, said, "Up to now they have made flour without wheat; now there is a new group of people in our public life that wants to make flour with wheat."[3]

From the beginning, the writings of the principal nationalist ideologues and the content of the nationalist parties' programs make clear that Catalan nationalism was autonomist or federalist, not separatist. That objective was consistent with the interests of the social sectors that led the Catalan nationalist movement—those large segments of the Catalan high bourgeoisie and intelligentsia concerned to protect Catalan culture and to ensure that the economic policies they advocated would come to be implemented in Catalonia. These groups seldom demanded independence, because of their belief, expressed in the writings of Prat de la Riba, Rovira i Virgili, and other Catalan nationalists, that it was in Catalonia's economic interests to remain a part of Spain.

The Puzzle: Two Persistently Distinct Nationalisms

The Spanish Civil War broke out just when the Basque and Catalan nationalist parties had attained political dominance in their regions and had achieved for them a significant degree of political autonomy. After the war, however, General Franco sought systematically to erase all signs of cultural diversity within Spain, and in the process to annihilate the Basque and Catalan nationalist movements, as well as the nationalist consciousness that had developed in the two regions during the pre–Civil War period. During

Franco's dictatorship, opposition to his cultural-homogenization policies and fascist government became the chief catalyst for clandestine nationalist political mobilization in the Basque Country and Catalonia.

As in the preceding decades, however, the Basque and Catalan nationalist movements were radically different in character. ETA, the most active, most popular Basque nationalist organization during this period, continued to stand firm on the goal of separatism, but was subscribing now to the theses of the third world's revolutionary national-liberation movements and advocating violent tactics. The nationalist program espoused by ETA was thus no longer traditionalist, but its rejection of capitalism—this time using a socialist-revolutionary discourse—had deeper roots, in the program of nationalism Arana had promulgated so long before. The Catalan nationalist movement, meanwhile, continued to be generally pro-autonomy and procapitalist, reflecting, in fact, considerable continuity with the pre–Civil War Catalan nationalist leaders' motives and objectives.

In the years since democracy was restored to Spain, following Franco's death, the contrast between the Basque and Catalan nationalist movements has persisted, as demonstrated by the greater electoral success of separatist and revolutionary organizations in the Basque Country than in Catalonia. The persistence of the contrast between the two nationalisms is remarkable, for in any given period the nationalist organizations in these two regions have covered the gamut of political goals and ideologies: from decentralization to independence, from racism to the glorification of ethnic diversity, from traditionalist or socialist anticapitalism to the enthusiastic embrace of capitalist development. Thus the roots of the contrast between the two movements must lie not in their respective intellectual histories, but in the particular socioeconomic and political characteristics of the two regions. These characteristics have determined the relative sizes and influence of the social groups supporting separatist and anticapitalist goals in the Basque Country and in Catalonia, as well as the resources available to the nationalist political organizations promoting these goals.

Analyzing the two movements and their contrasting constituencies and histories is the purpose of this book. The Basque Country and Catalonia are two of the seventeen politically autonomous communities into which Spain has been divided since the promulgation of the 1978 Constitution. The Basque Country lies in northern Spain where the Pyrenees meet the Bay of Biscay, and comprises the provinces of Vizcaya, Guipúzcoa, and Alava. In 1989, the Basque Country numbered 2,157,598 inhabitants, most of them concentrated along the coast. With the exception of those living in the Vizcayan city of Bilbao—more than 370,000 inhabitants—and its metropolitan area, most of the population of the Basque Country resides in relatively small and midsize towns. Catalonia, both greater in area and more heavily popu-

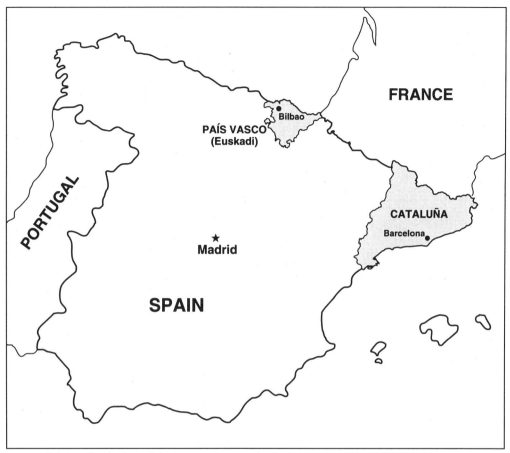

Map 1. Catalonia and the Basque Country in Spain

lated than the Basque Country, lies in northeastern Spain, and comprises the provinces of Barcelona, Gerona, Lérida, and Tarragona. In 1989, the population of Catalonia was 6,124,923, a great percentage of which is concentrated in the city of Barcelona—more than 1,600,000 inhabitants—and its surrounding metropolitan area.

The Basque Country and Catalonia enjoy similarly high levels of economic development. Catalonia, in the early nineteenth century, and then the Basque Country, in the last third of the nineteenth century, were among the first Spanish regions to experience the industrial revolution, and they remain, with Madrid, among the most industrialized Spanish regions. Since the end of the nineteenth century, these high levels of development have attracted thousands

Map 2. Catalonia

of immigrants from poorer Spanish regions, and today about a third of the population of the Basque Country and Catalonia were born outside the two regions, the immigrants represented disproportionately in the lower class.

The Basque Country and Catalonia, together with Galicia, the Community of Valencia, the Balearic Islands, and Navarre are linguistically distinct from other Spanish regions. Although fluency in Castilian is universal in all these regions, significant numbers of people consider another language to be their own. In the Basque Country, Castilian is spoken alongside Euskera (or Basque), a non-Romance language that has long puzzled linguists because of its seemingly untraceable origins. In Catalonia, Castilian coexists with Catalan, another Romance language.

The use of Euskera and Catalan extends, in fact, beyond the politico-administrative boundaries of the Basque Country and Catalonia. Euskera is

Map 3. The Basque Country

spoken, for instance, in some northern areas of the neighboring autonomous community of Navarre and in the French lands bordering the Spanish Basque Country. Catalan is spoken in the French area bordering Catalonia, and there has always been a heated debate over whether Valencian, the language spoken in the neighboring Community of Valencia, is really distinct from Catalan. Because in both the Basque Country and Catalonia there are two overlapping linguistic communities, and because the areas of usage of the regional languages are not congruent with the regional politico-administrative borders, language has become a significant symbol of collective identity and a politically manipulable cultural trait in the two regions. And since the two regions are alike in being linguistically distinct from the rest of Spain, language cannot be a significant factor in an explanation of the historical differences in the character of Basque and Catalan nationalism.

Thus, the contrast between the Basque Country and Catalonia is ideal because of their profound similarities in theoretically significant aspects, such as their shared cultural and linguistic distinctiveness within the larger polity and their high levels of economic development. The contrast therefore provides a unique opportunity to further the development of a theory to explain the success (or failure) of particular peripheral nationalist organizations and nationalist programs.

Because of the ideal nature of this comparison, the lack of a systematic comparative study explaining the contrast between the two movements is quite surprising.[4] A more comparative perspective would reveal the problematic nature of some of the explanations that have been offered for one or the other movement. Thus, explanations of Basque nationalism that stress the roles of social and identity crises induced by modernization[5] and of Francoist repression[6] fail to address the fact that Catalonia experienced similar levels of socioeconomic change and Francoist repression. Other studies of Basque or Catalan nationalism correctly identify differences in the social composition of the leadership of the two nationalist movements but fail to explain the *origin* of these differences, or to show how they have influenced the relative success of particular nationalist organizations.[7]

The puzzle thus remains unsolved. Thanks to previous studies we have some of the pieces of the puzzle—modernization, social composition, and repression—that are needed to explain the contrast between the two nationalist movements. Many of the pieces, however, are still missing, and, what is more important, we lack a master plan to put them together. Such a plan will be proffered below.

The Analytical Framework

The level of popular support attained by a radical peripheral nationalist organization can have immense consequences for the stability of the larger state. Needless to say, the risk of violence or even civil war is much greater when a peripheral nationalist movement is separatist and subversive of the social order than when it is "federalist" and conforms to the social order. Up to now, however, general sociological theories have focused more on the emergence and strength of peripheral nationalist movements per se than on explaining why particular nationalist political agendas (e.g. independence, autonomy) are more successful in some regions than in others. Although the factors emphasized by these theories—state centralization,[8] capitalist development,[9] relative deprivation,[10] regional overdevelopment relative to the rest of the state,[11] and ethnic competition[12]—offer valid insights into some features of the Basque and Catalan nationalist movements, they cannot explain why separatist and anticapitalist forms of nationalism have been more successful in the Basque Country than in Catalonia. Indeed, the two regions are identical in the variables emphasized by these theories: they have experienced state-centralization efforts in the same way and along the same time line; they are among the most industrialized regions in Spain; and they have attracted great numbers of immigrants who, though overrepresented at the base of society, can potentially compete for jobs with the native populations.

In the past decade, several authors have directly addressed the issue of secessionism.[13] In their view, a people's degree of support for independence is informed by cost/benefit calculations of the consequences of independence for themselves and their communities. This book will show, however, that although a cost/benefit explanation can be invoked to explain why support for political independence has remained generally low in both the Basque Country and Catalonia, it cannot explain why it has been far greater in the former than in the latter.

The lack of a theory explaining that variance is surprising, since the political instability that accompanies high levels of support for these organizations has undoubtedly been a major reason for the continuing academic and public fascination with the topic of nationalism. It is safe to say that if the IRA, ETA, the radical Serb nationalists, and the many other stridently radical nationalist groups had won less popular support, our interest in nationalism would have faded long ago.

Undoubtedly, one cannot begin to explain variation in the level of support attained by radical nationalist organizations unless a theory explaining the origins of nationalism and nationalist movements has previously been developed. Thanks to the collective efforts of many scholars over the past decade, the building blocks of this theory have been sketched out, and we can now devote our efforts to explaining the degree of radicalism of particular forms of nationalism. Liah Greenfeld's and Rogers Brubaker's work is sensitive to variation in the character of nationalism, but it focuses more on elites than on the population at large, and more on state-led nationalism than on state-seeking nationalism.[14] This book, then, moves to the mass level. Although I analyze the emergence of nationalist political organizations in the Basque Country and Catalonia, my focus is on explaining the different degrees of popular support won by these organizations.

The theories of peripheral nationalism just cited have tended to overlook the heterogeneity of political orientations within ethnoregional populations, and to focus exclusively on the explanatory roles of socioeconomic-structural factors and state-centralization policies. We thus need a more complex analytical framework. This book emphasizes the central roles played by the structure and dynamics of competition between social groups in mediating the relationship between socioeconomic structures and state policies, and in influencing political outcomes. The analytical framework I propose conceptualizes peripheral nationalist mobilization as influenced by conflict both between and within groups, and explores the roles that socioeconomic structures, political-competition structures, and historical processes play in levels of support for peripheral nationalist organizations. Each of the elements of this framework merits further discussion.

Divided Nations

Peripheral nationalist mobilization reflects two interrelated loci of conflict: that between the state and the peripheral nationalists and that within the population that the peripheral nationalists claim to represent. Since some segments of the nationalist organizations' potential support base identify with their claims and objectives while others do not, and may even actively oppose them, the "nations" in whose name peripheral nationalist organizations claim to speak are in fact *divided nations*.

An emphasis on divisions within "nations" characterizes some of the most important recent contributions to the study of nationalism in general.[15] These works show that although peripheral nationalism may in large part be a response to inadequate state representation of the interests of the periphery, the roots of center-periphery conflict often lie in social conflict within the periphery itself. The ideological manipulation of ethnic boundaries and the concomitant pursuit of political autonomy or independence are strategies through which members of a peripheral ethnic group can try to prevail over their local opponents, especially when the opponents have enlisted the state's cooperation. Thus, for instance, the emergence of Basque nationalism in the last decade of the nineteenth century can be linked to intense conflict between the ascending high bourgeoisie and other, declining social groups in Basque society, and to the strong ties the former established with the Spanish state, both of which persisted throughout the twentieth century. As a result, many sectors of Basque society see the Basque high bourgeoisie as alien to Basque society, despite its Basque origins and its members' claims that they are as Basque as anyone else.

Regional and State Socioeconomic Structures

Formulating and supporting nationalist programs are strategies that individuals can adopt to express their ethnocultural identity and to attain various material and nonmaterial objectives. These political choices are shaped by socialization experiences and economic interests that are closely related to people's social origins and current class status. To understand political behavior in peripheral regions, one accordingly needs to focus on the class structures of these regions.

The analysis of socioeconomic structures cannot, however, be limited to a static description of the distribution of the population across social groups and the level of economic development of a particular region relative to that of the state as a whole. Descriptions of that sort cannot account for political behavior,[16] unless they are complemented by thorough analyses of the problems and opportunities faced by different classes at the regional level, the relationships they maintain with each other, the socioeconomic structures in which they are embedded, and the degree to which they are economically dependent on the state's economy and the particular patterns of regional development. The focus on patterns, rather than levels, of development distinguishes this book from previous studies of nationalism and allows me to demonstrate that the contrast between the two nationalist movements is largely the result of the different patterns of development experienced in the Basque Country (combined and specialized in capital-goods production) and in Catalonia (endogenous and specialized in consumer-goods production) and the distinct social structures engendered by these patterns. (The terms "combined" and "endogenous" are explained in Chapter 2.)

The emergence of and support for peripheral nationalist parties depends to a large extent on the structural possibility of forming multiethnic political coalitions and on the potential efficacy of these coalitions in nationalist political mobilization. One can argue, for instance, that a significant reason why peripheral nationalism often develops in regions that are distinctly underdeveloped or overdeveloped (as predicted by Overdevelopment and Relative Deprivation theories) is that there is a marked difference between their social structures and those of the rest of the state, which works against the development of political alliances at the state level. As I show in this book, overdevelopment with respect to the rest of Spain contributed heavily to the emergence of peripheral nationalism in the Basque Country and Catalonia by making the formation of class-based political alliances at the state level highly problematic.

The Structure of Political Competition and the Viability of Nationalist Organizations

In seeking to explain peripheral nationalism, it is crucial that we recognize the autonomous role played by political structures. Studies that attempt to explain degrees of support for nationalist parties have often failed to consider the competition between different political alternatives and how it influences the political choices made by individuals. These studies tend to treat political competition within the communities under study as a black box situated between socioeconomic explanatory factors and the political outcomes they are supposed to explain. Instead, this book brings political competition to center stage, thus recognizing that in any given country or region there are always conflicting conceptions of national identity embedded in competing political programs.

The relationship between socioeconomic structure and political-competition structure is quite close, especially in periods of dramatic change—change engendered, for example, by industrialization—that lead to the emergence of new social classes and the decline of others. Over time, however, the structure of political competition can become relatively autonomous with respect to the social structure that generated it. Autonomy at that locus is especially significant in dictatorships, wherein free competition between political organizations is forbidden. Under a dictatorship, the oppositional political structure that develops is a distorted reflection of the socioeconomic structure of society, for it is heavily shaped by the capacities of different political organizations to operate clandestinely, and by the costs of political mobilization for different social actors. During the Franco dictatorship, as Part III of the book will show, the Basque and Catalan oppositional political structures differed greatly, despite significant similarities between their socioeconomic structures.

A focus on the role of competition between social actors demands particular attention to the political environment and to the resources different social actors are able to mobilize in order to promote their political agendas. Only recently have scholars begun to take into account the autonomy of the political sphere with respect to the socioeconomic-structural sphere, and their efforts thus far have been focused on the free-rider problem faced by nationalist organizations in trying to garner popular support.[17] Although this approach has offered interesting insights into the relative success of nationalist organizations, it fails to consider that a target ethnic group cannot simply be divided into participants and free riders; many of its members may not be interested in the collective goods promised by the nationalist organizations and therefore will not fall into either category.[18] Moreover, free-riding is not an important variable in the explanation of a secret, low-risk political activity such as voting for a particular organization, which is one of the central topics of this investigation. Unless they have the means to discover what party an individual has voted for, political organizations cannot use selective rewards and penalties to attract support for their cause.

The main problem faced by nationalist organizations is how to go about convincing members of the group they claim to represent that they should value the collective goods the organizations hope to attain. Competition between social movements or political organizations plays a crucial role in defining the terms of the political debate, in articulating people's interests, and in shaping people's perceptions of the desirability of different courses of political action. In this sense, it is not very relevant to know that support for independence hinges on people's assessment of the costs and benefits of independence, if what these assessments reflect is for the most part the success of political entrepreneurs in shaping these perceptions. Our understanding of nationalism will remain incomplete unless we explain what makes political entrepreneurs more or less successful in shaping people's perceptions.

This book, then, accords special attention to the political diversity or "structural conduciveness" of a particular environment.[19] It claims that the success of a nationalist organization is partly a function of the number of political organizations offering similar collective goods. Other things being equal, a separatist organization will be more successful if it alone promotes a nationalist program than if it competes against other nationalist organizations that are not separatist. Obviously, the separatist organization is more likely to attract nationalist but not separatist supporters in the former scenario than in the latter.

The degree of diversity of the political environment in a given region at any given time affects not only current political alignments among the population, but future ones as well. In Part III, I demonstrate that the differences between the Basque and Catalan political-mobilization structures during the Franco period have contributed decisively to the greater success of separatist and anticapitalist political organizations in the Basque Country than in Catalonia in the years since the restoration of democracy. The enduring effect of these Franco-period structures has of course been mediated by socialization and relatively autonomous historical processes, as we shall see in Chapter 11.

I also explore, in Part III, the connections between the political diversity of the environment and the political autonomy enjoyed by different social actors. This analysis is particularly relevant to explaining the structure of political mobilization under regimes that limit the public expression of political preferences. Political autonomy is defined here as people's ability to translate their political beliefs into political action. The literature on social movements has focused on this factor in studies of the political behavior of the so-called "revolutionary classes," such as the working class and the peasantry.[20] There is no systematic work, however, that explains variation in the degree of political autonomy enjoyed by the bourgeoisie or the intelligentsia, or analyzes the impact of political autonomy on the political behavior of these classes.

This book suggests that the political autonomy of the bourgeoisie and the intelligentsia is greater in economies specialized in consumer-goods production, such as the Catalan, than in those specialized in capital-goods production, such as the Basque. Largely in consequence, the political behavior of the Basque and Catalan bourgeoisies and intelligentsias differed greatly during the Franco regime, thus leading to the emergence of very different structures of political competition in the two regions during this period.

Historical Process and Nationalism

The final element of the book's analytical framework is its dynamic or historical approach. It would be naive to postulate a deterministic relationship between social and political structures or such a relationship between these two structural spheres and such political outcomes as the degree of support for particular nationalist organizations. A sociological analysis of peripheral nationalism needs to be sensitive to more than that; its needs to recognize, as well, the three elements that according to Sewell characterize "an eventful conception of temporality": path dependency, temporally heterogeneous causalities, and global contingency.[21] The first of these elements states that the range of possible outcomes at a point in time is constrained by the preceding sequence of events (e.g. Gerschenkron's account of paths toward industrialization).[22] The second element states that significant events can alter particular causal structures. The third element states that despite the durabilities displayed by history, "nothing in social life is ultimately immune to change."[23]

Following this approach, we can say that although extant social structures constrain the types of political structures that can develop in a particular state or region, the crystallization of a structure of political competition that adequately reflects those social structures is often mediated by a tortuous historical process. Thus despite the existence of conditions favorable to the emergence of the Basque and Catalan nationalist movements (e.g. the Spanish state's centralization attempts during the nineteenth century and the dissimilarity between, on the one hand, the Basque and Catalan social structures and, on the other, the social structure characterizing the rest of Spain), nationalist parties emerged in the two regions only after repeated attempts by their respective middle classes to influence Spanish politics through Spanish political organizations. The failure of these attempts, conditioned but not determined by social-structural factors, was decisive in the final adoption of nationalist politics by these social groups.

The relationships between socioeconomic-structural factors, political-structural factors, and the political outcomes one wants to explain (e.g. the degree of support for a particular nationalist organization) is also mediated

by historical processes and events that are largely autonomous with respect
to the socioeconomic and political structures. The demands of the Basque
and Catalan nationalist movements, for example, were decisively shaped by
the historical processes that contributed to their emergence, such as the
nineteenth-century Carlist Wars and the military defeats of 1898 that led to
the independence of Cuba and the Philippines. Moreover, the particular
political dynamics and events of the decade 1970–80 play a crucial role in
explaining why radical nationalist organizations have been more successful
in the Basque Country than in Catalonia since democracy was restored in
Spain. Whereas around 1969 the Basque population was significantly less
nationalist than the Catalan population, by 1980 it had become just as
nationalist and in fact more supportive of radical nationalist political organizations. Without examining the historical process that played out during
the 1970s, one cannot understand this dramatic and enduring transformation in the political attitudes of the Basque population.

Summary: The Study of Basque and Catalan Nationalism

In this book I show that the emergence of nationalist politics in the
Basque Country and Catalonia at the close of the nineteenth century corroborates those general explanations for the emergence of nationalism in other
European countries that emphasize the role of the development of the modern state and of capitalist expansion.[24] Of course, by the time Basque and
Catalan nationalism emerged, nationalism had already become a legitimate
style of politics across Europe, which was prone to territorial piracy.[25] Therefore, although one cannot argue that the emergence of the Basque and Catalan nationalist movements was *determined* by accelerated state-centralization
policies and capitalist transformations, it was rendered *possible* by the avail-
ability of nationalism as one among many alternative forms of political
mobilization that could be adopted in response.

The book focuses on an explanation of the enduring contrast between the
Basque and Catalan nationalisms, a contrast that can be explained only by
examining the different patterns of capitalist development experienced by the
two regions, their different structures of political mobilization, and their particular histories.

Combined development and specialization in capital-goods production in
the Basque Country and endogenous development and specialization in consumer-goods production in Catalonia—again, the terms are discussed in
Chapter 2—facilitated the development of very different social structures,
very different attitudes toward capitalism and membership in the Spanish
state, and, consequently, very different political structures and degrees of

support for particular nationalist political organizations. Whereas Basques tended to support a form of nationalism that demanded independence and a return to precapitalist forms of social organization, Catalans favored a form that demanded political autonomy with the Spanish state and policies that would promote capitalist development.

During Franco's dictatorship, the banning of political competition and the consequent need for oppositional forces to organize clandestinely distorted the relationship between socioeconomic characteristics and political-competition structures in the two regions. The structural characteristics of the opposition movements during this period were shaped by other factors, too, such as differences in the political traditions and the degrees of political autonomy of the two middle classes. Thus, although the Basque and Catalan social structures became almost identical during the Franco years, the patterns of political mobilization and the character of nationalism in the two regions remained quite distinct. These differences in the structure of oppositional politics during the Franco regime, and differences between the political processes that unfolded in the two regions during the 1970s, explain why separatist and anticapitalist political organizations have achieved greater support in the Basque Country than in Catalonia since democracy was restored, despite growing similarities between their social structures and political-competition structures.

The book is divided into three parts. The first (Chapters 1 and 2) provides indispensable background material for the understanding of political and socioeconomic developments in the Basque Country and Catalonia during the last two centuries. It focuses on the process by which the Basque provinces and Catalonia became part of Spain, and on the types of economic and political ties that the Basque and Catalan middle and upper classes established with the rest of Spain before industrialization in the nineteenth century. These ties played an important role in the development of political and cultural orientations among the Basque and Catalan socioeconomic and political elites, which would in time shape their disparate attitudes toward nationalist mobilization.

Part II focuses on the industrialization processes in the two regions during the nineteenth and early twentieth centuries (Chapter 3) and on how they influenced Basque and Catalan prenationalist politics (Chapter 4) and the character of early Basque and Catalan nationalism (Chapters 5, 6, and 7).

Finally, Part III analyzes Basque and Catalan nationalism in the years during and since the Spanish Civil War (1936–39); the different elements of the analytical approach that I propose for the study of peripheral nationalism will be most evident here. Chapter 8 presents an overview of development patterns and their effects on the social structure of Catalonia and the Basque

Country during the period 1939–1992. Chapters 9 and 10 offer a historical overview of the Basque and Catalan nationalist movements during the Francoist period, with particular emphasis on their social bases. Finally, Chapter 11 analyzes the influence of the social and political contexts described in the preceding chapters on the character of Basque and Catalan nationalism in democratic Spain. The book closes with a brief concluding chapter.

INTEGRATION AND CULTURAL IDENTITY IN THE EARLY SPANISH STATE

The first part of this book focuses on the political and economic histories of the Basque Country and Catalonia prior to the nineteenth century. This historical background serves to contextualize the nineteenth-century political and socioeconomic transformations that led to the rise of nationalist movements in these two regions. It also helps to explain the attitudes of the Basque and Catalan upper classes toward these movements.

People's political behavior is to some extent shaped by rational calculations grounded primarily in economic and political interests. Such calculations tend to be informed by past personal experience and by political and cultural orientations, for when there are alternative paths toward desired goals social actors often lack the information needed to predict the strategies that will be most successful in achieving those goals. Their prior experience and orientations thus provide a blueprint for their interpretation of events and shape their political behavior. Moreover, political and cultural orientations tend to be transmitted intergenerationally unless major socioeconomic or political upheavals force people to reevaluate their goals and beliefs.

The two chapters that follow focus on the economic and political ties that the Basque and Catalan upper classes have forged with Spain since the Middle Ages, and suggest that they have played a significant role in the development of their political and cultural orientations. As the literature has repeatedly pointed out, the Basque upper class has been powerfully oriented toward Spain, both politically and culturally, and has never opposed the Spanish state or sponsored nationalist movements. The Catalan upper class, by contrast, has repeatedly challenged the domination of the Spanish state since the seventeenth century and has been a major force in Catalan nationalist mobilization since the late nineteenth century. Contemporary differences between the Basque Country and Catalonia in the use of language attest to the different cultural orientations of the economic elites of the two regions. Survey data collected in 1988, for example, reveal that ability to speak the regional language was much lower in the Basque Country (20 percent) than in Catalonia (52 percent). Although patterns of language use have surely changed over time, the contemporary contrast in attitudes toward language use reflects the attitudes of the Basque and Catalan upper classes since the Middle Ages. For whereas the Catalan language became a literary language, Euskera (as the Basque language is known) remained—notwithstanding its enduring fascination for comparative linguists—a language spoken mainly by the peasants and some members of the lower clergy. Only recently has use of Euskera by broader segments of Basque society begun to increase, thanks to the efforts of the Basque autonomous government.

The two chapters analyze how the Basque Country and Catalonia came to be integrated into Spain; they also analyze the particular economic and political ties that the Basque and Catalan elites established with the Spanish economy and polity prior to industrialization in the nineteenth century. The analysis shows that, from an early date, the Basque upper classes developed closer economic ties with Spain than did the Catalan upper classes. I argue that the great persistence of these different levels of economic and political interdependence with Spain facilitated the development of more pro-Spanish political and cultural orientations among the Basque upper classes.

CHAPTER I

State-building in
the Iberian Peninsula

This chapter focuses on how the Basque provinces and Catalonia came to be parts of Spain, and compares the degrees of autonomy the two enjoyed before and after the unification of the kingdoms of Castile, Aragón, and Navarre under the Catholic Kings, at the close of the fifteenth century.[1] It also examines the economic and political ties that the Basque and Catalan socioeconomic elites established, first, with the kingdom of Castile and, then, with the Spanish Crown during this period. The political consequences of these ties are explored in Chapter 2.

The Unification of the Spanish Kingdoms

Catalonia and the Kingdom of Castile

The Principality of Catalonia, occupying the northeastern corner of the Iberian Peninsula, emerged out of the unification of a group of independent counties that had been created by the French Carolingian kings in the eleventh century. Unification was achieved by Ramón Berenguer I (1035–1076), who acquired sole authority over the counties of Barcelona, Gerona, and Ausona (Vich) and then ensured that the Counts of Ampurias, Urgel, Besalú, Cerdagne, and Pallars recognized his suzerainty.

During this period, Catalonia became a major power in the Mediterranean region. By about 1060, it had already established powerful commercial links with Italian and other Mediterranean ports and had built a strong commercial fleet. The rise of Catalonia was based mostly on agricultural prosperity and on tribute paid in gold by surrounding Muslim kingdoms, which then occupied a large part of the Iberian Peninsula.

In 1137, Catalonia became part of, and the dominant power within, a larger confederation of kingdoms known as the Crown of Aragón. Strengthened by this union, it continued its military and commercial expansion in the Mediterranean, especially between 1238 and 1358. Catalonia exported wine, dried fruits, salt, animal products such as leather and furs, coral, raw materials for shipbuilding, and manufactured products such as glass and textiles. It imported luxury goods from the East, such as spices, sugar, paper, precious metals, and fine textiles. Although the value of imported goods generally exceeded that of exported goods, Catalonia balanced its payments by engaging in the slave trade and exacting tribute from the neighboring Muslim kingdoms.[2]

In the second half of the fourteenth century, however, plague epidemics decimated the Catalan population and halted Catalonia's rise to power. As Vilar pointed out, in 1962, this demographic crisis played a primary role in Catalonia's economic and political decline during the fifteenth and early sixteenth centuries. The lowered production levels engendered by demographic decline also brought about an acute social crisis that pitted feudal lords against peasants and was not resolved until King Ferdinand enacted the Sentencia de Guadalupe in 1480. This Sentencia eliminated seignorial abuses and granted freedom of movement to the peasantry. During the fifteenth century, as a result of its decline, Catalonia gradually fell within the sphere of influence of the kingdom of Castile, and Castile's growing dominance of Catalonia's affairs was sealed in 1469 with the marriage of Isabella, heir to the kingdom of Castile, to Ferdinand, heir to the Crown of Aragón.

The Basque Provinces and the Kingdom of Castile

While Catalonia was enjoying political autonomy and economic splendor in the late Middle Ages, the Basque provinces during this period were already linked intimately to Castile. During the eleventh and twelfth centuries, Castile formed a political union with another western kingdom, León, and together they annexed the three Basque provinces of Alava, Vizcaya (which became a lordship with substantial feudal immunity), and Guipúzcoa. Although Alava and Guipúzcoa later reverted to the third pillar of Spanish unification, the kingdom of Navarre, they were re-annexed to Castile during Alfonso VIII's reign in the twelfth century.

From roughly 1250 to 1350, Castile enjoyed economic transformations much like those experienced by Catalonia. The ascent of Castile was linked to the development of European trade and to the special role that Castile played as a producer of wool for export to the market centered in the Low Countries. Sheepraising became an essential part of the Castilian economy, regulated and encouraged by the Castilian kings. As part of their intervention in the wool trade, the Castilian kings tightened their control over the Cantabrian (north-central) coast, where they founded numerous chartered towns to encourage trade with the rest of Europe. In the process, the Basque provinces (also on the Bay of Biscay, between the Cantabrian Coast and the Pyrenees) became integrated into the Spanish economy, through participating in the wool trade between Castile and Flanders and contributing warships to the Castilian navy.

The Decentralization of Power in Early Spain

The dynastic unification of Spain under the Catholic Kings did not imply the emergence of a centralized state. A state bureaucracy was slow to emerge, and laws and political institutions continued to vary across the Spanish territory. How the Basque provinces and Catalonia were politically integrated into this emerging state is the question we address next, and the answer requires a step back in time.

Feudalism in the Iberian Christian Kingdoms

Feudal influences had been felt clearly in the Christian Spanish states since the eleventh century. Small estates were replaced by large ones, as powerful lords appropriated land from free peasants, as free peasants relinquished their land in exchange for protection, and as kings gave broader and more frequent immunities. In general, by the end of the Middle Ages the influence of feudalism had been sufficiently pervasive to deprive the Crowns of the Christian kingdoms not only of their jurisdiction over large portions of their territories, including the Basque provinces, but even of their ownership of them.

The Castilian and Aragonese kings, sensing the danger that some of these autonomous seigniories represented for their authority, undertook a process of re-annexation of some of these seigniories (e.g. the County and Land of Alava and the Seigniorie of Vizcaya). Annexation, however, did not mean political and juridical homogenization, and Alava and Vizcaya, for example, maintained their own political organizations.

Respect for preexisting institutions was greater under the Crown of Aragón than in Castile, which attempted to extend the power of certain central institutions and to create new institutions encompassing the whole realm. Thus, whereas in Castile a single Cortes (the name of the Parliament in the Iberian kingdoms) represented almost the totality of its territory (except such areas as the Basque Provinces and Galicia), each kingdom or principality under the Crown of Aragón (Aragón, Catalonia, Valencia, the Balearic Islands, Sicily, and Sardinia) retained its own parliament. This practice of preserving territorial political and juridical institutions was the one adopted when Castile and Aragón united in the late fifteenth century.

The Cortes of Castile and Aragón, and the Brotherhood Associations

During the Low Middle Ages (roughly the twelfth to fifteenth centuries), monarchs reversed the feudalization of society by annexing seigniories and strengthening the consultative institutions of their kingdoms. The most important of these institutions were the Cortes and the Brotherhood Associations.

Integrated by the king and the three estates, the Cortes (Parliaments) were the major organizations through which the estates participated in government and defended their interests. Although a Cortes was not exactly a legislative body, its functions were more than merely consultative. Royal power was limited by territorial law and tradition, and the Cortes, through its consideration of grievances and petitions to the king, ensured to some extent that the king would respect these laws and traditions. Two types of Cortes, differing in their structure and in their sphere of competence, can be distinguished: those of the Castilian type and those of the Aragonese type.

In the Cortes of Castile, the three estates were not clearly defined. Instead, the major political cleavage was between, on the one hand, the king and his closest counseling body (integrated by the nobility and the clergy), and, on the other, the popular representatives of cities and towns. Eventually, however, the Castilian Cortes were attended only by representatives of certain cities located in areas of royal jurisdiction. In time, their main functions came to be voting on extraordinary subsidies requested by the king and establishing rules for how to collect these subsidies and how the king should spend them.

In the Aragonese Cortes, the differentiation between the estates was more clear-cut. Another difference was that in the Aragonese Cortes the king had to satisfy the estates' grievances before presenting his own demands. Finally, the Cortes of the kingdoms belonging to the Crown of Aragón had full legislative powers of their own. In Catalonia, for instance, laws of a general character had to be enacted by the Cortes with the approval of all the estates. When the Cortes were not in session, their permanent delegation, the Generalitat, watched over the collection of taxes and the execution of the Cortes's decisions.

Despite their increasing importance in the government of the various kingdoms, the Cortes were not the only institution through which the estates participated in government. Since the twelfth century in Castile and the second half of the thirteenth century in Aragón, municipalities had been joining together to form Brotherhoods (or Hermandades). The internal regime of the Brotherhoods was regulated by constitutional documents, called Brotherhood Charters (Cartas de Hermandad), approved by the Brotherhoods' governing assemblies, the Juntas de Hermandad.

It is through these Brotherhoods that the Basque provinces, which had no need to attend the Castilian Cortes sessions because of their political and jurisdictional immunity, organized the representation of their own interests. The Hermandades constituted a political body ruled by traditional norms and privileges that the kings swore to abide by and to maintain.

The Junta de Hermandad met to deal with community affairs, to decree the norms for good government, to maintain public peace, and to ensure the defense and strict application of the Fueros, or common law. The Junta had legislative power and thus functioned in some ways like the Cortes of Castile.

But whereas the Juntas of Alava and Guipúzcoa included only the chartered towns in these regions, the Junta of Vizcaya included representatives from rural areas, as well. In fact, the Seigniorie of Vizcaya enjoyed greater jurisdictional powers and a greater degree of political institutionalization than did either Guipúzcoa or Alava. In 1452, for instance, the Junta de Hermandad of Vizcaya agreed to set down Vizcaya's laws in a document called the Fuero Viejo de Vizcaya. This event had important political implications almost four hundred years later, when the Spanish Crown once again stepped up the process of centralization. The existence of this written document conferred upon Vizcayan autonomy a degree of legitimacy that other autonomous regions lacked.

The Spanish State after the Union of Castile and Aragón

The Union of Aragón and Castile effected by the marriage of Isabella and Ferdinand did not imply profound state transformations. Neither the Catholic Kings nor their successors, up to the seventeenth century, seriously attempted to eliminate the medieval elements of the state they had inherited. During this period, Spain remained a patchwork of legal and jurisdictional constitutions, and because the system of internal customs remained intact, goods were heavily taxed as they crossed from region to region. Within Castile, this conception of power favored the persistence of two distinct political and legal systems, one for Castile, the other for Aragón. It also meant the persistence of the juridico-political singularity of the Basque provinces, which had a relatively more formal constitution than did other semiautonomous areas of Castile.

The patrimonial conception of power held by the early modern Spanish rulers led them to view Castile and Aragón as distinct possessions. The distinction was evidenced in their treatment of the American territories, which were administered solely by Castile. Although the territories of the Crown of

Aragón, and of Catalonia in particular, were not excluded from participating in commerce and emigration to America, in practice the Catalans were treated like other foreigners trying to benefit from American wealth and opportunities. Basques, by contrast, as members of the kingdom of Castile, were able to participate in the conquest of America unrestrained.

Basque and Catalan Ties with the Rest of Spain: From the Catholic Kings to the Early Habsburgs

During the sixteenth century, Castile maintained strong economic links with both Northern Europe (particularly the Low Countries) and America. In fact, the American and Northern European commercial routes were closely linked, for products and treasures from America went to Northern Europe, and textiles from Northern Europe eventually found their way to America. The North Atlantic economy—that between Spain and Northern Europe—was based, as in the period preceding Spanish unification, on sheepraising for the export of wool and on the development of the textile sector. The Basques and Catalans played very different roles in these economic exchanges.

The Basques and the Empire

Basques were active in both the North Atlantic and the Transatlantic economies. Bilbao, the chief Vizcayan city, played a pivotal role in the wool trade with the Low Countries, which by the middle of the sixteenth century absorbed nearly half of Spain's export trade and sent a third of their exports to Spain. The wool-trade route had its base in the interior of Castile, where wool was prepared for market; from there the wool went to Burgos, the main trade center in northern Castile, and from Burgos it went on to Bilbao; finally, from Bilbao, it was shipped to Flanders. The centrality of Burgos (itself not a port) in this system was constantly challenged by Bilbao, which was unwilling to accept Burgos's monopoly over wool exports from the Cantabrian ports. Bilbao, a thriving port in its own right, was the center of the Vizcayan iron trade, which was one of the major industrial components of the Castilian economy. Pressure by Basque merchants finally won the day when, in 1511, King Ferdinand authorized a special trade consulate in Bilbao for Vizcaya.

Wool exports benefited the other coastal Basque provinces, as well, because they favored the growth of the merchant fleet, which was built in the Cantabrian ports. The Basque provinces offered good opportunities for shipbuilding because of their ample supplies of local timber and iron and their location on the trade route between Castile and the Low Countries. The

Catholic Kings encouraged this local development by offering subsidies toward the construction of ships weighing over 600 tons, and by requiring that Castilian goods be exported in Castilian ships. Although Seville had a monopoly on trade with the American colonies, the north of Spain (especially Vizcaya) had a monopoly on shipping, for it supplied—particularly from 1520 to 1580—almost all of the Spanish vessels in the Indies trade.

Iron production and export, together with shipbuilding, were the main indigenous industries in the Basque provinces. Iron production for export gave rise to a prosperous merchant sector, which then sold Basque products instead of merely trans-shipping products from other regions. In exchange, these merchants imported cloth and food for the local population.

In general, the sixteenth century was a prosperous one for the commercial and industrial sectors of the Basque provinces, for they were tightly integrated into the Castilian economy. Their intense trade activities allowed them to import grain, which was chronically in deficit in the Basque Country because of low land productivity and steady urban growth. Trade, shipbuilding, the iron industry, and limited firearms manufacturing flourished, though all were highly dependent on foreign markets and the Spanish Crown. Already in this period Basque development depended almost less on Spain than on the Spanish Crown, since the latter demanded firearms, ships, and manpower for the development of trade with the Low Countries and America. Only iron producers and those merchants engaged in exporting iron were dependent more on foreign markets than on the Spanish Crown.

The Catalans and the Empire

During the sixteenth century, Catalonia continued to experience economic and political decline. Although the cause of the decline lay chiefly with the demographic crisis brought on by the plague of the fourteenth century, in the long run the shift of the center of economic activities from the Mediterranean to the Atlantic played an even greater role.[3] But during the post-unification period the patrimonial and feudal character of the Spanish monarchy, which treated Castile and Catalonia as autonomous political and jurisdictional entities, also contributed to Catalonia's decline. In consequence of these inequitable policies, Catalonia failed to benefit from the opportunities opened by Castilian prosperity and by the conquest of America.

Treated as foreigners by the kingdom of Castile and lacking financial power, Catalans were unable to compete with the Genoese merchants, who truly *were* foreigners. The pact of 1528, for instance, between Emperor Charles V and his banker Andrea Doria, gave the Genoese an advantage in the competition for control of the spice, cloth, and corn trades in the

Mediterranean. Under this pact the Genoese were granted privileges that allowed them to sell textiles in the Spanish possessions of Sicily and Naples, which had been the traditional markets for Catalan industry. Catalans were also outbid by the Genoese even when competing for the Castilian market. The Genoese had established a solid alliance with the Spanish Crown and had settled in Córdoba, Cádiz, and Seville, where they succeeded in controlling wool exports from Spain's southern ports. Together with Flemish artisans, they were encouraged to settle in Spain for long periods without being required to pay taxes.

That the Genoese prevailed over the Catalans when competing for the Spanish market demonstrates that Castile made no political distinction between Catalans and foreigners, and the Catalans lacked the financial power to extract favors from the Crown. Catalans were refused direct trade with America and even permission for a consulate in Seville or Cádiz, the southern centers of Castilian trade with America. When they turned their efforts toward markets in Castile, the gateway to America, they faced severe competition from Flemish, English, and French clothiers: whereas these foreign producers were allowed to place their goods directly in the ports of Seville or Cádiz on payment of moderate customs duties, Catalan exporters to Castile were confronted by numerous fiscal barriers: customs duties, transit dues across Aragón, and entrance duties at the "dry ports" of Castile (customs posts located inland).

In sum, the historical evidence available for the fifteenth and sixteenth centuries demonstrates that by the time of the Catholic Kings' reign, Catalonia had already achieved a higher degree of political, institutional, and cultural development than other Spanish communities had. The Basque Country, for its part, essentially did not exist at this time as a political or even cultural entity. What most distinguished the Basque provinces from other Spanish provinces were probably their written Fueros and their somewhat more developed political institutions. Their vividly distinct language was routinely subordinated to the Spanish tongue. But the history also reveals the early existence of conditions favoring a cultural and political identification of the Basque upper classes with Castile. Since the late Middle Ages, economic and political ties with the rest of Spain were stronger in the Basque provinces than in Catalonia. One major consequence of these closer ties was that the Basque provinces initially benefited more from trade with America than did Catalonia. Vis-à-vis the Basque provinces, the political and economic histories of Catalonia were less tied to those of the rest of Spain, and the development of a regional ethnic identity among its elites was more advanced.

In the next chapter we shall see a telling illustration of how the economic and political ties established by the two regions came to affect the attitudes of the Basque and Catalan sociopolitical elites toward the Spanish Crown.

Fiscal Crisis, Centralization, and Rebellion

We need now to analyze the first attempts at political centralization undertaken by the Spanish state, and the different reactions these steps provoked in the Basque provinces and Catalonia.[1]

Fiscal Crisis and the First Centralization Attempts

Although the sixteenth century saw great military and economic achievement in Spain, the seeds of crisis were already being sown during the reign of Charles V (1516–56). Growing fiscal problems, a key concern, motivated the first attempts to centralize economic policy in Spain. Such efforts would lead eventually to the full integration of Catalonia and the Basque provinces into the Spanish politico-institutional system of government.

Failure to centralize had been a major reason for the Crown's chronic inability to collect revenues sufficient to fund its wars. The great diversity of laws and institutions in Spain's various kingdoms hindered attempts to mandate uniform contributions, and for the most part Charles had to rely on money provided by the Low Countries and, later, by the kingdom of Naples. Once these Spanish possessions became unable or unwilling to pay for the costs of maintaining the Empire, the Spanish Habsburgs had no choice but to turn to Spain.

The kingdom of Castile bore the brunt of the burden because only there could the Spanish monarchs circumvent the Cortes when raising new taxes. In the kingdom of Aragón, by contrast, the approval of the Cortes was strictly required, and obtaining it was no small hurdle, since the Cortes of Aragón generally opposed new taxes on the questionable grounds that their regions did not have sufficient economic resources.[2]

Gaining the approval of the Crown of Aragón was also a long process, one that required the prior redressment of the Aragón Cortes's grievances toward the king of Spain. In practice, then, the burden of financing imperial policy fell chiefly on Castile. In 1616, Castile paid for 73 percent of the imperial costs, while Portugal, the Low Countries, Naples, and Aragón paid for 10, 9, 5, and 1 percent, respectively.

The first steps toward redressing this situation were not taken until well into the reign of Philip III (1598–1621). The "arbitristas," a rising intelligentsia, began to propose measures for rationalizing the collection of revenue, measures that involved chiefly increased contributions by the Crown of Aragón and the Spanish nobility. Such reforms were strongly opposed, however, and the Spanish Crown continued to rely on Castile, on the selling of offices and jurisdictions, and on monetary devaluations. These measures were both insufficient and harmful at a time when Dutch piracy was rampant and silver arrivals were diminishing.

Both Philip III and his successor, Philip IV, delegated most of their political decisions to highly visible advisors who came to be called *validos*. It was precisely Philip IV's valido, the Count-Duke of Olivares, who finally attempted to force all of the Spanish territories to contribute equitably.[3] In his famous project of 1624, the Unión de Armas, he dictated that all the Spanish kingdoms would contribute to the raising of an army. Any kingdom finding itself under attack by foreign armies could immediately call upon the seventh part of this reserve army—that is, 20,000 infantrymen and 4,000 cavalrymen—for help. The Cortes of Aragón opposed the plan, and in so doing ignited one of the major crises of the seventeenth century: the revolt of the Catalans in 1640.

This revolt was matched by the Motín de la Sal (Salt Mutiny), which broke out in the Basque province of Vizcaya in 1631. But although both incidents were precipitated by repeated royal attempts to increase the fiscal contributions of Spain's constituent territories, and although both resulted in the defeat of the rebels, the attitude of the leading sectors of Catalan society toward tax increases differed from that of the leaders of Basque society. Closer examination of these two episodes, and the ways in which they differed, will be instructive.

The Revolt of the Catalans in 1640

The Catalan opposition to his Unión de Armas did not discourage Olivares, and in 1626 he proclaimed it for the rest of the Empire. Nonetheless, during the succeeding two years the economic situation did not substantially improve. And to make matters worse, Spain embarked on a war against the

French in Italy (1628–31). Fiscal reform, now crucial, could not be implemented, because the Spanish nobility opposed all reforms that might threaten their tax exemptions. And because they monopolized positions in the various councils and controlled the cities' representation at the Castilian Cortes, the nobility were a force to be reckoned with. Olivares was thus forced to resort to ruses that would help him circumvent the Cortes in the collecting of new taxes.

The war against France, which resumed in 1635, presented Olivares with the excuse he had been waiting for to raise the Catalan contribution to the Spanish treasury. In 1639 he announced that the Spanish army would invade France via Catalonia, and he chose the siege of Sasles, on the far side of the Pyrenees, as the occasion to have Catalans participate in the Unión de Armas. He succeeded, though in doing so he systematically violated the Catalan constitution, thereby provoking further outrage.

In 1640, after the victory at Sasles, Olivares decided to exploit the presence of the armies billeted in Catalonia: he would use them to coerce the Catalan Cortes into contributing funds to the Crown, and into participating further in the Unión de Armas. Predictably, his policies found no sympathy from the Cortes of Aragón, which refused meeting under these conditions, nor from the Catalan population, which rebelled against the occupying forces and assassinated the Crown's Catalan Viceroy, Santa Coloma. After almost two hundred years of monarchic unity, the Crown was now fighting a war against Catalonia.

The war between the Crown and Catalonia revealed the weakness of the Spanish monarchy. As the Crown dispatched troops to Catalonia, Portuguese nobles seized the opportunity to proclaim their independence from Spain, a status not threatened since. Other regions, such as Andalucía, Aragón, and Naples, followed suit, though less successfully. Meanwhile, led by the canon of the Catalan town of Urgell, the Catalans sought French support and became a dependency of France.

Of the several rebellions, that in Catalonia persisted longest, but after twelve years of war, the Spanish campaign against Catalonia succeeded. France, now engaged in fighting the Fronde, in the north, could no longer protect its newly acquired prize. And in any case, inclusion in France proved to be no more attractive to Catalans than inclusion in Spain, particularly for Catalonia's merchants, who could not compete against the French products that flooded the Catalan market. Moreover, scores of the Catalan aristocracy, fearing popular rebellion and unsure about French intentions, crossed into Spain and aided the army in its efforts to recover Catalonia for the Spanish Crown. Ultimately, an epidemic of plague fell upon Barcelona, precipitating Philip's final victory, in 1652.

The price of victory was high, however, and Spain was in no condition to impose onerous terms upon either the Catalans or the French. Thus although Catalonia retained its political constitution, France, through the Treaty of the Pyrenees, obtained the Roussillon and the French Cerdagne, Catalan-speaking extremities that would never again be returned to Catalonia.

The Salt Mutiny of 1632 in the Basque Country

Many rebellions afflicted the Spanish monarchy during the third and fourth decades of the seventeenth century. Of these, the Salt Mutiny, which took place in 1631 in the Basque province of Vizcaya, offers the most interesting contrast with the Catalan revolt of 1640. Both rebellions were eventually defeated; but whereas in Vizcaya the upper class was willing to meet the Crown's demands, in Catalonia the upper class energetically opposed them.

A royal petition for a large "voluntary" contribution, addressed to the Junta General de Hermandad of the Seigniorie of Vizcaya in 1629, initiated the conflict called El Motín de la Sal. Until the seventeenth century, the Basque provinces had traditionally been tax-exempt, and these voluntary contributions—called *donativos*—were a relatively new tax-collection measure. The Junta had been accustomed to deciding whether to contribute, and, if so, how their contribution would be collected. This Junta was dominated by the large landowners, who, from the early years of the century, had sought to deny the peasantry their due representation.

On September 11, a special commission named by the Junta agreed to provide the King a large sum of money, two manned warships weighing 600 tons each, and six months' salary for 200 sailors. To collect the necessary funds, the commission members planned to tax certain commercial activities and consumer goods, notably wine and fish. In exchange, they requested certain royal favors, such as the appropriation by the Junta of taxes paid to the Crown for the export of iron (traditionally, the mines were part of the royal or seigniorial patrimony) for a ten-year period. These agreements were met with much popular discontent because the new taxes affected basic food products whose prices were already too high as a result of monetary policies previously enacted by the Crown.

The Crown's attempts to raise additional funds did not cease here, for in 1630 new taxes on commerce were decreed, and this time the peasants were required to make donations in silver coin instead of the traditional transactional coin (*moneda de vellón*), which had less monetary value. It was under these circumstances that in 1631 the Junta authorized a new military draft, a tax on salt, and a "gracious" donation. The new measures incited great popular turmoil because salt was a basic ingredient in the preservation of fish, and fish was an essential part of the Basque diet.

In October 1632, a mutiny against the new taxes erupted in Vizcaya. The mutineers, in most cases people of humble circumstance, initially presented to the city of Bilbao, in Vizcaya, a document demanding the suppression of taxes affecting commerce. As time passed, however, the movement became more radical, and the rebels began to question even Vizcaya's system of government. In particular, they demanded a more representative system, one that would not deny the propertyless election to the Junta. Upon learning of these demands, the small merchants, who until then had supported the rebels, withdrew their support and petitioned the King to restore order, punish the leaders of the rebellion, and suppress the salt tax and various other taxes on commerce. In May 1634, six leaders of the movement were captured and sentenced to death. In this same year, the King decreed an amnesty and a tax reduction.[4]

The event symbolizes the acquiescing character of the Junta General when confronted with the King's demands. Fernández de Pinedo explains it in this way:[5]

> The unanimity with which the Junta accepted the new and repeated demands by the King reflects the role this nobility played within the Spanish monarchy. The Basque Country was a poor region; the non-inheriting offspring of aristocratic families had to become merchants, priests, military officers, or, more often, bureaucrats at the Court. In Madrid, they constituted an important and compact group, and much of their income depended upon the Royalty. Thus when asked for money by the King, the provincial Juntas barely complained: they had to please the King, especially since it would be the peasants, fishermen, and merchants who would pay, and not the representatives who approved the donation.

Contrasts in the Catalan and Basque Rebellions

In both the Catalan case and the Basque case, it was the popular sectors that led the rebellion against the Crown. In the Basque Country, however, the Crown received the support of the local notables, whereas in Catalonia the local leaders opposed the King's demands. As the preceding chapter showed, there was greater commonality of interests between the Basque elite and the Crown than between the Catalan elite and the Crown. This disparity explains the different behaviors of the two elite groups in the two situations just described.[6]

The War of Succession (1702–13)

Although the Spanish Crown managed in the end to appease both the Basques and the Catalans, it failed to increase the financial contribution of either area. It would take Spain more than a hundred years to eliminate the political and jurisdictional obstacles that had allowed the Catalans and the Basques to avoid contributing to the Spanish treasury in proportion to their relative wealth. Of the two regions, Catalonia, after the War of Succession of 1713, was the first to be fully integrated into the Spanish state.

The Treaty of Munster, by which the United Provinces gained independence, and the Treaty of the Pyrenees, which sealed the Spanish-French border in the Pyrenees, merely signaled the onset of the Spanish Empire's decline. In the years that followed, France became a major European power, steadily depriving Spain of each of its possessions beyond the Pyrenees and repeatedly trying to capture an outraged Catalonia.

In Spain, there was economic and political chaos. Philip IV died in 1665 and was succeeded by the physically and mentally unfit Charles II (1665–1700), who during his reign allowed others to rule and was routinely manipulated by various cliques. Spain became a pawn in the hands of foreign powers, who, realizing that Charles would die heirless, put forward different candidates to his succession.

Thus although Charles II, in his last will, offered the Crown to Louis XIV's grandson, Philip of Anjou, the Archduke Charles, son of the Austrian Emperor, also claimed the inheritance of the Crown, with the backing of England and the Netherlands. The dispute would be resolved only on the battlefield, soon after Charles's death, when Philip of Anjou, who had become Philip V of Spain, was forced to defend his rights against the alliance that had supported the Archduke Charles. The war, begun in 1702, ended in 1713, when a series of shifts in international alliances facilitated Philip's victory. The Treaty of Utrecht, signed in 1713, certified not only Philip's victory but also the demise of Spain's European Empire. Henceforth, the Spanish kings ruled over an empire that included only Spain and its American and Asian possessions.

An indirect consequence of the war was that Catalonia was stripped of its political institutions and fully integrated into the Spanish state. Although political centralization had been a paramount goal of the Spanish kings since the early seventeenth century, the immediate impetus for Philip's stripping of Catalonia's political autonomy was that Catalans had taken Archduke Charles' side during the War of Succession. They had done so fearful of French centralism and resentful toward the French because of their repeated attempts to invade Catalonia in previous years. One year after the signing of the Treaty of Utrecht, Catalonia surrendered to Philip, who then enacted the decree known as the Decreto de Nueva Planta as part of the peace agreements. This decree imposed upon Catalonia both Castilian laws and the official use of the Castilian language,[7] the removal of customs barriers between Catalonia and the rest of Spain, and the military occupation of Catalonia by the Spanish army. The Castilian fiscal system, however, was not implemented in Catalonia; rather, a single tax contribution was decreed for each of the three Aragonese kingdoms, each contribution proportional to the resources of that kingdom.

Thus, by 1716, Spain was considerably more centralized and, relieved of the cost of empire, it now collected its revenue from a much wider territorial base, one that included the now prosperous Catalonia. In all, there were good reasons to anticipate the economic recovery experienced by Spain during the eighteenth century. Full centralization, however, had not yet been achieved. Both the Basque provinces and Navarre retained their autonomy, their particular laws (Fueros), and their institutions, and they remained tax-exempt—perhaps as rewards for the support they had given Philip during the War of Succession.

The Virtues and Costs of Incorporation

This chapter has shown that in the period preceding capitalist industrialization the Basque elites had established more cordial relationships with the Spanish Crown than did the Catalan elites, chiefly because the Basque merchants and nobility depended so heavily on opportunities offered by the Spanish Crown. With the exception of their iron reserves, which afforded them commerce with other Spanish regions and other countries but did not become a valued asset until the final quarter of the nineteenth century, the Basque provinces were a small and relatively resourceless region. Not even their privileged location on the Bay of Biscay, the chief reason for Castile's interest in this area, gave Vizcaya and Guipúzcoa significant bargaining power. Castile needed an exit to the sea in the north, for access to the Northern European markets, but Bilbao and San Sebastián were by no means the only choices available; the nearby Castilian port of Santander offered many of the same possibilities. There is indeed evidence that Castile used Santander to threaten Basque interests during the eighteenth century, when Castile began to authorize free trade with America from certain northern ports. In 1778, for example, the Crown authorized shipments to America from Santander, to the detriment of Basque commerce and industry, in order to pressure the Basque provinces into surrendering some of their autonomy.

The Catalan case is different. Catalonia, as an independent political entity and hegemonic power in the Crown of Aragón, had developed a commercial mini-empire across the Mediterranean in the period preceding the Great Plague of the fourteenth century. From a sociological viewpoint, the major consequence of this apogee was the development of a culturally and politically conscious bourgeoisie. Though established in Barcelona, this group maintained close ties with the Catalan countryside, which provided much of the goods traded in the Mediterranean markets. The leading Catalan groups aspired to remain independent and to regain their own economic power without surrendering their autonomy. This stance proved to be highly disadvantageous, for it denied them some of the advantages the Basques enjoyed, such as full trading rights with America and influence at the Court.

Nevertheless, traditionally, it had more sense for the class-conscious Catalan elite to resist full integration into the centralized Spanish state than it had for the Basques: their territory was larger and their economic resources greater (Vilar shows that by the end of the sixteenth century the Catalans were already recovering from the crisis of the fourteenth-century). Further, the Catalans paid a heavy price for their incorporation into the Spanish state structure, for in the process they lost their elaborate political and juridical institutional structure, one that had provided them ample bureaucratic career opportunities. There is evidence suggesting that many members of the Catalan ruling classes favored integration into Spain during the seventeenth and eighteenth centuries, because of the commercial advantages it offered. But the sentiment was not unanimous, as it had been in the Basque Country.

In summary, whereas the Basque bourgeoisie and intelligentsia emerged as a result of incorporation into Spain, the emergence of the Catalan bourgeoisie and intelligentsia preceded incorporation; and whereas the viability of the Basque bourgeoisie and intelligentsia was almost inconceivable without integration into Spain, the same cannot be said of Catalonia. One might argue that the different attitudes of the two elites toward Spain were shaped by these structural conditions, but it is equally apparent that their attitudes were intensified by the passage of time. As Basque merchants and nobles participated increasingly in Spanish economic and political affairs, they developed political connections and networks of relationships that probably strengthened their commitment to Spain. As Catalan merchants and nobles faced exclusion both from trade opportunities in America and from political influence, and as their own political activities and networks of relationships came to be centered in Catalonia, their commitment to Catalonia may also have increased.

The different involvement of Basques and Catalans in the Spanish economy and finances, on the eve of the economic and political transformations leading to the emergence of nationalism in the Basque Country and Catalonia, can be seen in data recently collected for a doctoral dissertation on the Madrid economic and financial elite.[8] Analyzing the regional origin of

Madrid's merchants during the period 1750–1850, Jesús Cruz shows that 62 percent of these merchants (124) came from either the Basque Country or the neighboring province of Santander, whereas only 2 percent (3) came from Catalonia or Aragón. During the same period, 57 percent (13) of Madrid's bankers came from what the author calls the North region (Basque Country, Navarre, Rioja), whereas none originated in Catalonia. It is clear that ties between Basques and the Spanish economy (Basque bankers were in Madrid because the state administration was the major borrower) were stronger than those established by the Catalans. Cruz stresses that these in-migrants formed close-knit communities that identified strongly with their communities of origin; that sense, however, was perfectly compatible with their defense of state interests, when necessary, and with their adoption of Castilian culture.

Part II of this book analyzes the influence of industrialization on the Basque and Catalan elites' attitudes toward nationalism, and on the distinctive character of nationalism in the two regions. It is important to stress, however, that history predisposed the Basque elites to an antinationalist (pro-Crown) feeling when pursuing their own interests, whereas it predisposed Catalan elites to a more nationalistic outlook.

PATTERNS OF DEVELOPMENT AND NATIONALISM BEFORE THE CIVIL WAR

Although distinctive cultures and languages and different histories of political autonomy facilitated the development of the particular nationalisms of the Basque Country and Catalonia, and provided the raw materials for the "invention" of the Basque and Catalan nations, they do not explain the timing of these nationalist movements. For that, we must look to the ideological imports from beyond Iberia that helped to engender a nationalist discourse during the nineteenth century.[1] The influence of these imports is revealed in the references that Basque and Catalan nationalist ideologues made to foreign philosophers (e.g. Herder) who had written on the national question, or to nationalist movements themselves, elsewhere in Europe. The immediate factors, however, that led to the emergence of the Basque and Catalan nationalist movements and shaped their character, were the political and economic transformations that took place in the two regions during this period. These transformations, and their contribution to the emergence and character of Basque and Catalan nationalism, are the focus of the second part of this book.

Contrary to what scholars in the Relative Deprivation theory tradition (e.g. Modernization theory and the theory of Internal Colonialism) and other theoretical traditions would predict,[2] nationalism in Spain burgeoned in its most developed areas, the Basque Country and Catalonia, not in its least developed areas, such as Galicia. This finding is more consistent with Overdevelopment theory. For Nairn, for instance, *uneven* development is the primary explanation of nationalism and, therefore, peripheral nationalism is as likely in overdeveloped as in underdeveloped peripheral areas.[3] Nairn sees uneven regional development as an inevitable outcome of capitalist expansion, an outcome that leads inevitably to peripheral nationalism wherever regional inequalities coincide or overlap with ethnic differentiation.[4] Like

Linz and Douglass,[5] Nairn posits that having imperial possessions keeps states from seeing a need to build national identities, or to pursue thorough-going centralization, largely because they are able to extract large revenues from their colonies. According to these authors, so long as empires last and, as such, do not weigh too heavily on the peripheral regions of the core state, the peripheral regions tend to accept subordination to the core. But when empires begin to unravel, the peripheries rebel against the new financial, political, juridical, and military demands imposed by the core.

Nairn emphasizes the role of uneven development as a mobilizing force when state membership no longer presents advantages. In underdeveloped regions nationalist movements mobilize the population to demand an end to ethnic economic inequality, while in overdeveloped regions nationalist movements mobilize the population to demand state reforms that will pro-mote still further regional development.[6]

The Spanish case fits Nairn's explanation well. The rise of Basque and Catalan nationalism was in part an indirect consequence of Spain's loss of its chief imperial possessions. The impact of that loss should not be overempha-sized, however, for it cannot account for the programmatic features of the two nationalist movements. Neither Nairn nor other authors in the Overde-velopment tradition can explain, for example, the separatist and traditional-ist character of early Basque nationalism, which differed so dramatically from the procapitalist and generally nonseparatist character of Catalan national-ism.[7] Only the Catalan case fits his expectations about the character of nationalism in an overdeveloped region.

More generally, differences in the character of Basque nationalism and Catalan nationalism also reveal the limitations of previous sociological work on the relationship between economic development and nationalism (e.g. Relative Deprivation theory, Overdevelopment theory, Ethnic Competition theory, the Cost-Benefit approach). None of these theories can suffice here, since both regions were overdeveloped, highly dependent on Spain, and characterized by similar levels of ethnic competition.

To account for the distinction between the two regional nationalisms, I stress the role of class interests in mediating the effects of development on nationalist mobilization. I also analyze how development processes shaped Basque and Catalan nationalism by creating constellations of class and ethnic interests that determined both center-periphery relations and class relations within the two regions. But unlike previous work on the relationship between development and nationalism, I stress *patterns* of development rather than *levels* of development. My explanation pays particular attention to two contrasts: that between combined development and endogenous devel-opment and that between capital-goods development and consumer-goods development.

The concept of *combined development* rests on the coexistence, within a country or region, of an advanced and highly concentrated industrial sector and an economy that remains largely traditional.[8] This dual economic structure is typical of industrial latecomers, where capitalist development is induced by the state and by financial and foreign investment, and it leads to the rise of a small but economically powerful capitalist class (generally linked to the capital-goods production sector) that maintains strong ties to the state. The development of this small capitalist class precedes and stunts the formation of a commercial and industrial bourgeoisie. It also sweeps away various preindustrial social groups, such as small-scale manufacturers and artisans, and leads to the rapid proletarianization of the peasantry.

Endogenous development, by contrast, stems from capital accumulated in agriculture, which is then invested in industry. This pattern, which generally takes form over a longer time span than does combined development, facilitates the emergence of a large bourgeois class and the gradual integration of preindustrial classes, including the peasantry, into the process of capitalist industrialization.

The character of capitalist development, however, whether endogenous or combined, is not the only factor influencing the social structures that developed in the Basque Country and Catalonia, nor does it explain the different roles played by different social groups in the development of Basque and Catalan nationalism. We need also to examine the main industrial sectors in which the two regions specialized.

General accounts of European economic development have shown that industrialization moved through two major initial phases: consumer-goods industrialization (mostly textile production) and capital-goods industrialization (mostly the production of iron and steel).[9] How these two sectors developed and where they found their financing depended on whether they took root in economically advanced, moderately backward, or extremely backward countries.

The textile industry, with small capital requirements, did not depend on investment by banks, the state, or foreigners for its development, and its rise was thus not conducive to the emergence of a powerful banking system. The textile industries of the latecomers to industrialization (e.g. Spain) differed from those of the early industrializing countries (e.g. England) in tending to be less competitive in foreign markets, and their leading organizations, in response, developed much more protectionist demands.

The steel industry, historically, required large sums of capital for its expansion. In Great Britain, capital was supplied by industry itself, thanks to the profits accumulated during the preceding phase of industrial development.[10] Latecomers, however, because of the later development and modest initial scale of their textile industries, relied to a greater extent on the banking system (e.g. Germany) or on the state (e.g. Russia). New types of banks, the "mobilier," which made only long-term loans and investment, and the "general" bank, which both lent and invested, acquired a pivotal role in these late-developing economies, promoting the initiation and concentration of the steel sector and other sectors of the capital-goods industry.[11] Although there was a good deal of interpenetration between banking and industry, through interlocking directorates, this relationship cannot be described, in general terms, as one of domination of "industrialists" by "bankers," but rather as one of institutional domination of industry by the banking sector.[12]

In the second part of this book I give priority to the effects of the social-structural context on the character of Basque and Catalan nationalism. For despite superficial similarities in the two regions (e.g. level of development, arrival of large number of immigrants), their patterns of development and resulting social structures differed demonstrably. I demonstrate the relevance of the combined/endogenous and capital goods/consumer goods dichotomies for Basque and Catalan nationalism. While the Basque Country experienced combined development based on the capital-goods sector, Catalonia experienced endogenous development based on the consumer-goods sector. I show that the effects of these distinct patterns on nationalism were mediated by three factors: the extent to which traditional societies were able to benefit from capitalist development; the strength of the ties established by emerging capitalist elites with the state's economy and polity; and the relative size and political autonomy of the local bourgeoisie.

CHAPTER 3

Capitalist Industrialization

Traditional explanations of Basque nationalism have emphasized the disruptive effects of modernization in the Basque Country. Explanations of Catalan nationalism, meanwhile, have emphasized the frustration of the Catalan bourgeoisie over the policies that consistently denied them serious influence on state policy. But these observations do not explain why modernization was less disruptive in Catalonia than it was in the Basque Country, or why the Basque bourgeoisie were less frustrated than were the Catalan bourgeoisie. Those who have pointed out that the Basque capitalist elite maintained closer ties with the Spanish state than did the Catalan capitalist elite have failed to show why that should be so. Scholars have focused too much on the role of capitalist elites in the rise of nationalism in the two regions, too little on the role of the local bourgeoisies (the latter defined as the segment of the bourgeoisie whose economic and social horizons were largely bounded by the community's limits). In sum, although these traditional explanations are not incorrect, they are incomplete. In seeking to address these shortcomings, this chapter analyzes the patterns of economic development in the Basque Country and Catalonia during the nineteenth century and the early years of the twentieth century. It focuses on the timing, the pace, and the intensity of development in the two regions, and on the economic sectors in which each region specialized. It also analyzes the different social structures that developed in Catalonia and the Basque Country, and the ties that the socioeconomic elites established with the Spanish economy and polity. The different patterns of development and the different social structures thus engendered contributed to the creation of two different political dynamics and two different nationalist projects.

The Collapse of the Spanish Old Regime

In 1808, French troops commanded by General Murat crossed the Pyrenees with the apparent goal of cutting Portugal off from England, thus strengthening Napoleon's continental blockade. King Charles IV seemed unperturbed by the French presence in Spanish territory, but the Spanish people, not sharing his sentiments, forced his abdication in March, following the Mutiny of Aranjuez, on May 2 and demonstrated violently against the French troops in the streets of Madrid. Spanish volunteers, aided militarily by better organized British troops, fought the invader for almost five years, combining guerrilla warfare with open combat. The war in Spain ended when Napoleon, hard-pressed to strengthen the Russian front, chose to withdraw from Spain.

Behind the battle lines, important political developments were unfolding. Provincial resistance organizations, called the Juntas provinciales, formed throughout Spain and called for a special parliamentary session to be held in Cádiz, for the purpose of writing a new constitution. The deputies who gathered in Cádiz for the first time in 1810 were mostly liberal priests and members of the intelligentsia and the military. Imbued as they were with the ideals of the French Revolution, they proclaimed national sovereignty, sought to move forward in administrative centralization, created a conscript army, and abolished the Inquisition. The Cádiz legislators also decreed reforms concerned with fostering industrial development. In particular, they suppressed the monopoly over production so long enjoyed by guilds, and removed restrictions on industrial activity.

Arguably the most important decision made by the Cortes de Cádiz was to initiate the de-entailment of the land—the termination of various practices that withheld land from general use. Population and production increases during the eighteenth century had led to land scarcity and to rising land prices. Land had become a coveted commodity for poor laborers, rich landowners, and the commercial bourgeoisie, whose members were either repatriating capital from America or, in the context of the trade disruption created by the Napoleonic wars, seeking more profitable investments.

At that time a very large portion of productive Spanish land was off the market, owned by absentee landlords not interested in increasing its productivity. One kind of entailed property, the Mayorazgos, was a common-law institution dating back to the fourteenth century. An important source of rent for their owners, the Mayorazgos were transmitted undivided from generation to generation. A second group of entailed properties belonged to the Church. The Church's patrimony had increased since the time of the Catholic Kings, and canonic law prevented the placement of Church property on the land market. Finally, municipalities owned very extensive properties that were either leased or exploited as communal land. The lack of a market for land discouraged investment to raise land productivity above its very low levels.

Given this scarcity of land, it is not surprising that the bourgeoisie urged the de-entailment of land, and their demands were met with sympathy by reform-minded administrators who saw that nationalizing entailed land and selling it back to private owners would be a potentially substantial source of revenue.

The measures adopted by the Cortes de Cádiz represented only the first attempt to dismantle the Old Regime in Spain, and right from the start they encountered trouble. Upon his return from exile, Ferdinand VII, son and heir of King Charles IV, reverted to absolutism for most of his reign, revoking the Cádiz legislation. The ensuing struggle between liberals and absolutists, spanning two-thirds of the nineteenth century, was shaped by both internal factors and international pressure, and resulted in an endless succession of governments and two civil wars (1833–40; 1872–76).

The Road to Industrialization in Catalonia

Catalonia's industrial transformation began to take root in the eighteenth century, earlier than in most Spanish regions. Its economic growth resulted primarily from the combination of agrarian development with the full integration of Catalonia into the Spanish state.

In 1716, in the wake of the War of Succession that brought the Bourbon royal dynasty to Spain, Catalonia was fully incorporated into Spain by the Decreto de Nueva Planta.[1] Full integration vastly increased the market for Catalan producers, for Catalonia was able now to participate more directly in trade with the rest of Spain and with the colonies of Latin America.

Catalonia had the resources it would need in seeking to benefit from the new trading opportunities. The most important of these resources were agrarian wealth and low population density. The Sentencia de Guadalupe, enacted by Ferdinand of Aragón in the sixteenth century to eliminate seigniorial abuses and to grant freedom of movement to the peasantry, had favored the development of a prosperous peasantry in Catalonia.[2] Although peasants were not the sole owners of their land, seigniorial rights were sufficiently restricted, and land-tenure contracts sufficiently permanent, to encourage investments in productivity. Indeed, because of low population densities, the seigniors reaped greater benefits from promoting increases in land productivity than from land speculation based on periodic rent increases. Low population densities also favored the development of mid-sized farms from which great numbers of peasants were able to extract pro-

duce sufficient not only for the payment of rents and for their own suste-
nance, but also for the market.[3]

The development of a commercial agriculture in Catalonia can be traced
back to the eighteenth century. In response to growing demographic pressure on land resources, many landless peasants rented marginal land from
more prosperous tenants and began to occupy unpopulated lands close to
the Catalan coast. It was in these newly cultivated lands that, encouraged by
commercial opportunities in Latin America, peasants planted vineyards and
specialized in the production of wine and eau-de-vie (brandy) for export,
under increasingly capitalistic forms and relations of production.[4]

For two centuries, eau-de-vie and, later, wine were the chief Catalan
exports, and Latin America was their biggest market. This export-oriented
economy encouraged the development of a dynamic commercial sector, a
thriving shipbuilding industry, and, from the early 1800s, a modern textile
industry.

Throughout this period, the Catalan countryside prospered. The peasantry
now had the means to buy manufactured products and sufficient capital to
invest in commercial and industrial activities. Sensing this rising demand for
manufactured products, and looking for ways to break with the strict guild-
production regulations of the cities, merchants promoted the production of
wool textiles in the countryside. Raw wool, purchased in Aragón and
Castile, was processed in rural areas and then sold in rural and urban markets
at prices lower than those of goods produced under the guild system.
Although merchants played a major role in these innovations, peasant households were not passive participants; the inheritance system prevailing in Catalonia facilitated the direct transfer of capital from the countryside to the city,
and from agriculture to commerce and industry. This system was one of
impartible inheritance (inherited parcels could not be partitioned), whereby
those who did not inherit land—the "fradristerns"—received an economic
compensation. As peasant households prospered throughout the eighteenth
century, the value of these economic compensations increased, and fradristerns were able to invest them in urban commercial or industrial activities.
This process ensured a relatively fluid transition from a rural to an urban
society and favored the development of a cultural and economic affinity
between rural and urban Catalonia. In the nineteenth century many members of the Catalan high bourgeoisie proudly claimed to descend from peasant families.[5]

The textile industry, whose development is also owed to the preexistence
of a proto-industrial urban sector, was the backbone of Catalan industrialization.[6] From the 1830s to the 1850s the Catalan textile industry underwent a
technological revolution that raised it to European standards. This progress
is indicated by Catalonia's index of industrial production, which trebled

between 1840 and 1860. By 1860, the Catalan textile industry had captured about 80% of the Spanish textiles market, and in that same year, when Catalonia constituted 11% of the Spanish population, the value of its production represented 13% of the Spanish GDP (see Table 1).

The growth potential of this dynamic sector was limited, however, by the modest strength of the Spanish market and by high production costs, which curtailed the ability of Catalan industry to compete abroad. In 1856, for instance, industrialists suggested that English production was 90% cheaper than Catalan production.[7] Catalan competitiveness was hindered by the need to import coal and by the relatively high cost of labor, brought on by the high price of grain and, in turn, bread. To solve these problems, Catalans embarked on an ambitious project of investment in railroad construction, with two goals in mind: to connect textile areas to the only place in Catalonia where producers hoped to find abundant coal (San Juan de las Abadesas), and to improve communication between the Spanish interior and Catalonia, thereby reducing the cost of importing Castilian grain for bread and, consequently, the cost of labor. The crisis of the 1860s revealed the failure of this approach. The mines in San Juan de las Abadesas were not the promised Eldorado, the price of bread remained high, and the railroad companies in which Catalans had invested went bankrupt.[8] Most authors concur that the financial crisis that afflicted Catalonia in 1866 signaled the end of the Catalan bourgeoisie's aspirations in the world market. It also marked its shift toward a conservative stance aimed at closing the Spanish market to foreign penetration—in consequence of which the Catalan capitalist sector came to depend on protectionist legislation enacted by the Spanish government.

Table 1. Gross domestic product, population, and gross domestic product per capita for the Basque Country and for Catalonia, 1800–1930

	Basque Country			Catalonia		
Year	GDP	Population (millions)	GDP/capita	GDP	Population (millions)	GDP/capita
1800	2.0	2.7	0.7	8.3	8.1	1.0
1860	3.0	2.7	1.1	13.3	10.7	1.2
1900	4.0	3.2	1.3	16.3	10.6	1.5
1920	4.8	3.6	1.3	18.7	10.8	1.7
1930	5.4	3.7	1.5	21.4	11.4	1.9

Note: These are estimates made by Albert Carreras "La producción industrial Catalana y Vasca" (1985). Accurate absolute estimates are not yet available.

In Carreras's tables, GDP and population are expressed as proportions of the total for Spain. The GDP/capita included in his tables is, therefore, only an approximation, with no real substantive meaning. At the same time, however, the ratio between the GDP/capita for one of the regions and that for the other gives an exact measurement of the *difference* between their GDP/capita figures.

Apart from periodic reductions in the level of import tariffs (significant cuts in these tariffs were operative during the 1870s and 1880s), the Catalan textile industry remained protected for the entire period preceding the Spanish Civil War.[9]

The Establishment of Iron-Based Industry
in the Basque Country

At the outset of the nineteenth century, the Basque provinces seemed to be less poised for economic development than were other Spanish regions. With almost 3% of the Spanish population in 1800, the Basque Country produced only 2% of the Spanish GDP and was one of the poorest regions in Spain.[10] This condition reflected the limits of Basque agriculture as well as the commercial and industrial crises created by the Napoleonic Wars, by the loss of the Latin American colonies, and by the loss of markets for iron owing to more competitive Northern European production.

In the following decades, the Basque commercial bourgeoisie followed different strategies to adjust to these new realities. It made low-risk investments in public debt and real estate, lobbied for the privatization of mining, took steps to mechanize iron production, and favored the transfer of customs houses, traditionally located on the border between Castile and the Basque provinces, to the coast. These transformations were so successful that between 1800 and 1860 the Basque Country's GDP increased faster than that of any other region except Madrid and Catalonia.[11] The Basque commercial bourgeoisie had succeeded in redirecting its economic activity, thereby establishing the foundation for a smooth, ordered transition to industrial capitalism.

Unlike development in Catalonia, however, development in the Basque Country was of the combined sort. In the Basque Country, development in commerce and industry proceeded despite crisis in the agricultural sector, and even at the expense of agriculture. Whereas Catalan capitalist development was initiated in part by broad segments of the peasantry, Basque capitalist development brought great harm to the peasantry.[12] Land speculation and the privatization of municipal land and of mining, in particular, resulted in the concentration of landholdings. As a result, the proportion of peasant households in Vizcaya occupied by landowners, about 60% in 1704, had already declined to less than 30% by the early decades of the nineteenth century.[13] The harmful effects of modernization fostered deep unrest among the Basque peasantry. (The political implications of these developments are analyzed in the next chapter.)

The 1856 discovery of the Bessemer process, for the production of steel by the "direct method," revolutionized the iron industry. The Bessemer process, which allowed for the production of iron at very low cost and in very large quantities, required the exclusive use of hematites, with very low phosphoric content, which were more abundant and closer to the surface in the Basque Country than almost anywhere else in Europe. The immense international demand that followed created great incentives for both improvements in mining infrastructure and the elimination of tariffs.[14] As a result of the increased demand, iron production skyrocketed: in the five-year period between 1866 and 1870, the number of tons of iron ore extracted was double that of the previous five-year period.

Mining in the Basque Country was rapidly colonized, however, as it was in the rest of Spain.[15] The transportation and export of iron were in the hands of foreigners, and two of the three largest producers, the Orconera and the Franco-Belge companies, were also foreign-owned. Between 1876 and 1898, as a result of these high levels of colonization, foreigners captured between 40% and 66% of the sector's profits.[16] Although it is impossible to estimate the actual amount of these benefits, even the lower estimate indicates unequivocally a tremendous presence of foreign capital in the Basque Country.

The only area where indigenous dominance was undeniable was mine ownership. Two official state measures supported local ownership: the special provisions that had granted exclusive rights to Basque miners until 1841, and a prohibition on exporting iron ore that persisted until 1863. These measures directly benefited a very small number of capitalist firms—nine or ten, largely Basque—which gained control over 66% of the capital accumulated by Spanish miners. These firms were, in turn, controlled by a slightly greater number of families.

Although iron-ore exports were controlled almost entirely by foreign interests, they generated an extensive economic activity in the Basque Country itself. The spillover effect of mining activity on other sectors was almost immediate, attracting the investment of Basque and Spanish capital in other vertically or horizontally related activities.[17] Unlike mining, all of these activities, including the steel industry, metallurgy, and naval construction, were controlled by Spanish, typically Basque, investors. The nascent Basque industries, like the Catalan industries, needed protection; because they lacked a cheap source of coal, which they increasingly imported from England, rather than from neighboring Asturias, their industrial products were too expensive to compete in foreign markets. But despite these structural problems, between 1860 and 1930 the Basque GDP grew faster than that of any other Spanish region, from 3% of the Spanish GDP to 5% (see Table 1).

This spectacular rate of industrial growth had dramatic social consequences. For whereas an almost minuscule group within the traditional Basque commercial and landowning elites benefited, most commercial capi-

talists, iron producers, and big landowners were completely displaced by foreign capitalists. The displaced preindustrial elites would later form a political
alliance with the disgruntled peasantry, and, together, they would reject the
whole modernization project.

Patterns of Development and Bourgeois Segmentation

We see here two very different patterns of development: endogenous,
based on consumer-goods production, in Catalonia; and combined, based
on capital-goods production, in the Basque Country. In analyzing the two,
my primary source has been the 1922 Directory of Spanish Corporations and
Financial Institutions. Since by 1922 the corporation had already become a
major institution in both Catalan society and Basque society, the Directory
provides a good approximation of the essential differences in economic
structure between the two regions.[18]

The information in this directory shows that in overall strength, Basque
capitalism and Catalan capitalism were very similar: accumulated nominal
assets throughout Catalan and Basque corporations and financial institutions
amounted to approximately the same figure (see Table 2). Moreover, in both
communities, the number of very large companies (with nominal assets
above 10 million pesetas) was about the same: 49 in the Basque Country and
41 in Catalonia. Finally, the Basque Country and Catalonia, along with
Madrid, were Spain's leading capitalist communities at the time. Indeed,
among the 200 largest Spanish corporations, 55 were Basque and 50 were
Catalan. Exchanging economic power for political power and ennoblement,

Table 2. Distribution by nominal assets of Basque and Catalan corporations, 1922

Ntile capital	Nominal assets, Basque Country	Cumulative percent of Basque capital they represent	Nominal assets, Catalonia	Cumulative percent of Catalan capital they represent
10%	100,000	.109	10,000	.027
20%	229,000	.450	25,000	.110
30%	350,600	1.088	60,000	.312
40%	524,500	2.170	100,000	.720
50%	1,000,000	3.876	250,000	1.540
60%	1,500,000	6.383	500,000	3.435
70%	2,500,000	10.707	800,000	6.064
80%	4,363,194	18.457	1,500,000	10.800
90%	10,000,000	32.651	3,500,000	21.062
		Total accumulated assets		
	2,342,054,947		2,367,928,087	

Source: Ibáñez and Gardóqui, *Anuario Financiero y de Sociedades Anónimas* (1922).

many owners of the largest corporations were steadily incorporated into the Spanish power bloc, which included the most powerful members of the landed aristocracy, forming what Moya has called the "financial aristocracy."[19]

Beyond these similarities, however, the Basque and Catalan capitalist structures differed in important ways. The distribution of corporations by size, for example, was very different in the two communities, for capital was far more concentrated in the Basque Country than it was in Catalonia (see Table 2). Moreover, as Table 3 shows, the average corporation size in Catalonia in 1922 was half that in the Basque Country.

An analysis of variance included in this table demonstrates that only 11% of this difference in corporation size can be explained by the different economic specializations of the Basque and Catalan corporations. The remaining variance depends on the relative average size of Basque and Catalan corporations within sectors of the economy. These data provide overwhelming support for the assertion that, before the Civil War, small-firm capitalism characterized Catalan development while large-firm capitalism characterized Basque development. One can see, for instance, that even in the leading sector of Catalan industrialization, the textile sector, Basque corporations had more capital assets than did Catalan corporations.

What better describes the contrast between Basque and Catalan capitalism, however, is the average size of Basque and Catalan financial institutions (see Table 3). This comparison simultaneously reveals the difference in economic power of the two capitalist elites. In 1922, there were 99 financial institutions in Catalonia compared with 23 in the Basque Country, but cumulative nominal assets in these institutions were 21% greater in the Basque Country than in Catalonia. The importance of these banks—in injecting Basque capitalism into the rest of Spain, in enhancing the lobbying power of Basque capitalists, and in promoting the development of other economic sectors—cannot be overstated. Maluquer de Motes has noted, for instance, the decisive role that Basque banks played in the development of the electrical sector.[20] By the 1920s and 1930s, electric companies subordinated to the Banco de Bilbao (e.g. Saltos del Duero) and to the Banco de Vizcaya (e.g. Hidroeléctrica Española) controlled most of the Spanish market. Meanwhile, in Catalonia, the largest commercial electric companies were controlled by foreign capital, and many textile mills generated their own electricity on a small scale.

In sum, since one can assume that in early twentieth-century Spain the levels of capital concentration and economic specialization were indicators of the strength of involvement in the Spanish market, Basque capitalism was clearly more oriented toward the rest of Spain than was Catalan capitalism. Thus whereas in both communities there was a strong high bourgeoisie, the relative weight of the local bourgeoisie was much greater in Catalonia than

Table 3. Mean corporation assets by region and sector, 1922 (in pesetas)

	Mean	Mean after adjusting for composition by sector	N
Basque Country	4,495,307.0	4,337,257.6	521
Catalonia	2,182,422.2	2,258,315.0	1,085
Grand mean:	2,932,741.603		

	Mean corporation assets (pesetas) (with number of corporations)	
Sector	Basque Country	Catalonia
Agriculture	556,900.1	715,255.1
	(8)	(32)
Mining	2,975,588.1	2,148,671.5
	(109)	(67)
Water, gas, electricity	6,807,635.6	7,361,386.4
	(44)	(83)
Food, beverages, tobacco	1,665,893.9	1,580,627.2
	(33)	(114)
Textiles	2,277,500.0	1,883,312.0
	(9)	(83)
Leather, clothes, shoes	383,750.0	394,122.3
	(4)	(47)
Paper, printing, graphic arts	3,014,685.7	411,991.3
	(35)	(46)
Chemical	8,259,749.6	940,275.0
	(20)	(100)
Ceramics, glass, cement	1,896,666.7	1,161,625.0
	(12)	(16)
Steel	31,750,000.0	2,000,000.0
	(6)	(3)
Metallurgy	2,136,678.9	867,122.49
	(74)	(206)
Construction	1,229,354.8	1,132,916.7
	(31)	(36)
Transport, communication	4,924,769.7	4,831,256.5
	(92)	(90)
Commerce	0.0	3,367,777.8
	(0)	(9)
Financial	21,485,000.0	4,337,500.1
	(20)	(83)
Hotels and similar	1,950,000.0	1,248,916.7
	(3)	(6)
Diverse services	859,772.7	437,608.7
	(11)	(46)
Foreign banks	0.0	1,589,597.6
	(0)	(8)
Foreign mining	5,843,832.0	1,260,040.0
	(10)	(10)

Source: Ibáñez and Gardóqui, *Anuario Financiero y de Sociedades Anónimas* (1922).
Note: Branches of the Bank of Spain have not been included.

in the Basque Country. Similarly, the economic distance between groups representing capitalism and groups representing traditional society was much greater in the Basque Country than in Catalonia.

The fact that major capital owners still tended to be members of the boards of their companies in this period (they also participated in political contests) justifies further analysis of the data contained in the 1922 Directory. In the absence of information on the place of origin of all directors, my analysis has used information on the provinces where corporations were located to compare the numbers of directors belonging to the boards of both Basque and non-Basque corporations (those outside the Basque Country) with the numbers of directors that belonged to the boards of both Catalan and non-Catalan corporations. Of 7,581 directors throughout Spain, 238 (14% of all directors in Basque companies) belonged to the boards of both Basque and non-Basque corporations, compared to just 158 (8% of all directors in Catalan companies) who belonged to the boards of both Catalan and non-Catalan corporations (see Table 4). This difference suggests that the ties between Basque and non-Basque capital in Spanish corporations were stronger than the ties between Catalan and non-Catalan capital.

To gauge somewhat better the extent to which Basque and Catalan capitalists tended to be involved in economic activities outside their regions, I have ranked separately the directors in Catalan and Basque companies according to the accumulated assets of the Catalan or Basque companies with which they were associated, and selected the top 100 directors in each of the two communities. Because of their intense involvement in Basque or Catalan economic activities, one can define these top 100 directors as Basque or Catalan, regardless of place of birth. More to the point, linking the names included on these lists with biographical information available on these persons, along with my personal knowledge of typical Catalan and Basque names, suggests that these people were indeed Basque or Catalan by ethnic-

Table 4. Distribution of directors of Spanish corporations and financial institutions, by location of corporations in which they serve, 1922

Location of corporations	Number of directors
Basque	1,474
Basque and other	238
Catalan	1,881
Catalan and other	158
Others in Spain	3,887

Note: The total number of directors is 7,581; the sum presented above does not add up to this number because 20 directors belonged to the boards of Catalan, Basque, and other Spanish corporations simultaneously and 35 belonged to the boards of Catalan and Basque corporations simultaneously.

ity as well as by intensity of economic involvement in the region. Of the top 100 directors in each of the two regions, 43 were directors in both Basque and non-Basque corporations, while only 16 were directors in both Catalan and non-Catalan corporations. Similar findings were obtained by ranking directors according to the numbers of directorships they held and selecting the top 100 in each region. In sum, support is very strong for the hypothesis that Basques were more involved in capitalist activities outside their community than were Catalans, and that Basque/non-Basque capitalist links were greater than Catalan/non-Catalan links. Further support for the hypothesis lies in the fact that, overall, the number of companies and directors in the Basque Country was much smaller than that in Catalonia.

Finally, this review of the linkages between Basque and Catalan capitalism and the rest of Spain considers the strength of the economic ties that Basque and Catalan capitalists maintained with the Spanish state apparatus, for these ties conditioned the political attitudes of Basque and Catalan capitalists toward the Spanish state. The literature shows that Basque industry depended in greater measure upon state purchases than did Catalan industry,[21] a dependence undoubtedly related to the economic sectors predominant in each community—namely, capital-goods production in the Basque Country and consumer-goods production in Catalonia. Consumers of Basque products were typically other industries or the state, whereas the main consumers of Catalan products—principally textiles—were, with the exception of army clothing, typically private individuals. During the dictatorship of Miguel Primo de Rivera (1923–1930), commercial relations between the state and Basque industry intensified because of a vast program of public works. These relations became so close that when the dictatorship collapsed in 1930 and a new finance minister decided to halt infrastructural reforms, an economic crisis in Vizcaya, more severely hit by this reversal than was any other province, immediately followed.[22]

In summary, in the period that preceded the Spanish Civil War, the Basque Country and Catalonia established themselves as the leaders of Spanish industrialization. During the process, the wealthiest Basque and Catalan capitalist families were incorporated into the Spanish power elite. The liberal aristocracy that still ruled Spain, pressed by budget needs and unwilling to conduct the necessary fiscal reforms that would increase state revenues, chose a particularistic approach that best suited its patrimonialist conception of power.[23] This approach entailed borrowing from rich capitalists who then were rewarded with noble titles and monopolistic economic concessions. A typical story is told by Pérez Regúlez, about Juan Manuel de Manzanedo y González de la Teja:[24] Of humble origins, he emigrates to Cuba, where he makes a fortune. In the 1840s he comes back to Spain, where he embarks on many industrial and financial adventures; these multiply his wealth so quickly that when speaking of a wealthy man, people begin to say "he is as wealthy as Manzanedo." Don Juan Manuel develops a reputation for generosity after donating to orphanages, founding schools, and, most important, making loans to the government that he does not bother to reclaim (e.g. 2 million pesetas during the "War of Africa" in which Spain was briefly involved). In reward for his generosity, the Crown finally names him Marquis of Manzanedo and Duke of Santoña.

Being named a marquis, however, was not an exceptional honor. Between 1874 and 1931 the Crown ennobled 214 marquis, 167 counts, 30 viscounts, and 28 barons. Among these one finds many members of Basque and Catalan families, such as the Güell in Catalonia or the Chávarri in the Basque Country. As has often been remarked about other societies, the "financial aristocracy" to which Basque and Catalan oligarchs belonged was highly endogamous.[25] Consequently, these people formed a group apart, within the bourgeoisie. Greatly involved in Spanish economic and political affairs, they generally supported the Liberal and the Conservative Monarchic parties, the two ruling parties of the period.[26]

Beyond rough similarities, however, the economic structures of the two regions differed quite substantially. Basque capital was more powerful, more concentrated, more oriented toward the rest of Spain, and more closely dependent on the Spanish state. From a sociostructural standpoint, the results of this situation were (1) the existence of a far more numerous local bourgeoisie in Catalonia than in the Basque Country and (2) the development of stronger economic linkages between Basque and non-Basque capitalism than between Catalan and non-Catalan capitalism.

To sum up, the Basque Country and Catalonia experienced very different patterns of development. Combined development based on the capital-goods sector excluded large segments of the Basque population from the benefits of capitalism and led to the emergence of a very small local bourgeoisie and a very powerful capitalist elite. Endogenous development based on the consumer-goods sector benefited large segments of the Catalan population and led to the emergence of a large bourgeois class and a capitalist elite less powerful than that of the Basque Country. These divergent patterns shaped the attitudes of the Basque and Catalan populations toward capitalist development, the levels of social cohesion within the Basque Country and Catalonia, and the ties between Spain and their respective capitalist classes. The political implications of these developments are explored in the next three chapters.

CHAPTER 4

Patterns of Development,
and Traditionalist Reaction

In Spain, as in other European countries, capitalist development and the growth of the bourgeoisie created irresolvable social tensions within the Old Regime. Conflict between liberals and absolutists, particularly intense in the Basque Country and Catalonia, spanned most of the nineteenth century and culminated in the two Carlist Wars (1833–40 and 1872–76). This chapter explains why support for Carlism was so intense in the Basque Country and Catalonia, and why it was more intense in the former than in the latter. The focus is on the triangular relations developed during this period between the emerging capitalist bourgeoisie in each community, the persisting social classes of the Old Regime, and the state. The patterns of conflict and affinity that developed between these broad social groups greatly influenced the type of nationalist movement that would eventually develop in each community.

As a basis for better understanding the Carlist Wars, the contrasts between the Basque Country and Catalonia are ideal. For although the regions shared many socioeconomic characteristics, support for Carlism remained stable between the two wars in the Basque Country but declined dramatically in Catalonia. This historical scenario is optimal for testing alternative hypotheses.

Thus far, the voluminous literature on the Carlist Wars, including Karl Marx's journalistic impressions, has explained the peculiar intensity of Carlism in the Basque Country as resulting mainly from the secularization and centralization measures undertaken by the Spanish state during the nineteenth century. Long overdue, however, is a sociological treatment of the Carlist Wars along the lines of Tilly's explanation of counterrevolution in France.

This chapter demonstrates that support for the traditionalist forces grouped around Carlism was stronger in the Basque Country than in Catalonia because development was combined in the former and endogenous in the latter.

Liberalism and Absolutism: The Basis for the Carlist Wars

The conflict between the absolutist state and the constitutional or liberal state, which pervaded the entire nineteenth century, was expressed in the Carlist Wars. Following the withdrawal of French forces from Spain, King Ferdinand VII moved swiftly toward absolutism, by nullifying the legislation that had been enacted by the Cortes de Cádiz between 1812 and 1814. The fiscal institutions of the Old Regime were inadequate, however, for solving the financial crisis faced by the restored monarchy. War-related destruction, the loss of the traditional monopoly of trade with Latin America, and the economic recession in Europe had all aggravated existing fiscal problems, and drastic reforms were demanded if state revenues were to be raised. Nevertheless, on the strength of his own convictions, and with the encouragement of the Church and the traditional elites, Ferdinand stubbornly opposed all changes in the traditional structures.

From 1814 to 1820, then, the government adopted absolutist policies that only further impoverished the taxpayers and contributed to greater popular discontent. Liberals thus had little difficulty regaining power. In 1820, after a successful insurrection, they forced King Ferdinand to reinstate the Constitution of 1812. Over the following three years, known as the Liberal Triennium, liberal legislators pursued the radical reforms they had initiated in 1812: they moved toward a constitutional monarchy, limited the economic and political power of the Church, and centralized administration.

The liberal legislators failed, however, to complement these drastic measures with reforms that would redistribute wealth in favor of the peasantry. Much of the land that was nationalized and auctioned did not change ownership, or came under capitalist ownership; holders of small and midsize properties, as well as landless peasants, rarely benefited from these sales. For farmers who rented the land they worked, the shift in ownership may even have been detrimental, since new owners tended to charge higher rents than the Church had. In sum, devoid of social policies, the liberal reforms actually harmed the peasantry, which soon became the Church's and the traditionalist elites' main ally against liberalism.

Throughout the Liberal Triennium, supporters of absolutism, known as Royalists, staged repeated uprisings. The most serious took place in Catalonia and Navarre, but there were also uprisings in Aragón and the Basque Country. The rebellions, typically led by the clergy or disenchanted army officers, and widely supported by peasants, generally arose in rural areas.

What was decisive, however, for the eventual success of the Royalists' rebellion, was foreign support. In 1822, the Congress of Vienna authorized France to form an army to assist Royalist volunteers in overthrowing Spain's liberal government. This army, popularly called the "One Hundred Thousand Sons of Saint Louis," invaded Spain in 1823 and, encountering little popular opposition, soon restored absolutism.

The remaining ten years of Ferdinand VII's reign were a repetition of the turmoil that had preceded his restoration. The experience of the 1814–20 period suggested that the fiscal crisis could be remedied only by reforms in the archaic structures of the Old Regime, but the experience of the Triennium had also demonstrated that the bulk of the Spanish population opposed radical measures devoid of social reforms. Ferdinand, under pressure from the occupying French forces, who did not want him to move too far to the right, searched for a middle road. Most indicative of this positioning were his decisions not to reestablish the Inquisition, not to purge liberals from public administration or from the army, and not to integrate the royalist volunteers into the regular army. He also relied for counsel on a mixed group of moderate royalists and moderate liberals who attempted to balance the monarchy's budget and run the Spanish economy more efficiently.

One consequence of the King's moderate approach was the alienation of sectors within the extreme Right and the extreme Left. The former berated Ferdinand for failing to restore the Church's full authority; the latter, for not going far enough in limiting the power of the Church. While the Right, supported by the peasantry, rebelled against the monarchy in rural areas, as did many Catalan peasants (known in Catalonia as the "malcontents"), leftist militants burned churches in Barcelona and other big cities. The final break between King Ferdinand and the radical royalists, or "apostólicos," occurred immediately after the rebellion of the malcontents in 1827. By then, the most traditionalist elements in the absolutist camp were already gathering around Ferdinand's brother Carlos, who claimed to be his legitimate successor and urged a traditionalist political program.

Carlos's claims to the Spanish Crown were not unfounded: after Philip V was crowned, in 1700, the French Salic Law, which denied women the right of succession to the throne, was introduced in Spain. Although King Charles IV revoked the law in 1789, it was not until 1830 that his action was made public by King Ferdinand, after his third wife, María Cristina, gave birth to their only child, Isabel. For the last three years of Ferdinand's life, the Carlist camp and the Cristino camp (named for María Cristina, who held the regency until Isabel's majority) defended their respective claims of succession. Meanwhile, María Cristina's entourage was placing trusted friends in high military and administrative positions and attempting to cut off the funding of the royalist volunteers, who were readying themselves to fight for

Carlos's claims. By the time Ferdinand VII died, on September 29, 1833, no progress had been made in reconciling the two camps, and war was inevitable.

The First Carlist War

Hostilities began in October with a series of Carlist insurrections across Spain. Although the wide distribution of these uprisings attests to the statewide support for Carlism, it was in the Basque Country and Navarre that Carlism took its firmest hold, and it was from there that the Carlists launched expeditions into other parts of Spain. Between 1836 and 1839 the Carlist army made important progress in Aragón and Catalonia, and by 1838 it controlled the Basque countryside, the provinces of Teruel and Castellón, and large areas of Zaragoza, Valencia, Cuenca, Tarragona, and Guadalajara. But because of their failure to obtain financial, military, or diplomatic support from foreign powers, the year marked a reversal for the Carlist forces. Thereafter, the scarcity of resources gradually embittered relations within the ranks of the Carlist army and between Don Carlos and his generals, and Carlist forces began to lose ground to the Spanish army. Finally, in 1839, an exhausted Basque Carlist army signed an armistice with the regency (the Tratado de Vergara). The terms of the armistice were generous: confirmation of the Basque Fueros and the freedom to join the Queen's army, with ranks confirmed and back pay made up.[1] The salient victory for the liberal camp was the transfer of customs houses from the border between the Basque provinces and Castile to the coast.

By all accounts, Carlism enjoyed wide support within the Spanish population. The First Carlist War should thus be seen as part of the political and military turmoil that characterized the first three decades of the nineteenth century. Support for Carlism was stronger, however, in the Basque Country and in Catalonia than in most other Spanish regions, and stronger in the former than in the latter.

The literature has emphasized the role of high levels of religiosity and of anticentralist sentiment in explaining why Carlism received greater support in these northern regions than elsewhere. Authors have remarked that the peasant revolts of the 1820s and 1830s, as well as support for Carlism, drew their strength from a powerful alliance between the lower clergy and the peasantry, an alliance made possible because in northern Spain, as contrasted with other regions, the clergy was poor, and imposed few economic demands on the peasantry. In fact, the priests earned very low salaries, since the tithe generally reverted to higher Church authorities or to tithe farmers, or tax farmers. In these regions of midsized and small estates, where the population tended to live in isolated farms, Sunday Mass was the meeting ground for villagers, and the priest was the main source of information and indoctrination. Rural priests thus had little difficulty in mobilizing the peasantry to oppose liberal reforms.[2]

The second factor mentioned in explanations of support for Carlism in the Basque Country and Catalonia is anticentralist sentiment. In Catalonia, the state's centralization measures inspired nostalgia for the autonomy previously enjoyed by Catalans and favored the development in rural areas of what Vicens Vives has called "provincialism," an ideology that romanticized traditional life and celebrated Catalan singularity. Royalist propaganda, capitalizing on this mood, openly supported the traditional Catalan rights and laws, and even promised to broaden their scope.[3]

Anticentralism, triggered by a perceived threat to the Fueros, also played an important role in the Basque Country, although recent research has demonstrated that it was not the primary factor in support for Carlism.[4] Throughout the eighteenth and early nineteenth centuries, the state put pressure on the Basque provinces to move their customs houses to the coast as a way of increasing revenue. Initially, these measures faced unanimous opposition from the Basque population. Urban and rural social groups maintained that it was necessary to maintain the customs houses in the interior because of the limitations of Basque agriculture, which forced the Basque population to import much of their food. Moreover, Basque merchants benefited from this arrangement, because it facilitated the highly profitable smuggling of imported products into Castile.[5]

Immediately after Spain's Latin American colonies gained their independence, in the early decades of the nineteenth century, the Basque bourgeoisie reoriented its economic activities toward the rest of Spain, and no longer saw an advantage to keeping the customs houses where they were. The rest of Basque society, however, continued to oppose a transfer. Royalist and Carlist propaganda began to portray the cities and the Basque bourgeoisie as the chief foes of the Basque Fueros. In fact, this was a distortion, for the Basque liberals sought not to abolish the Fueros but merely to modify them in such a way as to promote their economic interests.

Anticentralist sentiment, then, and a convergence of interests between the peasantry and the clergy, explain why Carlism was stronger in northern Spain (including the Basque Country and Catalonia) than in central and southern Spain. These factors cannot explain, however, why it was stronger in the Basque Country than in Catalonia. To address this question, one needs to focus on the nature of capitalist development in the two regions.

Most research on Catalonia shows that Carlism was strongest in what Vilar calls the Mountain Region, an area that lies between the littoral and the Pyrenees.[6] This was an area of midsized landholdings—the "Mas"—where subsistence farming predominated. It differed markedly from the scantily populated Pyrenees, where bare subsistence farming still prevailed; from the coastal areas, where specialization in viticulture had developed, with a reliance on wage labor; and from the larger cities, like Barcelona and Reus, where industrial and commercial activities predominated, and where there was already a sizable industrial labor force.

Although the seigniors officially held title to the land in the Mountain Region, in practice the farmers were the owners, for they had virtually perpetual rights over the land they worked in exchange for very small feudal dues. As the population of the area increased during the eighteenth century, these farmers began to rent out marginal land from their estates to other peasants, under long-term contracts stipulating the payment of rent in kind and in cash.[7] In general, while landlords produced crops for their own consumption, tenants grew commercial crops such as grapes and olives. Over the course of the eighteenth and early nineteenth centuries, the peasantry of this area (especially the tenants, or "masovers") grew increasingly dependent on the market.[8]

Catalan Carlism thus gained most of its support from an area engaged in a transition toward commercial farming while still largely reliant on production for private consumption. Underlying Carlism's success in this area, then, is the economic crisis that struck the Catalan economy during the early decades of the nineteenth century.

The loss of the Latin American market had very detrimental effects on Catalan exports of eau de vie and wine.[9] Masovers, in particular, were among the hardest hit, for they typically specialized in export agriculture on their small tenancies. Lower prices for their products meant that, after payment of rent and seigniorial dues, they were often short of cash to purchase food for themselves. Their living conditions were further worsened by the 1820 decree forbidding the import of grain, which forced vine growers to purchase Castile's more expensive grain, and by increased fiscal pressure during and after the Liberal Triennium. In sum, burdened by taxes and bankrupt, many peasants who lived in the Mountain Region of Catalonia came to oppose capitalist transformations.[10]

Such factors can also be invoked to explain the overwhelming support for Carlism in rural areas of the Basque Country. The combination of demographic pressure and limited farming potential contributed to a deterioration of the peasantry's standard of living in the late eighteenth and early nineteenth centuries. These problems were further aggravated by the economic behavior of the Basque commercial bourgeoisie in response to statewide economic crisis, and to the movements for independence in Latin America. The commercial bourgeoisie directed its investments toward the purchase of real estate and the capitalist transformation of Basque rural areas. The detrimental effects that these capitalist transformations had on the living standards of the Basque peasantry have already been described: increasing land value, higher rents, higher taxes, shifts from long-term tenure contracts to short-term ones, lower prices, speculation in grain, the privatization of communal land and of mining, and a decline in traditional iron production. These developments generated intense class conflict throughout the nineteenth century, and peasant support for the Carlist army.[11]

In sum, on the eve of the First Carlist War, market forces were clearly making inroads into the Basque and Catalan countrysides. The imperfection of market mechanisms, lower food prices, and higher fiscal pressure in the early nineteenth century resulted in cash shortages among the peasantry, and provoked unrest in both the Basque Country and Catalonia. In the eyes of the peasantry, the culprits were the ideology of liberalism and the cities where it had developed. It was in the cities that taxes were collected, rents were payable, and profits from irregular commercial practices were invested,[12] and peasant unrest was compounded by popular dissatisfaction with the way in which many liberals were treating the clergy. It is because of these various sources of discontent among the peasantry that we can say that, in John Coverdale's words, "what was at stake in the First Carlist War was an entire way of life, a social and cultural identity which included economic, political, and religious elements, but which was something more than a mere sum of these elements."[13]

Nevertheless, market forces affected the Basque and Catalan countrysides differently. In Catalonia economic tension, resulting primarily from the disruption in trade brought on by independence in Latin America, was temporary. In the Basque Country, where the crisis was caused by structural factors, it was more intense, having to do with the inability of the countryside to sustain the growing population. In the Basque Country, therefore, Carlism was not, as Coverdale put it, the reaction of a society that "could still satisfy its members' needs and desires well enough to make it worth defending."[14] It was, rather, the reaction of a society that could satisfy the spiritual needs of its members, but not its economic needs. Not surprisingly, Carlism gained more strength and lasted longer in the Basque Country than in Catalonia.

The Second Carlist War

The Second Carlist War followed a different course of events but was brought on by many of the same factors. Between 1840 and 1868, Spain was ruled by a series of class coalitions, formed by members of the aristocracy and the bourgeoisie who believed in a constitutional monarchy but opposed democratization. Successive governments were subject to pressure from both absolutist and democratic groups, a dynamic that mirrored Spain's disjointed process of development—a periphery undergoing industrialization while the interior remained anchored in traditional agriculture. For most of this period, however, the Left was more active than were the traditionalist forces in opposing the government. Several times during this period, industrial workers in Barcelona and other cities took to the streets demanding better living conditions and political enfranchisement. The mobilization efforts of these groups were crowned with success in the Revolution of 1868, which forced the abdication of Queen Isabel II.

The "Glorious Revolution" opened a new and short-lived period of political innovation in Spanish history. A coalition of intellectuals and high-ranking army officers, backed by the urban proletariat, attempted to establish a democratic government based on universal suffrage, civil rights, the separation of Church and State, and freedom of religion. The experiment culminated in 1873 with the proclamation of the First Republic.

Organized on federalist principles of Proudhonian origin, the First Republic proved to be premature. The members of the bourgeoisie, few in number and ineffectual, were unable to control the social forces unleashed by their actions: the working class and the peasantry rioted; federalism degenerated into cantonalism; and traditionalist forces took to rebellion, in the form of a Carlist military insurrection. Cornered by both conservatives and radicals, the Republican government was toppled by a new, more moderate coalition, only a year after coming to power. Shortly thereafter, the new coalition proclaimed a constitutional monarchy, to be headed by Queen Isabel's son, Alfonso XII.

In the 28 years that followed the First Carlist War, moderate governments had pursued policies that liberal legislators had promoted since the period of the Cortes de Cádiz, such as de-entailment and centralization at all levels. Relations between the state and the Church gradually improved after the First Carlist War, reaching a high point with the signing of a Concordat in 1851. In the years preceding the Second Carlist War, however, and during the revolution itself, they cooled again, following such measures as the enactment of freedom of religion, the recognition of the Kingdom of Italy in 1865, the institutionalization of civil marriage, and the enforcement of the suppression of the mandatory tithe.

These liberal-secular measures, among others, triggered the mobilization of Carlist forces against the revolutionary government. In general, however, the Second Carlist War once again reflected the opposition between capitalist and traditional society, and between city and countryside. The forces around Charles VII (grandson of the previous pretender, Charles V) were supported by peasants and artisans and led by old officers from the First Carlist War, representatives of the small rural nobility, and clergymen. Opposing them were the bulk of the upper aristocracy, the bourgeoisie, and the industrial working class, with its own revolutionary agenda.

The war began after the proclamation of the First Republic in 1873 and ended in 1876, soon after the coronation of Alfonso XII. In sharp contrast to the First Carlist War, the Second was almost totally confined to the Basque Country and Navarre. Some indication of support for Carlism throughout Spain can be drawn from an analysis of the general election results from the years immediately preceding the war. The only areas where the Carlist Party obtained a majority of seats in the general elections of 1869, 1871, and 1872 were the Basque Country and Navarre. In Catalonia, support for the Carlist Party was greater than that in other communities but never large enough to ensure that its candidates would be elected.

The religious factor is an unlikely explanation for differences in support for Carlism between the Basque Country and Catalonia. The literature on both communities stresses the intense religious faith of the rural population and the harmonious relationship between peasantry and clergy, and although census data from 1887 show that the number of inhabitants per priest was considerably lower in the Basque Country than in Catalonia (see Table 5), it was also

Table 5. Regional socioeconomic characteristics and support for Carlism in the 1871 general elections

Region	Median number of inhabitants per priest	Median percent men employed in agriculture	Number of Carlist candidates elected over total number of candidates	Proportion of Carlist deputies over total
Andalucía	628.8	75.6	0/74	0.00
Extremadura	608.1	79.9	2/17	0.12
Castilla la Nueva	373.3	75.5	2/30	0.07
Valencia	532.8	77.2	3/32	0.09
Catalonia	236.6	58.0	6/42	0.14
Aragón	311.4	80.2	3/23	0.13
Castilla la Vieja/ León	249.6	78.5	5/53	0.09
Basque Country	135.1	60.2	9/10	0.90
Asturias	593.4	73.7	4/14	0.29
Galicia	372.3	79.2	5/45	0.11
Murcia	564.1	76.3	1/10	0.10
Canary Islands	759.3	79.7	0/ 6	0.00
Balearic Islands	283.4	68.9	4/ 7	0.57
Madrid	280.7	64.2	0/12	0.00
Rioja	181.4	74.8	0/ 4	0.00
Cantabria	291.2	68.3	1/ 5	0.20
Navarre	204.5	76.9	6/ 7	0.86

Source: Socioeconomic data: Instituto Nacional de Estadística, Censo de 1887; database provided by David Reher. Electoral results: Martínez Cuadrado, Elecciones y Partidos.
Note: These regions include the provinces that currently belong to them.

very low in Catalonia compared to the rest of Spain. Moreover, contrary to what one would expect, support for Carlism in the Basque Country was not highest in districts where the number of priests per inhabitant was the lowest. Finally, one can assume that the number of priests per inhabitant in Catalonia, and the mobilizing capacity of the clergy, remained fairly constant between the First and the Second Carlist Wars.

The different impacts that state-centralization policies had on the Basque Country and on Catalonia offer another attractive explanation for differences in the level of support for Carlism between the two regions. Whereas Catalonia lost its political autonomy in 1716, the Basque Country remained autonomous until the end of the Second Carlist War. Attempts by the liberal governments to increase taxation and to levy armies must therefore have been viewed much more critically in the Basque Country than in Catalonia, for such actions were direct violations of the Fueros, and were presented as such by Carlist leaders.

Nevertheless, although the Fueros question was important in the mobilization of Carlist volunteers in the Basque Country, Carlism was a Spanish cause, not simply a Basque cause. In his study of Carlist ideology, Garmendia stresses this point and demonstrates that Carlist leaders tried not to let the defense of the Fueros take priority over the main elements of the Carlist creed: "God, Country, and King."[15] The only group that clearly prioritized the preservation of the Fueros over more general Carlist aims was the Basque rural nobility, for the Juntas and the Fueros were the basis of their power.

One must look, then, for factors that explain the different degrees of involvement of the peasantry among Catalans and Basques, for it was they who formed Carlism's material and financial base. From this perspective, the threat to the old Fueros seems an unlikely explanation, since there is evidence that the Fueros were cherished as much by Catalan peasants as by Basque peasants.[16]

The relative degree of prosperity of Basque and Catalan rural areas is in fact the most likely foundation for an explanation of differences in Carlist support in the Basque Country and Catalonia. The preceding analysis of the First Carlist War has suggested that Carlism obtained more popular support in the Basque Country than in Catalonia because Basque agriculture had adapted less successfully to the forces of capitalism, and that the greater strength of Catalan support for Carlism during the First Carlist War (than during the Second) can be attributed in part to a temporary crisis in Catalan agriculture at about the time of the war.

Between 1840 and 1873, Basque and Catalan agriculture followed very different paths of development. Basque agriculture continued to suffer from past structural limitations and from competition with Castilian grain, whereas Catalan agriculture recovered well from the crisis of the early nineteenth century.[17]

An analysis of the relationship between levels of electoral support for Carlism, in the Basque Country, and economic conditions there in the 1880s, both factors measured at the judicial-district level, shows that support tended to be greater in the most heavily agricultural areas and in areas where emigration was highest (see Table 6). This finding corroborates exhaustive analyses by both Extramiana and Garmendia of documents from the Second Carlist War, which demonstrate that socioeconomic grievances fueled peasant support for Carlism in northern Spain.[18] In fact, liberals often referred to Carlism as "white socialism" because in areas dominated by Carlists the wealthy were taxed heavily and their houses and property were expropriated. As Extramiana and Garmendia have pointed out, anger toward the wealthy and anger toward the big cities, where the wealthy were concentrated, were almost synonymous. In this sense, in the Basque Country the Carlist Wars both reflected and further widened a political gulf between the rural peasantry and the urban bourgeoisie.

Although industrialization proceeded at a faster rate in the Basque Country than in Catalonia during the years surrounding the Second Carlist War,

Table 6. Socioeconomic characteristics and percentage of total votes for Carlist parties in provincial elections by electoral district, in the Basque Country (circa 1887)

Province and district	Percent Carlism	Year	Percent agriculture	Percent net migration (1887–1900)	Inhabitants per priest
Guipúzcoa					
Azpeitia	77.1	(1888)	60.49	−0.8	115.2
Tolosa	69.2	(1888)	59.81	−0.6	201.2
Vergara	44.0	(1888)	43.66	−0.5	89.2
San Sebastián	22.0	(1886)	34.66	0.4	151.0
Alava					
Amurrio	20.6	(1888)	78.07	−0.6	125.7
Laguardia	57.9	(1886)	71.88	−4.2	301.3
Vitoria	52.0	(1884)	56.66	−1.2	99.4
Vizcaya					
Bilbao	35.5	(1890)	17.59	2.7	133.8
Durango	49.4	(1888)	66.44	−0.5	136.4
Guernica	40.0	(1886)	73.36	−0.2	209.2
Marquina	49.5	(1888)	71.88	−0.4	123.2
Valmaseda[a]	0.0	(1884)	19.58	2.3	213.3

Source: Socioeconomic data: Censo de 1887; I thank David Reher for lending me the database containing these data. Electoral data: Cuesta, El Carlismo Vasco (1985).

[a]Valmaseda was a mining district. Ramon de la Sota, the owner of many of the mines, controlled political power in this district. The Carlist Party did not present candidates in Valmaseda. Instead, the only pro-Fueros candidates were Sota's, and they participated as independent "Fuerista" candidates. They favored the restoration of the Fueros without being Carlist and attracted the majority of the votes (56.2% in 1884).

the Basque industrial sector was still too small to absorb the rural population surplus, the peasantry's standard of living continued to decline, and many Basque peasants were forced to emigrate to Latin America.

In contrast to Basque agriculture, Catalan agriculture experienced a cycle of prosperity between the two wars, because of a normalization of trade with Latin America, technical innovations in agriculture, rising world prices, and the beneficial effects of the Crimean War on demand for Catalan agricultural products.[19] In this period, Catalan rural areas also benefited from intense industrial development and mechanization in both urban and rural areas, which provided an outlet for surplus agricultural labor.[20] In particular, rural industry offered an opportunity for farmers to supplement their incomes, and fostered the development of a capitalist mentality. The linkage between cotton imports from the U.S. South and wine exports to Latin America, with Cuba as the node for this traffic, symbolized this symbiosis between industry and agriculture.

Industry and commercial agriculture developed sufficiently in Catalonia during the nineteenth century to reconcile large segments of the peasantry with liberalism. Although clericalism remained high, and although grievances against the state over its centralization efforts arose periodically, what most distinguished Catalonia from the Basque Country during this period were its higher rural prosperity and its greater capacity for absorbing labor into industry. The Basque Country, meanwhile, experienced a combined form of development, characterized in part by the decline of agriculture. Whereas Catalonia's endogenous development facilitated the rural population's adaptation to capitalism, the Basque Country's combined development prevented this adaptation. Thus although the different roads to capitalism traveled by the two regions do not explain Carlism per se, they do contribute to our understanding of why Basque peasants found capitalism more threatening than their Catalan counterparts did, and why they supported Carlism more energetically. In the Basque Country, the Carlist Wars were, as Manuel González Portilla put it, "to some extent, the outcome of the imbalance between population and production in the context of an agrarian system that had changed little since the eighteenth century. Population growth without production growth leads to underconsumption and to a deterioration of the peasantry's economic standing, especially that of the small peasant who has no other alternative than to emigrate or sink deeper into poverty. These conditions favor the development, among peasants, of political attitudes tending to maintain what was 'before,' or, in other words, traditionalism."[21]

The Carlist Wars had major consequences for the development of nationalism in the two communities, which, as Garmendia has pointed out, have generally been ignored in scholarly research.[22] Struggles against centralization provided both Basques and Catalans with symbols and myths that were later adopted by nationalist ideologues. The influence of the two wars was greater, however, in the Basque Country. There, the population's support for Carlism was nearly unanimous, which meant that most of the liberal troops battling Carlism in the Basque Country had to be recruited from the rest of Spain. For Basques, this created the feeling that they were being invaded.[23] The disgruntled rural and urban classes formed a political constituency susceptible to the appeals of platforms proclaiming the virtues of traditional society and the evils of capitalism. This situation forged a deep hostility between traditional society and the small but growing Basque industrial and commercial bourgeoisie, a hostility that constitutes one of the enduring features of Basque politics and nationalism.

CHAPTER 5

Basque Nationalism, 1876–1936

Although the forces of liberalism defeated the Old Regime in the Second Carlist War, the socioeconomic conditions that had ensured Carlism's appeal in the Basque Country endured, and they continued to affect Basque political life until the Spanish Civil War (1936–39). This chapter analyzes the impact of the Carlists' defeat on the rise of Basque nationalism, and recounts the process by which nationalism came to dominate political thinking in the Basque Country in the years immediately preceding the Civil War.

The literature on Basque nationalism has traditionally focused on the motivations of Basque nationalists and on the Basque capitalist elite's disinclination to support a nationalist program. Little emphasis, however, has been placed on the role played by the local bourgeoisie. This chapter gives due consideration to divisions *within* the Basque local bourgeoisie and analyzes the limited extent of its influence on the programmatic content of Basque nationalism. Whereas Chapter 3 has suggested that the limited influence of the local bourgeoisie was due to its small size, this chapter analyzes, as well, the influence of the predominantly Spanish orientation of this social class, which can be explained by three factors: the elites' traditional orientation toward Spain; the political ascendance of the Spanish-oriented oligarchy; and, especially, ideological conflict between the local bourgeoisie and the old middle classes, the latter of which formed the social base of Basque nationalism.

The Fragmentation of the Basque Carlist Community

The Second Carlist War significantly enhanced Basque ethnic consciousness because the overwhelming concentration of Carlist military support in the Basque provinces had implicitly turned this war into an enduring conflict between the Basque provinces and the rest of Spain. The conflict was exacerbated immediately after the war, when the state, pressed by fiscal needs and lobbied by centralist politicians, abolished the Fueros, in July 1876.

The institutional consequences of the decree were dramatic. Among the most important changes it brought about were compulsory military conscription; taxes from which the Basque Country had previously been exempt; and the replacement of its main legislative and executive bodies, the Juntas Generales, with Diputaciones Provinciales—the main governing bodies in the 52 Spanish provinces until the 1980s, when Spain was divided into seventeen regions, or "autonomous communities," and the Diputaciones lost most of their previous functions and power. In contrast with the Juntas Generales, which enjoyed substantial political autonomy and were elected through procedures that privileged the traditionalist rural areas, the Diputaciones Provinciales were elected democratically, by direct ballot, and subordinated to the central government.

Basque society unanimously condemned the abolition of the Fueros. In the years immediately following the Second Carlist War, numerous cultural organizations and publications emerged in support of traditional Basque institutions and a Basque cultural revival. Although interest in Basque history and culture had preceded the abolition of the Fueros, the decree abolishing them was a powerful impetus for this cultural and historiographical movement.[1]

The abolition of the Fueros also prompted political mobilization of forces favoring their restoration. This movement was joined both by members of the emerging industrial oligarchy and by traditionalist members of the declining old order. Because the Spanish state was still largely controlled by rich landowners, the degree of political and administrative autonomy provided by the Fueros was undoubtedly appealing to the rising Basque industrial and commercial bourgeoisie. The old petty bourgeoisie and the rural nobility, for their part, saw the Fueros and the Juntas as the vehicle through which they could exert power over Basque society, and as a shield against industrialization, secularization, and political liberalism. And for the general populace, finally, the Fueros meant relatively low fiscal contributions and exemption from military service. It is not surprising, then, that the defense of the Fueros became a rallying cry for all political factions competing in municipal, provincial, and general elections in the Basque Country between 1876 and 1882.

The enactment of the Conciertos Económicos (Economic Agreements) in 1882 ended this period of unusually broad consensus in Basque society. The Conciertos allowed the Diputaciones Provinciales of the Basque provinces to determine procedures for collecting taxes autonomously, provided they transferred a yearly sum (the "Cupo") to the state. The replacement of traditional political institutions by democratically elected Diputaciones Provinciales, and the enactment of the Conciertos Económicos, which allowed the Basque Diputaciones to shift the tax burden to the lower classes through indirect taxation, greatly satisfied the rising industrial oligarchy. Thus, the Basque industrial and commercial upper classes transferred their allegiance to the statewide Liberal or Conservative parties (known as the dynastic parties) that had become dominant in Spain since the restoration of the monarchy, and eventually dropped their demands for the restoration of the Fueros.

The renunciation of the restoration of the Fueros by the Basque upper classes coincided with a similar shift in attitudes among broad sectors within Carlism. Carlists had sought to restore a Spanish monarchy that would be faithful to the sociopolitical structures characteristic of Spain before the age of liberalism and democracy. These aspirations were largely met under the Bourbon monarch Alfonso XII, whose reign preserved, in Javier Cuesta's words, "the great majority of the values for which Carlists had fought: peace, order, private property, morality, family, and, in general, the foundations of a conservative social order."[2] Carlists and Conservatives, the latter at that time the dominant political party, differed on only three main issues: who had the right to reign in Spain; what to do with the Fueros; and how clerical the Constitution ought to be. Generally, Carlists deplored the laical character of the 1876 Spanish Constitution, which instituted freedom of religion, but they were themselves divided on the clerical question. Carlism eventually split over this decision into two parties, the Integrists, who stressed religious fundamentalism, and the Carlists, who emphasized the defense of the Fueros. The Carlists' defense of the Fueros was merely symbolic, however; in practice, they accepted the new political order.[3]

Thus, by 1882 the defense of the Fueros became—in the electoral platforms of Carlists, liberals, and conservatives alike—either an irrelevancy or a hollow promise. The defense of the Fueros thus could not have been the basis of support for Carlism in the Basque Country during the Second Carlist War. Following the approval of the Conciertos Económicos in 1882, Basque political life was dominated by conflict between traditionalists and liberals/conservatives, an opposition gradually superseded by conflict between liberals/conservatives and socialists.

Bourgeois Nationalism: Ramón de la Sota y Llano

Although the signing of the Conciertos Económicos generally satisfied the Basque bourgeoisie, a small group among them maintained the "Fuerista" flame. The group organized itself around the Sociedad Euskalerría of Vizcaya, led by Fidel de Sagarmínaga, and the Asociación Euskara of Navarre, led by Juan Iturralde. Both associations combined cultural activities with political programs centered on the restoration of the Fueros. According to most authors, the members of the associations were moderate liberals who belonged to what the authors call the "jauntxo" class, a segment of the urban bourgeoisie owning extensive rural and urban property but not involved in the emerging capitalist industrial sector.[4] Politically, the jauntxo constituted the core of the loosely organized Unión Vasco-Navarra. The Unión Vasco-Navarra presented itself as a Basque alternative to the dominant Spanish parties. It was, in fact, the first association in Basque history to attempt to represent the interests of all the Basque provinces.

The Unión's program, focused solely on the Fueros, had limited popular appeal, as revealed by its poor electoral performance. The 1880 provincial election, which accorded it many votes, particularly in Vizcaya, was its only victory.[5] In the following years, lack of electoral success, disagreement among its members about how much emphasis to place on religion and on defending the Fueros, and defections of militants who were satisfied with the Conciertos Económicos, gradually led to the dissolution of the Unión Vasco-Navarra. The Unión's supporters then transferred their allegiances to either the dynastic parties or the traditionalist parties. Those who were satisfied with the Conciertos and who de-emphasized religion in their agenda ended up supporting the dynastic parties; those whose emphasis was on religion shifted their support to the traditionalist parties; and only a very small group remained faithful to the "Fuerista" cause represented by the Sociedad Euskalerría and the Asociación Euskara.

During the 1880s the two societies slowly diverged in their activities. The Asociación Euskara, centered in Navarre, a rural, Castilianized province, embarked on a program to revitalize Basque culture. Removed from politics, its members espoused a religious program very like that of the traditionalists. The Sociedad Euskalerría, centered in Vizcaya, was more active politically, albeit quite unsuccessfully.

Two factions competed for control of the Euskalerría association over the course of the 1880s, one led by Fidel de Sagarmínaga, a proprietor of urban and rural real estate, and the other by Ramón de la Sota y Llano, a mine owner and industrialist. The Fueros and the religious question were the dividing lines between the two groups: Sagarmínaga espoused a more clerical stance, Sota y Llano a more secular approach and an intense pro-Fueros position. Conflict between the two eventually forced Sota's group to abandon the Sociedad Euskalerría in the early 1890s and to try to form a nationalist party. Sota and his son, Ramón de la Sota Aburto, in time came to lead the capitalist faction of the Basque nationalist community, until the Civil War.

Sota y Llano came from a prosperous family involved in both mining and commercial activities. Although much of his mining activity was centered in the province of Santander, adjacent to Vizcaya, he owned substantial property in the electoral district of Valmaseda in westernmost Vizcaya. During the 1890s, Sota complemented his mining activities with investment in shipping, shipbuilding, and insurance companies. By the 1880s he was already a powerful figure in Vizcaya, and despite the electoral defeats of the Sociedad Euskalerría, he always managed to gain substantial support for his candidates in the district of Valmaseda. To ensure the victories of his candidates, Sota relied on political practices quite as corrupt as those employed by the "caciques" of the Liberal and Conservative parties, as Sabino Arana, founder of the Basque Nationalist Party, himself noted.[6]

In Corcuera's view (not thoroughly documented), Sota's entourage represented a sector of the urban industrial bourgeoisie[7] falling between the industrial and financial elites and the jauntxos led by Sagarmínaga. Their political program was not clearly defined, and they lacked an ideologue who would have injected coherence and clarity into their agenda. Through content analysis of the newspapers that Sota controlled, scholars have attempted to delineate the main traits of his group's political program.[8] Their analysis has shown that Sota's group sought the kind of political and administrative autonomy for the Basque provinces within the Spanish state that the Fueros had provided, and a strengthening of Basque identity through the promotion of the Basque language. Little is known, however, about the motivations behind their political stance.

Some authors suggest that economic interest was the force that pitted Sota and his group against the bourgeoisie aligned with the dynastic parties.[9] They suggest that Sota's group represented free traders whose main activities were mining, metallurgy, and shipping, while dynastic-party supporters represented the protectionist interests of the steel and shipbuilding sectors. Empirical support for this hypothesis remains scanty and inconclusive, however,[10] and other arguments seem more plausible: Sabino Arana, for instance, interpreted conflict between Sota and the Basque bourgeoisie that supported the Liberal or Conservative parties as a power struggle between two local caciques, Sota and Victor Chávarri.[11] Another interpretation is suggested by the fact that some of the major political figures surrounding Sota were of foreign origin, such as the bourgeois nationalist senators Pedro Chalbaud (of French origin) and José Horn Areilza (of Czech origin) (Ybarra, 1947).[12] This observation raises the possibility that Sota's group attracted sectors of the bourgeoisie that had yet to be assimilated by the Basque financial and industrial elite.

The social roots of bourgeois nationalism in the Basque Country can be approximated from information contained in the Directory of Spanish Corporations and Financial Institutions of 1922. I have matched this information with the names of nationalist leaders who, according to various sources, were still alive in 1922 and either belonged to the Sociedad Euskalerría or had ideas close to Sota's.[13] In the Directory, only twelve of the 22 nationalist leaders politically close to Sota appear as members of boards of directors. Of these twelve, only six are present in three or more boards of directors: Ramón de la Sota y Llano himself, his son Ramón de la Sota Aburto, his son-in-law Pedro Chalbaud, José Horn Areilza, Federico Zabala, Rafael Picavea, and Domingo Epalza. Among them, only Sota and Epalza could be considered members of the Basque oligarchy; the rest can hardly be compared with the likes of the Ibarra, Chávarri, Gandarias, Zubiría, Aznar, or Arteche families, which numbered many well-known members of the Basque oligarchy and supporters of the dynastic parties.

Therefore, the calls for decentralization made by the few local capitalists who turned to nationalism can be seen as a strategy employed by those who had been excluded from state-level political institutions, to increase their power share. Such a strategy may be inherent in the expansion of peripheral capitalism, because of the lack of opportunities for upward mobility for some members of the local capitalist class.[14] Of course, one cannot rule out genuine ideological motivations on the part of the local bourgeoisie, whose sociocultural world was the Basque Country and for whom the cost of supporting nationalism instead of a dynastic party was lower than it would be for the industrial and financial oligarchy. Nevertheless, the available information about the Sociedad Euskalerría's membership, and about electoral support for this political organization, shows that, throughout the Restoration (Alphonso XII's reign), the bulk of the Basque bourgeoisie supported the dynastic parties. Sota's group never obtained substantial electoral support in Vizcaya and received none at all in the other Basque provinces.[15] Moreover, very few members of the rising bourgeoisie joined this group. The Sociedad Euskalerría failed because of the local bourgeoisie's small size and Spanish cultural and political orientations. Its lack of success in attracting the bourgeoisie's support eventually forced Sota to form an alliance with the Basque Nationalist Party founded by Sabino Arana.

Traditionalist Nationalism: Sabino Arana

Carlism's second military defeat in 40 years dashed the hopes of those who wanted to preserve the Old Regime's social organization, political institutions, and way of life. Moreover, by the end of the nineteenth century, traditionalist forces had new enemies to contend with. Industrializing areas suddenly experienced a massive influx of immigrants from culturally different areas. Since the immigrants had not yet been socialized to respect the local Basque social hierarchies, and tended to identify with socialism, they represented a threat for those in the Basque middle classes who had not yet reaped the benefits of capitalist development and faced the prospect of pro-letarianization.

During the 1880s and 1890s, the Basque traditionalists joined forces with traditionalists in other Spanish regions and participated in Spanish politics by supporting the Carlist and Integrist parties. This strategy, intended to reverse the course of pervasive social transformations, failed, because support for traditionalism was significant only in the Basque Country, and even in this region the dynastic parties were far more successful than the traditional-ist parties had been.[16]

The Founding of the Basque Nationalist Party

The traditionalist parties' lack of electoral success, both in the Basque Country and in Spain generally, motivated some of their Basque supporters to mobilize for political independence. To justify this goal they simply refor-mulated their ideas in the language of their time: the language of national-ism. As Arturo Campión, addressing a nationalist audience in 1906, said:

> We proudly called ourselves "Fueristas" in riskier times than today's. However, given that there is a new term, which is more graphic, more intense, and thor-oughly expressive, and that this term does not allow the faint-hearted or those who see themselves as sophisticated (which amounts to the same thing) to take refuge under it, I declare, without renouncing my past, without subscrib-ing to new ideas, without adopting new attitudes, and, instead, in agreement with my own modest history, that I renounce the old label and from now on will call myself a nationalist.[17]

It is worth noting that Sabino Arana, the founder of the Basque National-ist Party, "converted" (he always used this religious vocabulary) from Carlism to nationalism in 1882, one year after a disastrous electoral perfor-mance by the traditionalists, in which they obtained only five of 392 seats allocated throughout Spain, and three of the five represented Vizcaya, Guipúzcoa, and Alava. Writing of his conversion and referring to his older brother Luis, who was the agent of his conversion, Arana wrote:

> . . . and he made such an effort to demonstrate to me that Carlism was an unnecessary, inconvenient, and destructive way to prevent Spanish influence, to break our ties with Spain, and even to recover the seigniorial tradition, that my mind, understanding that my brother knew history better than I, and that

he was incapable of lying to me, started to doubt, and I resolved to start studying with serenity the history of Biscay, and to adhere firmly to the Truth.[18]

Luis and Sabino Arana had concluded, by 1882, that Carlism was both unnecessary and harmful to their goals. It was unnecessary because a nationalist movement that would obtain independence for the Basque Country would achieve the same goals. It was harmful because, according to the Aranas, Spanish society was already too much influenced by secularism for religious reforms to have any effect on people's thinking. The two brothers thus concluded that the only way to save the Vizcayan people from contact with the heretical Spaniards was through political independence.

A brief sketch of Sabino Arana's life and ideology illustrates the social origins and worldview of the majority of the early Basque nationalists. Sabino de Arana Goiri (1865–1903) was the son of a typical jauntxo. Santiago Arana, his father, combined traditional industrial activities, shipbuilding and shipping, with the ownership of rural and urban property. He was also mayor of Abando, a small town close to Bilbao, and deputy at the Junta General of Vizcaya. During the Second Carlist War, Santiago Arana lent financial support to the Carlist cause and suffered exile in France until war's end, in 1876. Having lost much of his fortune during the war, Santiago Arana, like many others, was unable to adapt to the capitalist transformations ensuing in the Basque Country. In particular, he lacked the resources to shift from the construction of wooden ships to the construction of steel ships. Nevertheless, the Aranas remained a well-to-do family, and it is partly because of their small capital accumulation that Sabino Arana was able to support himself and to initiate many nationalist activities in the period before his group and Sota's group fused, in 1898. For Arana's family, liberalism and capitalism became synonymous with social decline.

Sabino Arana attended a Jesuit high school in the town of Orduña, as did the sons of many other jauntxo families. Some of his classmates, such as Gregorio de Ibarreche, later became nationalist or Carlist leaders themselves. Arana's father died in 1883, and from then until 1886 he lived with his family in Barcelona and studied law. Most accounts suggest that he was never a good student, and that he was not at all influenced by the nationalist atmosphere developing in Catalonia at the time. Instead he became an autodidact, immersing himself in Basque history and culture, as did so many others of his generation.[19] He published several works related to Basque language and grammar but did not attain the scholarly standing of other researchers in his field and was not academically successful.

Arana began his political career in 1890, two years after having been denied a position to teach Basque language at the Instituto de Bilbao. In that year he published *Cuatro Glorias Patrias* (retitled *Bizkaya por su Independencia* in 1892), in which he reviewed "four glorious battles" in which, according to him, Vizcayans fought for their independence. From June 1893 to August 1895, he issued the journal *Bizcaitarra*, at his own expense; its publication was eventually banned by state authorities. In 1893, Sota and other ex-members of Euskalerría organized a dinner for the presentation of Arana's ideas. Arana's speech (the "Discurso de Larrazabal"; see the Introduction) was considered a failure, even by Arana himself, for most of the hosts opposed his ultra-religious program and his aggressive stance toward the Sociedad Euskalerría.

In 1894, Arana founded a political organization, Euzkeldún Batzokija. He and his brother furnished the association with a flag, an anthem, and a new name for the province of Vizcaya, Euzkadi (Basque Country), which would later be used to describe the Basque Country as a whole. The association's program, which incorporated Arana's main political ideas, has been summarized by Corcuera:[20]

Organization of Vizcaya as an independent Roman Catholic state.
Legislation based on Vizcaya's traditional law.
Restoration of Vizcaya's traditional mores.
Exclusion of those who did not belong to the Basque race.
Institution of Basque [Euskera] as the official language.
Complete harmony between the religious and political domains.

The organization of the association itself was a reflection of Arana's political agenda. The Euzkeldún Batzokija was a very closed association: only people whose four grandparents had Basque last names could belong, and membership rules favored those who spoke Basque over those who did not. In July 1895, an assembly of the Euzkeldún Batzokija founded the Bizkai Batzar, an organization structured along the same lines as the Euzkeldún Batzokija that was to deal with every issue concerning Vizcayan nationalism.

In less than five years Arana had founded a nationalist association with a program that promoted independence and the constitution of a state organized on religious and linguistic principles, a newspaper, and the essential symbols (name, flag, and anthem) of a nationalist movement. Political support was scarce, however, because of the rigid rules for membership he had promulgated and the movement's limited economic resources.

Although as an organization it was small, the Bizkai Batzar did represent a potential political threat to the state, which had already been put on its guard by political turmoil in the Basque Country during the nineteenth century and by the independence movements in Latin America. This background explains why Arana's movement was so severely suppressed as soon as it began to gain popularity. In the second half of 1895, the Euzkeldún Batzokija and the journal *Bizkaitarra* were banned and Arana was imprisoned, from August to January. After his release, Arana continued his nationalist activities and published a new journal, *Baseritarra*, that was also banned, after just three months in existence. In August 1897, Arana dissolved the Euzkeldún Batzokija; and on October 22nd of that year he founded the Bizkai-Batzara, a clandestine political association. This date is viewed as the official founding date of the Basque Nationalist Party.

The social base of the Basque Nationalist Party (BNP) was the lower middle class. Corcuera's analysis of the social composition of the early pre-nationalist organizations founded by Arana reveals that although they included some members of the working class and some members from well-to-do bourgeois families, most of the early adherents were artisans, salaried workers, clerks, salesmen, and small-scale merchants.[21] This is the social composition that prevailed in the BNP until the Civil War, although a few members of the emerging intelligentsia unconnected to the capitalist world also adhered to it. The organization known as Aberri, a group within the BNP that would defend Arana's orthodoxy in the 1920s, illustrates the lower-middle-class origins. (A focus on the Aberri group is useful, because the BNP would eventually be joined by Sota and his followers, who represented a different social class.) Out of twenty of Aberri's leaders, only two were members of the board of directors of any company: Salvador Echeita and José de los Heros, each in only one company.[22] Out of seven other renowned nationalist leaders sharing Sabino Arana's ideas, all of whom I have been able to ascertain were alive in 1922, only Baltasar Amezola was a member of the board of directors of any Spanish corporation or financial institution (in two companies).[23] Instead of powerful capitalists, what one finds among these nationalist leaders are pharmacists, doctors, engineers, lawyers, clerks, and accountants—educated members of the Basque middle class. On the party rolls one finds only a few members of the upper class, such as Manuel Sota Aburto, who chose not to share the ideology and activities of his father and brother.

Ideological Principles of the Basque Nationalist Party

Arana presented his program for Basque independence as a struggle for the religious salvation of the Basque race. Salvation was to be won through complete isolation from other peoples, especially the Spaniards.[24] Language, for instance, just as political independence, was to be a shield; as Arana put it: "One cannot merely see the Basque language as a beautiful language, worthy of being used in literature: it is the symbol of our race, and the safeguard of the piety and morality of our people."[25]

Arana's nationalism, which pervaded Basque nationalist discourse until the Civil War, was in the main a defensive reaction against what he viewed as the corrosive influence of liberalism in Basque society.[26] The bulk of his writings may be interpreted from this formally religious perspective. I say "formally religious" because Arana invested the entire traditional Basque way of life with religious qualities. His negative attitudes toward Spanish immigrants, for example, can be traced to the changes they were producing in a social order that he and his adherents held in the deepest regard. Immigrants were important agents of change in the Basque Country; they represented views more secular than those prevailing among the Basque population, and they generally supported the Socialist party instead of adhering to a "religiously founded" system of paternalistic relations between employer and worker. Arana's political program thus specified that in a future Basque state there would be no room for Spaniards:

> What, then, does the nationalist program say about racial purity? It can be summarized as follows:
>
> 1. Foreigners would be allowed to establish themselves in Bizkaya under the tutelage of their respective consuls; but they could not be naturalized. As for the Spaniards, the Juntas Generales would decide whether to expel them, forbidding them to enter the territory of Bizkaya during the first few years after independence, to erase more easily any trace that their domination could have left in the character and the traditions of the people of Bizkaya.[27]

The racism of Arana's discourse was not motivated primarily by economically determined ethnic competition. Although he and other nationalists sometimes accused the immigrants of lowering general salary levels, the defense of the native working class played a subsidiary role in Arana's writings and in the program of the BNP. His discourse was motivated, rather, by culturally and class-determined ethnic competition between immigrants, who supported a more secular lifestyle and represented a challenge to property relations, and the Basque petty bourgeoisie, who resisted secularization and staunchly supported private property.

Arana's equally vicious attacks on those groups of Basque origin who had facilitated the penetration of liberalism into the Basque Country make it clear that his attacks on immigrants were related to their secular values and to the changes they were introducing in the Basque Country. The targets of his attacks were the economic, political, and cultural elites of Vizcaya:

> Pro-Spanish [Españolismo] attitudes have been present in our rulers; pro-Spanish attitudes have been present in our historians; pro-Spanish attitudes have been present in our jurists; and with pro-Spanish attitudes have our

people in general been inadvertently infected, by learning from those sources.[28]

Just before he died, in 1902, Arana showed an inclination to abandon his independence program.[29] He began to advocate a broad autonomy and a renewed effort to recover the distinctive traits of Basque culture, which, in his view, embodied true religious values. Among other things, he stressed the promotion of the Basque language.[30] Because he was seriously ill at the time, and because he offered only fragmentary and ambiguous evidence regarding the moderation of his political agenda, the reasons for his shift in attitude have been debated since he died. As a result, both those who sought independence and those who preferred autonomy were able to legitimize their claims by relying on Arana's authority, and in the years immediately preceding the Civil War, the Basque nationalist movement remained deeply divided on the issue of independence. The concern, however, was for the immediate political goals of the BNP; regarding the long-term goal of independence, the party remained united.

The Fusion of Bourgeois and Traditionalist Basque Nationalisms

On ideological and programmatic matters, the Sota and Arana groups differed in many ways. For Sota and his followers, political autonomy (symbolized by the Fueros) was an end in itself; for Arana, independence was a means to an end, a path toward moral regeneration. Sota's bourgeois nationalism was procapitalist and moderate Catholic; Arana's traditionalist nationalism was anticapitalist and fundamentalist Catholic. For the "euskalerriacos," the unity of the Basque Country was indisputable; for the "sabinianos," it depended on the will of the confederated provinces.[31] Sabino Arana always spoke of the Sota group in derogatory terms, calling them "Phoenicians," for instance. In 1894, Arana himself pointed out, in unmistakable terms, what differentiated the two nationalist groups:

Basque nationalists [Euskerianos nacionalistas] despise Spain, because it has trampled the laws of their Homeland, profaned and demolished their temple, and delivered their Homeland into the grip of the most infamous enslavement, and it is corrupting their Homeland's blood, which is the Basque race, the Basque language, and will ultimately drive their national feelings from their hearts. What about the pro-Spanish Basque nationalists [Euskerianos españolistas] who claim to despise Spain? why do they despise it? Ask them. Because Spain, in economic terms, is at the level of Greece and Italy, and in civilization, at the depths of Morocco and Turkey; because it lacks agriculture, industry, and commerce; because its army has fled the Moroccans, and even in diplomacy do Moroccans surpass Spaniards. In a word, [they despise Spain] because they would like to see it big and powerful, and instead they see it humiliated and emaciated.[32]

Despite the lack of a common nationalist vision, the two nationalist camps established an alliance, merging under the banner of the Basque Nationalist Party in 1898. The reason for the alliance is simple: neither of the two groups was attracting significant numbers of supporters alone. Indeed, popular support for Arana's group was no greater than that for Sota's. Although Arana refused to participate in elections, this paucity of support can be verified by indirect means. According to Arantzadi, there were only 265 subscribers to the journal *Baserritarra* in 1897. In the same year Arana himself referred to the meager support he was receiving: "We admit it without joy: the number of nationalists, that is, of affiliates to the party, and who, as such, fulfill faithfully their patriotic duties, is very small. To deny it would be foolish."[33]

Soon after Sota's group was absorbed into the BNP, Basque nationalism began to attract greater support. It remained, however, a very small party. Within Vizcaya, it was relatively strong only at the municipal level, and outside Vizcaya it had hardly any support at all. Although the ideology of the BNP and the party apparatus itself were controlled by Arana and his followers, Sota's group began to exert control over the selection of electoral candidates. Despite the BNP's radical rhetoric, in practice it became more moderate, particularly with respect to its aspirations to independence. This inconsistency allowed the BNP to avoid governmental repression and to broaden its electoral appeal.

In 1917 and 1918, the Basque Nationalist Party attained its greatest electoral successes, gaining control over the Diputación Provincial of Vizcaya, with Sota's son Ramón de la Sota Aburto as its president, and seeing all of its candidates elected to the Spanish parliament. These victories at the national level were Sota's, since most of the BNP's electoral candidates came from his faction within the BNP. One year later, however, the two dynastic parties regrouped as a single political entity, the Liga de Acción Monárquica, and handed the BNP a resounding defeat. The speed with which talk of nationalism then ceased is indicative of the instability of the BNP's political base and of the corrupt nature of politics during those years, for which both nationalists and non-nationalists could share the blame.

Between 1898 and 1923, which marks the onset of Miguel Primo de Rivera's dictatorship, the BNP remained a minor political force in the Basque Country, but during those years its political strength increased steadily. The influence of the BNP on Basque society also increased, and the party extended its organization to the province of Guipúzcoa. It also launched several major publications, each representing a different viewpoint within the party (*Euskalduna*, *La Patria*, *Euzkadi*, *Aberri*), and it opened a major cultural center, El Centro Vasco, that was controlled by the party. Finally, it created Basque Youth (Euzko Gaztedije) for the socialization of young nationalists.

Ideological conflict continued to flourish within the party. The chief sources of conflict were the separatist content of the program and the authoritarian character of the party. While the moderates controlled the nomination process and, to some extent, the party, the "sabinianos," with Engracio de Arantzadi and Luis Eleizalde as their ideologues, maintained their ideological hegemony. Eventually, however, divisions emerged in this second group regarding strategy. Arantzadi and Eleizalde, labeled as "posibilistas," began to emphasize the core of Arana's doctrine—the cultural regeneration of the Basque people through full adherence to religious principles—at the expense of the goal of independence. New cohorts of nationalists from Basque Youth, dissatisfied with this new approach, advocated the need to struggle for independence. These young dissenters also tried to attract the indigenous working class's support by criticizing the exploitive character of capitalism—always, of course, within the limits of traditionalist discourse.[34] The goal of this group, called Aberri, was essentially a society in which small industrial and agrarian properties would be the norm.

Conflict within the Basque Nationalist Party increased after World War I, reaching a peak in 1921, when the BNP expelled those members of the Aberri group who were led by Eli Gallástegui. The Aberri group, faithful to the radical legacy of Sabino Arana and joined by members of the old guard such as Luis Arana, kept the name Basque Nationalist Party, and the moderates within the Basque Nationalist Party adopted the name Comunión Nacionalista Vasca (Basque Nationalist Communion). In the Bilbao municipal elections of 1922, the only occasion on which the two parties competed against each other, the Basque Nationalist Party garnered slightly more votes than the Basque Nationalist Communion.

When in 1923 Miguel Primo de Rivera staged a coup, establishing a military dictatorship that held power for the remainder of the decade, the Basque nationalist community was as divided as it had been in 1898. In the Basque Nationalist Communion, Sota's group remained subordinate at the ideological level, but controlled the nominations. The group shared political power with the posibilista sector of the party, which supported a version of Sabino Arana's ideology that hewed to his main principles but was moderate in its strategy. The Basque Nationalist Party, on the other hand, remained faithful to Arana in both its ideological and strategic principles, while incorporating new elements that accentuated its antibourgeois stance and addressed working-class problems.

The dictatorship of Primo de Rivera, meanwhile, suppressed nationalism in all its forms. Although little is known about the activities of the radical nationalists during this period, what little knowledge we have reveals that they tried to confront the new regime and were either imprisoned or, for example Gallástegui, exiled.[35]

By the close of the dictatorship the political scene in the Basque Country had changed considerably. Seven years had been long enough, it appeared, to appease the spirits of the two contending factions of Basque nationalism. After the fall of the dictatorship, the Basque Nationalist Communion and the Basque Nationalist Party began talks that led eventually to their reunification, in November 1930. From an ideological viewpoint, the "Reunificación de Vergara"—as the merger of the two groups is known—symbolized the victory of orthodoxy, as evidenced by the doctrinal principles agreed upon by the two parties. As presented by La Granja, these were

First: Basque nationalism proclaims the Catholic religion as the only true religion and accepts the doctrine and jurisdiction of the Holy Catholic Church, Apostolic and Roman.

Second: Euzkadi, as well as each of the six historical ex-states that conform it, will be Catholic, Apostolic, and Roman in all the manifestations of life and in its relations with other nations, peoples, and states.

Third: Euzkadi is the nation and Homeland of the Basque people.

Fourth: Euzkadi, the Basque nation by natural law, historical right, God's design, and its own will, must be the absolute master of its destiny to govern itself, within natural law.

Fifth: Basque nationalism proclaims this right and intends to make it real, satisfying—as much as may be possible from now on, and completely once Euzkadi becomes master of its own destiny—

(a) the primary need to preserve and strengthen the Basque race, the essential base of the nationality;

(b) the preservation, diffusion, and refinement of the Basque language, the primary mark of our nationality;

(c) the reestablishment of the old practices and traditions, turning back the exotic practices that may distort our character and personality.

Sixth: Thorough reconstitution of the historical Basque ex-states of Araba, Bizkaya, Gipúzkoa, Nabarra, Laburdi, and Zuberoa, and their confederation into Euzkadi, will be ensured, without restricting their particular autonomy.[36]

Indeed, every principle of Arana's core doctrine is included in this program: independence, defense of religion, defense of the old social order, confederation of the Basque states, and race and language as the essence and mark of the Basque nation.

The honeymoon between posibilistas and the aberrianos did not last long. During the six years preceding the Civil War, the split between ideology and practice that had opened after Arana's death, and the ideological struggles that had previously led to the division of the party, remained as intense as they had been before. The Basque Nationalist Party's leadership shelved its demands for independence, and instead struggled to obtain a Statute of Autonomy like the one the Catalans had extracted with far less struggle (as we shall see). Old wounds reopened as a consequence of the leadership's moderation, and the group led by Eli Gallástegui, centered around the weekly newspaper *Jagi-Jagi*, abandoned the party.

Beyond differences in strategy, the two contending groups also disagreed in their social programs. Although the BNP's program became less traditionalist and thus closer to the Christian-democratic ideal, it remained closer to the interests of the middle class than to those of the working class.[37] Jagi-Jagi, by contrast, representing the most progressive social program within the Catholic Church, held to its ideology of a society of small rural landowners and industrial business owners, as well as to its focus on the working class.

A new nationalist group, Basque Nationalist Action, emerged during this period. This party, representing laical ideals within the Basque middle class, was the direct heir to a small group that had seceded from the Aberri group in the early 1920s. Its nationalist program was unique in its rejection of Arana's racism, his religious fundamentalism, and his goal of independence. Instead, its program was based on self-determination and on secular and autonomist principles. It differed on all these points not only from the Basque Nationalist Party, but also from Jagi-Jagi, although it shared with Jagi-Jagi a concern for the amelioration of the living conditions of the working class. This concern of Basque Nationalist Action for the working class, initially framed in paternalistic, non-Marxist terms, developed into increasingly anticapitalist positions.

During this period, notwithstanding all of these disputes and contenders, the Basque Nationalist Party obtained the greatest electoral support in its 35-year history (see Table 7). Its electoral success coincided with a sizable expansion of its organization, which included the formation of Euzko-Gaztedije (a Basque Youth unit), Emakume Abertzale Batza (a women's organization), Euzko-Gastetxu (a children's unit), and Euzko-Mendigoxale-Batza (an organization of mountaineers).[38] That the BNP was gaining in popularity was already clear in the 1931 municipal elections, when in coalition with all of the conservative political parties in the Basque Country it emerged victorious.

But it was in the 1933 general elections that the party achieved its clearest victory, obtaining 41% of the vote in Bilbao, 57% in the rest of Vizcaya, 46%

Table 7. Electoral results in the Basque Country, in general elections prior to the Civil War

Orientation and parties	(Percentages of votes for a given party, over total numbers of votes cast)[a]		
	1907	June 1931	Feb. 1936
RIGHT			
Conservative parties	64.07	12.40	16.23
Traditionalists	23.51	10.32	12.31
NATIONALISTS			
PNV	2.15	28.48	35.06
ANV		6.27	
CENTER AND LEFT			
Republicans[b]	4.27	22.56	13.24
Socialists	6.00	16.79	14.73
Communists and POUM[c]		3.18	8.44
Abstention	37.93	19.19	22.37

Sources: Martínez Cuadrado, *Elecciones y Partidos* (1969); Tusell, *Las Elecciones* (1971).
[a]It would be preferable to compute percentages on the basis of the number of elegible voters. However, since in some of these elections voters could choose several candidates, the number of votes always exceeded the number of voters. Therefore, I have been forced to compute percentages on the basis of the number of votes. (Abstentions are excluded from totals.)
[b]Under this label I have included several republican parties that competed in these elections.
[c]The POUM participated only in the 1936 election.

in Guipúzcoa, and 29% in Alava. In Vizcaya and Guipúzcoa, the BNP won more votes than did any other party. Conservatives, by contrast (including traditionalists) obtained 14% of the votes in Bilbao, 28% in the rest of Vizcaya, 23% in Guipúzcoa, and 58% of the votes in Alava. Finally, the Left obtained 44% of the votes in Bilbao, 14% in the rest of Vizcaya, 29% in Guipúzcoa, and 12% in Alava. The general elections of 1936 saw a general repeat of these voting patterns, although the voting percentages shifted slightly from the Basque Nationalist Party to the Spanish-level conservative parties.[39] Paradoxically, although Spain as a whole had sided with the leftist Popular Front in these elections, the Basque Country, which was one of the two leading industrial regions in Spain, saw the Left polling in the minority, compared to conservative forces (nationalists and Spanish conservatives).[40] Basque Nationalist Action, running independently in some districts or in alliance with the Left in others, drew insignificant electoral support.

In the 1933 and 1936 elections, Vizcaya and Guipúzcoa differed greatly from Alava in their voting patterns. In the former, nationalists and the Left (mostly socialists) received the greatest electoral support, while in Alava the

Spanish-oriented parties monopolized electoral support. Nationalism, then, was clearly successful in areas where it had a history of electoral support and a well-established organization.

The increase in the BNP's electoral strength resulted from a transfer of votes from traditionalist parties and dynastic parties. According to Heiberg, the transfer of votes came mainly from farmers. Because of industrial opportunities in the neighboring cities, these farmers had gained increasing economic independence, which freed them from the political hold of the small Carlist landlords who were active in village politics:

> The increased prosperity of the previous twenty years had helped to weaken the political links between many villagers and the Carlists by severing the economic ties between them. This factor explains why the villagers were able to exercise political choice. The "social programme" of the PNV [BNP], which many *baserritarrak* credit for enabling them to purchase land, was a major reason why many villagers chose Basque nationalism.[41]

If what Heiberg describes for Elgeta applies to other rural areas in the Basque Country, it reveals the failure of Carlists to deliver the social reforms—especially the protection of small property holdings—that they promised the peasantry during the Second Carlist War. In this sense, support for the BNP represented a fundamentalist return to the original Carlist principles. Peasants were experiencing, 30 years later, the same frustration with Carlism that had initially motivated Arana to create the BNP. These switches of allegiance from Carlism to nationalism came earlier to economically self-sufficient middle-class people like Arana, whereas farmers had to await the industrialization of nearby areas before they could gain enough economic autonomy to express freely their dissatisfaction with Carlism.

Although Heiberg's reasoning applies well to rural areas, the failure of Primo de Rivera's dictatorship may have been what motivated the Basque local bourgeoisie to loosen its political ties with the dynastic parties, which had supported the dictatorship. This is a topic for further research.

Drafting a Statute of Autonomy

During the Republican years, Basque nationalism was successful at the electoral level, but it faced great obstacles in its attempts to achieve Basque autonomy. These struggles are especially interesting for what they reveal about the ideological conflicts within the BNP. Like Catalan and Galician nationalists, Basque nationalists demanded and worked for a Statute of Autonomy. The first draft of the Statute had been developed by the Society of Basque Studies, which was closely linked with the BNP, and was then revised by the BNP, the traditionalist parties, and the nationalist union called Basque Workers Solidarity (Solidaridad de Obreros Vascos). Finally, it was submitted to a vote by an assembly of Basque municipal representatives from Alava, Guipúzcoa, Vizcaya, and Navarre. Once approved, the Statute was presented to the Spanish Cortes, in the summer of 1931.

The project met with a cool reception in Madrid, for the procedures by which the draft had been written violated the norms established by the newly elected Republican government. According to these norms, the provincial commissions should have done the groundwork, and their efforts should have been followed by a referendum in each Basque province to ratify or reject the project. Moreover, the assembly of Basque municipal representatives approved this first draft of the Statute on the basis of an undemocratic system that overrepresented small rural municipalities.

The first draft of the Statute reflected the BNP's intention to use political autonomy as a means to block the corrosive effect, on the Basque Country, of progressive reforms enacted in Spain. By including the three Basque provinces and Navarre as part of the Basque Autonomous Community, it satisfied the goal of those who favored a "greater Basque Country," by including Navarre from the outset, with, however, no consideration for the desires of the Navarrese. It also granted the Basque Country very broad autonomy, declared bilingualism, established a naturalization process that would greatly curtail immigrants' rights, and gave the Basque Country the right to regulate its relations with the Vatican independently. With the exception of the demand for independence, then, the project closely followed Arana's precepts. Indeed, it made it clear that, for most Basque nationalists, gaining independence was less important than ensuring a political landscape that would isolate the Basque Country from leftist influence. Not surprisingly, the Left-dominated Spanish Cortes rejected the Basque project.

After the rejection of the first draft of the Statute of Autonomy, Basque nationalists adopted a more pragmatic approach. They distanced themselves from other conservative forces in the Basque Country, who would have opposed any project with democratic overtones. This split had a lasting impact on support for Statute drafts in the four provinces. The second draft, with a more democratic content, was drafted in March 1932 following proper governmental procedures. Submitted for ratification by the municipal assemblies of the four provinces, it was supported overwhelmingly in the three Basque provinces but rejected in Navarre, which would have meant that a third draft had to be prepared. Instead, it was decided that the new project would include the provinces of Vizcaya, Guipúzcoa, and Alava only.

The third draft of the Statute, excluding Navarre, faced new obstacles. It was submitted in December 1933, soon after a Spanish conservative coalition, the CEDA (which included the Basque financial and industrial oligarchy), and another conservative party, the Radical Party, had come to power. These parties, intent on pursuing centralist policies, had strong misgivings about any Statute of Autonomy. Worse, in the referendum for the approval of the third draft, celebrated the previous month in the Basque provinces, only 46% of Alava's electorate approved it,[42] and the conservatives in Alava (the dominant electoral force in that province) therefore opposed the inclusion of their province in the Basque Autonomous Community. This lack of consensus concerning the status of Alava condemned the third project to failure.

In 1934, the Spanish Left renewed its revolutionary efforts through extra-parliamentary means that culminated in the general strike of October 1934. Repression by the conservatives was harsh, and a state of emergency declared by the government lasted until the dissolution of the Cortes in November 1935. Basque nationalists, still hoping to reach an agreement about the Statute of Autonomy, remained in the Parliament and offered their vote of confidence to the conservative government; support from the Basque nationalists, however, left the Spanish Right no better disposed toward Basque autonomy than before, and no progress was made on the Statute.

In November 1935 the Spanish Parliament was dissolved, and elections were called for February 1936. In these elections, the victory of the Left was overwhelming—except, as mentioned above, in the Basque Country. After this election, a fourth draft of the Statute was prepared, under the guidance of the Basque socialist leader Indalecio Prieto. The pragmatism of the Basque nationalists, who were by now desperate for a Statute of Autonomy, resulted in a document that was more moderate, more basic, more flexible to interpretation, and limited to Alava, Guipúzcoa, and Vizcaya in its proposed embrace. The document was finally approved, in October 1936, three months after the outbreak of the Spanish Civil War.

Five and a half years of difficult negotiations had led to the approval of a Statute that, ironically, did not have a chance to be implemented during peacetime. If one analyzes this long quest, with an eye to what it says about the Basque nationalist ideology, two conclusions emerge.

First, for Basque nationalists, nationalism was mainly a tactic for containing both the ascendance of big capitalism and the rise of the revolutionary working class in Basque society. When one analyzes the content of the first project drafted by the nationalists in 1931, that fact is clear. Later modifications sought pragmatically to ensure that the project would be approved by the leftist governments then in power.

Second, the Basque nation's boundaries, as imagined by Basque nationalists, did not correspond to popular sentiment. Neither the great majority of Navarrese nor the majority of the Alavans, very likely, hungered for an autonomous Basque community, a conclusion supported both by electoral results and by the outcomes of referenda for the approval of the second and third drafts of the Statute of Autonomy.

By 1936 Basque nationalism had become the most powerful political force in Vizcaya and Guipúzcoa by attracting substantial support from traditionalist forces and the local bourgeoisie. Analyses of the movement's ideology, of interparty and intraparty conflicts, of electoral results, and of political achievements suggest that Basque nationalism remained a predominantly traditionalist movement aimed at establishing a society of small-scale industrial and agrarian producers in which religious principles would inform most aspects of life. It was therefore the program of a conservative middle class whose most radical members placed independence at the forefront of their program.

One can also discern another form of nationalism, led by segments of the local bourgeoisie, that worked from within the BNP to turn the party away from separatist goals, but without great success. As Chapter 3 made clear, the local bourgeoisie was a relatively small sector of Basque society. It was also divided between a majority supporting Spanish political parties and a small element supporting Basque nationalist parties, in keeping with the traditional cultural and political orientation of the Basque bourgeoisie toward Spain. The two most determinative factors underlying this division, however, were the irreconcilable ideological differences between the local bourgeoisie and the old middle class, and the ascendance of the Spanish-oriented Basque capitalist elite at the expense of the local bourgeoisie. Both factors were indirect consequences of capitalist development—a development at once too rapid and too heavily based on capital-goods production.

Catalan Nationalism,
1876–1936

This chapter focuses on the relationship between economic development and the rise of nationalism in Catalonia. In particular, it examines how this relationship was mediated by the emergence of a particular social structure and a special constellation of class interests. The contrast between the rapid industrialization of Catalonia during the nineteenth century and the relative socioeconomic stagnation that characterized most of the rest of Spain created a wide gulf between the Spanish government, which represented non-Catalan landowning and financial interests, and Catalan society. This gulf was broadened by the cultural-homogenization policies enacted by the Spanish state during the nineteenth century, which were widely resented by the regionally oriented Catalan bourgeoisie and intelligentsia. The chapter reviews the various strategies followed by the these groups to protect their culture and their economic interests. We have already seen that the combination of endogenous development and industrialization based on the consumer-goods sector explains the political failure of traditionalist forms of nationalism in Catalonia. That combination also explains the Catalan bourgeoisie's and intelligentsia's lack of direct influence over state policies, and their consequent need to rely on nationalist politics to defend and promote their own interests.

Protonationalism

For most of the nineteenth century, Catalonia remained the only industrialized region in Spain. Industrialization in Catalonia brought about the rise of an industrial and commercial bourgeoisie, an intelligentsia, and an industrial working class. These transformations created new sources of conflict in

Catalonia. Capitalists were pitted against proletarians, and industrial society against agrarian society. Owing to the endogenous character of Catalan development, conflict of the latter type was not very intense. Conflict between capitalists and proletarians, however, attained tragic dimensions, partly because neither capitalists nor the working class had direct access to political power; Catalonia was an industrial island in the midst of an agrarian society still controlled by big landowners.

The Catalan industrial bourgeoisie was acutely sensitive to the political processes and decisions exercised at the state level, for example on trade policy. Since the Catalan textile industry was not competitive in international markets because of relatively high production costs, its survival and further growth hinged on protection from foreign competition in the Spanish market, on increasing consumption levels in the rest of Spain, and on low prices for imported grain, which had tended to keep industrial labor costs down. During the nineteenth century, then, Catalan capitalists, aware of their vulnerability, tried to influence the relevant state policies to their advantage.

The most serious sources of conflict between Catalan capitalists and the state concerned the import tariffs applied to grain and textiles. The agrarian bourgeoisie that controlled the Spanish government favored closing the Spanish market to grain imports and establishing low import tariffs for textile products, while the Catalan bourgeoisie demanded the opposite. Catalans argued that by prohibiting grain imports, the Spanish state would contribute to artificially high prices of bread, which in turn would push up industrial wages in Catalonia and make Catalan textile production less competitive. Moreover, they argued, lower import tariffs for textiles would reduce the Spanish market for Catalan textile products by encouraging foreign competition. For most of the nineteenth century and early twentieth century, both the Spanish cerealists and the Catalan industrial bourgeoisie showed a willingness to pull back from whichever of the two issues was less directly connected with their economic interests, and the outcome of these disputes, therefore, was that tariff levels for both grain and textile products remained high.

Although the Catalan bourgeoisie was frustrated by having to lobby constantly for higher import tariffs for textile products, it depended on the state to guarantee law and order within Catalonia. The profit margins of the fragmented Catalan textile industry—with its high production costs and its modest market—were too slim to allow flexible bargaining between employers and workers, and this zero-sum bargaining process led to periodic social crises that Catalan producers solved through state repression.

One indirect consequence of state repression was the mobilization of both conservative and progressive segments of the Catalan intelligentsia. The former interpreted repression as further evidence of increasing state centralization (Balmes, Torrás i Bages), while the latter sympathized with the working class's demands for improved working conditions. The progressive segment, influenced by prior political events in France, would begin to espouse republicanism as early as the 1840s.

Together with incessant conflict between the state, on the one hand, and both the Catalan bourgeoisie and the progressive segments of the Catalan intelligentsia, on the other, the early decades of the nineteenth century witnessed the blossoming of Catalan culture. Authors seeking to explain this phenomenon tend to stress the roles that foreign invasion (by the French, in 1808 and 1823), administrative and political centralization, and economic development played in this cultural awakening.[1] Catalan Romantic writers of the 1830s expressed in prose and in verse their love for their Catalan homeland, and searched medieval Catalan history for myths and legends expressing Catalan identity. Later, during the 1860s, the Jocs Florals (flower festivals) became an open forum in which writers and poets competed for popular acclaim by reading from their works, all written in Catalan. These festivals were an important vehicle for the diffusion of Catalan ethnic consciousness among the educated segments of Catalan society. The period of the Renaixença (Renaissance), between 1868 and 1876, represented the climax of this process of cultural renewal in Catalonia, a renewal that extended to all areas of scientific and humanistic endeavor.

The "Glorious Revolution" of 1868 was the culmination of the Catalan bourgeoisie's persistent attempts to assert itself politically. Launched from Catalonia, the "Pronunciamiento" that ultimately deposed Queen Isabel II opened the way for a very extensive participation of Catalans in the Spanish government, which afforded them a golden opportunity to enact the legislation that best suited their interests. This "bourgeois" revolution had the unintended consequences, however, of unleashing forces of reaction in the Basque region (igniting the Second Carlist War) and working-class mobilization in Catalonia. Unable to gather enough support from other social groups in Spanish society, the bourgeois government lost control of the situation and was soon deposed by more progressive groups, who proclaimed the First Republic in 1873. The fate of the republican government, which included many members of the Catalan intelligentsia, was no better, however, for it too was unable to deal with the Basque Carlist insurrection in the north, the working-class revolutionary activity in Catalonia, and the cantonalism that developed in many regions in Spain. The collapse of the First Republic in 1876 and the restoration of the monarchy, under Alfonso XII, marked the end of this brief interlude of Catalan hegemony in Spanish politics.

Two important lessons, the one obviously related to the other, were gained from these experiences: Spain lacked national cohesion and it was a geographical patchwork of disparate social formations. The Catalan bourgeoisie's and intelligentsia's attempts to mold the state according to their particular interests failed because most of Spain was still largely a traditional society. There was neither a Spanish bourgeoisie nor a Spanish working class. Instead, there were local bourgeoisies and local pockets of industrialization, concentrated for the most part around Barcelona. Recognizing this situation, the leading elements in Catalonia abandoned hopes to mold the Spanish state in their image and began to contemplate the idea of self-government. From the restoration of the monarchy to the outbreak of the Spanish Civil War, nationalism in Catalonia took two political forms: bourgeois nationalism and progressive nationalism.

Bourgeois Nationalism

The return to law and order brought about by the restored monarchy was welcomed by the Catalan bourgeoisie, who even sponsored the formation of a Catalan branch of the ruling Conservative Party. Nevertheless, Catalan capitalists never felt comfortable supporting a political party in which the leadership was mostly non-Catalan and the organization heavily centralized. These tensions erupted into open conflict after the disastrous losses of Cuba and the Philippines in 1898, which greatly damaged the Catalan economy. Thereafter, pressed by the need to restructure their economy and more conscious than ever of the specificity of Catalan socioeconomic structure, the Catalan economic elite began to lobby for political and administrative decentralization.

This is, of course, just what conservative segments of the Catalan intelligentsia had been doing since the 1830s. For almost 70 years, they had repeatedly opposed state attempts to undermine what was left of Catalan autonomy. Especially strong was their defense of Catalan civil law and of the Catalan language, whose survival had been threatened by laws that the Spanish government had enacted during the 1850s and 1860s. In 1881, the intelligentsia's opposition to further centralization crystallized in the foundation of the Centre Català (Catalan Center) by Valentí Almirall. The Centre attracted mostly conservative members of the intelligentsia, but also some progressives, whose common goal was to protect the Catalan language and Catalan juridical institutions. Their goals closely mirrored those of Catalan conservative intellectuals belonging to the group called Renaixença, who were revitalizing Catalan culture. In 1887, Renaixença and conservative members of the Centre Català merged to form a new Catalanist association called the Lliga de Catalunya. Later, in 1891, the Lliga launched another association, the Unió Catalanista, which sought to embrace every group and individual interested in promoting regionalism and in drafting a Catalanist political program. In its first assembly, the Unió Catalanista outlined a program, the Bases de Manresa, that sought to defend Catalan language, traditions, and institutions.

On the eve of the Cuban War, this small group of intellectuals, allied with other members of the intelligentsia who opposed centralization and sought to promote Catalan culture, took positions relatively independently of the business community. For instance, whereas the Unió Catalanista favored some form of autonomy for Cuba, the Catalan business community strongly opposed it.[2] The independence of Cuba, however, by triggering demands for decentralization among both the intelligentsia and the business community, facilitated the joint political action of these two social groups in the years that followed.

Immediately after the loss of Cuba, the Catalan industrial bourgeoisie played the Spanish card one more time, by supporting General Camilo Polavieja, a political outsider, in his bid for state power. In exchange for their support, Polavieja offered to grant to Catalonia the same fiscal autonomy enjoyed by the Basque Country. The Catalan bourgeoisie's hopes were again dashed, however, when the government headed by Francisco Silvela and Polavieja failed to deliver on its promise and, instead, approved a budget that increased direct taxation of capital gains. In response to these measures, the Lliga de Defensa Industrial i Comercial de Barcelona, which represented 146 trade and industrial guilds, refused to pay taxes. So did more than 7,000 retailers in Barcelona, despite the government's threats of repression. Eventually, the suspension of constitutional rights in Barcelona and the declaration of a state of war put an end to this episode.

After this doleful experience, Catalan capitalists veered resolutely toward regionalism. Members of the Catalan industrial bourgeoisie and many of the politicians who had seceded from the Unió Catalanista because of its political apathy formed a political coalition and participated in the 1901 general election. Their resounding victory in Barcelona, where they obtained four out of seven seats, led the coalition to form the first Catalan regionalist party: the Lliga Regionalista.

The Lliga was a conservative party whose supporters came from the industrial and commercial bourgeoisie, the petty bourgeoisie, and the intelligentsia. Its main political goals were to end political corruption and to establish a more decentralized state structure. Whereas the bourgeoisie attached primary importance to obtaining economic concessions from the government, the intelligentsia were more concerned with juridical and language issues.

From 1901 to 1936, the Lliga Regionalista remained one of the most powerful and influential parties in Catalonia. Until 1906, its influence remained limited to the city of Barcelona; elsewhere in Catalonia the major dynastic parties were still dominant. In 1906, however, a major political event provided the Lliga with the opportunity it needed to become the dominant force in Catalonia. Trying to satisfy the military, who, alarmed by the rise of nationalism in Catalonia, had been demanding repressive measures for some time, the government enacted a law giving the army jurisdiction over offenses against the armed forces and against the Spanish national symbols. As De Riquer has noted, the law was so vague that Catalan nationalists could be prosecuted in military courts simply for displaying the Catalan flag.[3] Catalan political forces were uniformly outraged, and, under the leadership of the Lliga, organized a coalition of parties called Solidaritat Catalana. This coalition included the Lliga, the Carlist parties, and a broad republican representation. In the general election of 1907, Solidaritat Catalana won all but three of the seats allocated to Catalonia. Moreover, the victory proved not to be provisional; although Solidaritat Catalana dissolved in 1910, the Lliga remained the dominant Catalan party until the dictatorship of Primo de Rivera.

Foremost among the achievements of the Lliga was the creation of the Mancomunitat Catalana. This institution, founded in 1914, was a supraprovincial organization with the power to coordinate the administration of the four provinces of the Catalan region. Although it fell short of providing political autonomy, it did return to Catalonia a sense of historical unity—a unity that had been severely undermined by the formal division of Spain into provinces in 1833.

Through the Mancomunitat, the Lliga implemented an ambitious program of economic, educational, and cultural reforms. It created a strong public-service infrastructure to facilitate economic development; it implemented policies to extend vocational training among workers; and it initiated an ambitious cultural program focusing on the promotion of the Catalan language and culture.[4] Such policies represented the goals of the principal groups behind the Lliga, namely the capitalist class and members of the intelligentsia.

During World War I, Spain's neutrality created economic opportunities that pushed the Lliga back into state politics. Conflict between the Lliga and the state followed the Lliga's proposal for the elimination of barriers to the import of grain. Although Catalan capitalists were benefiting handsomely from the war, they believed that this measure, by indirectly cutting labor costs, would allow them to take full advantage of the exceptional rise in demand for Catalan products created by shortages in the countries at war. The Lliga's proposal, however, faced the opposition of agrarian interests and was rejected. The Minister of Finances, Santiago Alba, instead proposed a law to tax the windfall profits made possible by the war. This additional revenue was to be invested in the development of agrarian production. The Lliga, however, found Alba's project unacceptable. Motivated by their position of economic strength and confident of obtaining the support of progressive military groups who were frustrated by state corruption, the Lliga decided to form an extraparliamentary assembly of deputies and senators. Seeing an opportunity to overthrow the monarchy, the progressive and leftist political parties went along with the Lliga's plan.

The King then tried to coopt the rebellious Lliga by inviting it to participate in a coalition government that would include two of the Lliga's leaders. The Lliga was put in a delicate position: on the one hand, it had for years opposed state policies and lobbied for a decentralized state; on the other hand, its ultimate goal, made explicit in Prat de la Riba's political manifesto "Per Catalunya i l'Espanya Gran" (1916), had always been to gain control over Spanish affairs. In the end, as when the Catalan bourgeoisie supported the overthrow of the First Republic, it was the social situation that determined its decision. Since these were years of intense social conflict in Catalonia, and because news of the Russian Revolution had galvanized the masses, the Lliga decided to withdraw from the Assembly of Parliamentarians and accept the offer.

Accepting the offer turned out to be an unfortunate decision, for two reasons. First, fruitlessness: within a year, the two coalition governments in which members of the Lliga had participated had fallen. Second, mixed signals: the Lliga's earlier withdrawal from the Assembly of Parliamentarians, which had included leftist Catalan nationalists, revealed that it had prioritized class and economics over nationalist interests. From 1919 to 1923, the Lliga attempted to regain the popularity it had lost by sponsoring a project of political autonomy for Catalonia. It was too late, however. Working-class unrest, which had reached unprecedented levels, along with the delegitimation of the Lliga after its participation in the Garcia Prieto and Maura governments, made it possible for leftist nationalists to seize the initiative. In June 1923, three months before Primo de Rivera's coup, the Lliga was electorally defeated for the first time by a leftist nationalist political group, Acció Catalana, which had been founded just the year before.

During the dictatorship of Primo de Rivera, the Lliga remained relatively dormant. Although Primo de Rivera suppressed the Mancomunitat and forbade the use and display of Catalan cultural symbols, including the Catalan language, the capitalist sectors of the Lliga were quite satisfied with the restoration of order brought about by the dictatorship. But in 1930, with the collapse of the dictatorial regime, the Lliga found itself diminished politically. Its loss of legitimacy, which preceded Primo de Rivera's coup, had been reinforced by its passivity between 1923 and 1930, in contrast to the visible opposition of leftist nationalist sectors led by Francesc Macià.

Thus, while the Lliga remained a major political force during the Second Republic, it ceased to be the dominant party in Catalonia. Torn between its class and nationalist identities, the Lliga at times sided with Spanish conservatives while at other times it sponsored nationalist demands. As revolution became increasingly likely, however, the Lliga sided resolutely with the right and eventually welcomed Franco's insurrection in July 1936. In Catalonia, support for the Republic and opposition to Franco's insurrection came from the other side of the nationalist political spectrum—from Esquerra Republicana (about which more later).

Progressive Nationalism

Beginning in the 1880s, a new form of nationalism developed in Catalonia, one that I will call progressive nationalism. It was sponsored by sectors of the Catalan intelligentsia, and its broadest characteristics were its republicanism, its federalism, and its socialist orientation.

Republicanism has a long tradition in Catalonia, dating back to the 1840s, when people like Abdó Terrades and Narcís Monturiol, influenced by Cabet, Saint-Simon, and Fourier, adopted republican ideas in their efforts to improve the economic and political conditions of the emerging Catalan working class. During the years preceding the Glorious Revolution of 1868, the development of Catalan republicanism mirrored the expansion of the working class and the growing inadequacy of the Spanish political framework for solving the problems of the proletariat. Republicanism, however, was largely a Catalan phenomenon, because of the disparity between the social structure of Catalonia and that of the rest of Spain. In the general election held just after the fall of Isabel II, for example, 76% of the deputies elected in Catalonia were republicans, compared with 18% in the rest of Spain. This concentration of republicanism in Catalonia partly explains the political failure of the First Republic, which was seen by many Spaniards as a Catalan conspiracy; from an ideological viewpoint, it explains why republicanism had a strong federalist component.[5]

From 1876 until 1900, republicanism languished in Catalonia. The efficiency of the liberal and conservative political machines of the Restoration, the demoralization of Catalan republican leaders after the failure of the First Republic, and the skepticism of the workers toward politics all made it difficult for republicans to play a major role in Catalan politics.

A major factor conditioning the success of republicanism in Catalonia was the great influence of anarchism among Catalan workers. This influence, by impeding the development of a socialist movement in Catalonia, redounded to the benefit of republican political organizations. The drawback of anar-

chist influence, however, was that it created great political apathy among
Catalan workers, which undermined the social bases of the various Catalan
republican groups. Nevertheless, republicans attracted working-class support
because of their show of solidarity with the working-class and their active
presence in working-class cultural associations (for example, choral associations).[6] Indeed, on many occasions between 1876 and 1936, anarchists and
republicans collaborated politically.

During the first two decades of the twentieth century, two types of republicanism, unitarian and federalist, flourished in Catalonia, though the two
evolved politically in very different ways. Under the leadership of Alejandro
Lerroux, a revolutionary type of unitarian republicanism attracted most of
the working-class vote. Lerroux's political parties, the Unió Republicana and
later the Partit Radical, were the major opposition parties to the dominant
Lliga Regionalista. Meanwhile, nationalist republicanism remained a minor
political force.

This failure of nationalist republicanism was due not to lack of support
within the intelligentsia. As early as 1904, some members of this social group
had seceded from the Lliga Regionalista to form a group named the Centro
Nacionalista Republicà. Later, they joined disenchanted members of Lerroux's party to form the Unió Federal Nacionalista Republicana (UFNR).
The UFNR's political program was federalist and democratic; it advocated
freedom of religion, promised to eradicate illiteracy, and favored the creation
of public institutions to protect workers. In 1915, a small group of UFNR's
members abandoned the party to form the Bloc Republicà Autonomista
(BRA), which adopted an even more leftist program. Finally, in 1917, the
UFNR and the BRA formed a new party named Partit Republicà Català.
Change of programs, change of names, change of electoral strategies: none
of these approaches succeeded for nationalist republicans. Republicans in
Catalonia preferred to vote for Lerroux's statewide republican party, Unió
Republicana.

The greater success of Spanish-oriented republican parties, as contrasted
with nationalist republican parties, has been interpreted as resulting from two
major factors. The first is the well-deserved stigma of "conservatism" that was
attached to nationalism during this period by the international labor movement; the clearly conservative character of the Lliga Regionalista certainly
reinforced this stigma in Catalonia. The second factor is the organizational
and logistic talents of Lerroux, whose perfect integration of ingredients—a
revolutionary discourse, anticlericalism, and anti-Catalanism[7]—made him
extremely popular among both the Catalan and the immigrant working
classes.

The major source of support for Catalanist republicans during this period
and thereafter was the emerging nonmanual labor force. In the Catalan lit-

erature, this group is more precisely called the "dependents del comerç i de l'indústria"; it comprised workers who, in exchange for a salary, worked for individual merchants or commercial firms, helping in all sorts of tasks. It also included nonmanual workers in industry.[8] In 1900, some 32,255 of the roughly 128,000 Catalan workers pursued these occupations. Using primary documentation as his evidence, Lladonosa has explained why members of the CADCI (the major organization created by this social group) became both nationalist and progressive. Nonmanual workers were a class-conscious group. They perceived themselves as socially distinct from manual workers, because of the type of jobs they performed and because of such status signs as their level of education and even the way they dressed. Their goal was to become members of the bourgeoisie by accumulating enough savings and skills to open their own retail shops or commercial firms, and the CADCI was in fact created for the express purpose of providing its members with the education they thought necessary to become members of the bourgeoisie: night classes (including the teaching of foreign languages), lectures given by prominent political and cultural figures in Catalan society, and libraries were all part of this strategy to achieve middle-class status. This goal also led the CADCI to incorporate the bourgeois nationalist ideal into its set of core values.[9]

Although nonmanual workers aspired to the bourgeoisie, they held progressive values consistent with their actual class situation. They worked without a fixed schedule and on very vaguely delimited tasks. In some ways, their working conditions were actually worse than those of manual workers, who with their longer history of political mobilization had in many cases secured for themselves a clearer set of work obligations and rewards. Nonmanual workers thus tended to support political programs, such as those of nationalist republican organizations, that contained clearly progressive proposals but did not challenge the institution of private property.

Despite their electoral appeal among the nonmanual working class, nationalist republican organizations were unable to secure widespread support until the close of World War I. It was then that growing social unrest, motivated by the rising cost of living during and after the war, facilitated the shift of electoral preferences toward nationalist republican and other progressive political parties.

After World War I, the Spanish anarchist union (the Confederación Nacional de Trabajadores, or CNT) reached a peak number of affiliates (more than 427,407 nationwide in 1917) and sponsored several general strikes that triggered a very violent response from the state and from employers themselves. Terror reigned in Barcelona as both employers and CNT members were assassinated by hired gunmen. Employers soon began to demand an authoritarian solution to the social crisis. In contrast, large segments of the

Catalan intelligentsia, not directly involved in these conflicts, proposed alternative solutions involving radical social reforms and a loosening of ties with a state that had long proved incapable of solving Catalonia's problems. These proposals were welcomed by the nonmanual workers, who, though they aspired to the bourgeoisie, found that their actual living conditions were deteriorating as a consequence of rising prices.

The most significant evidence of the growing support for radical change was the success of Acció Catalana, the liberal nationalist party founded in 1922, which defeated the Lliga Regionalista in the provincial elections of June 1923. But there were other symptoms of change. One was the formation of political parties, such as the Bloc Republicà Autonomista and the Partit Republicà Català, that represented a move from merely reformist to avowedly socialist positions. Another was the shift toward socialism in one of the oldest Catalanist organizations, the Unió Catalanista. A third symptom was the creation in 1919 of a new party, initially called Federación Democrática Nacionalista and renamed Estat Català in 1922, which was founded by Francesc Macià, an old sympathizer of the Lliga. The Estat Català's program defended Catalonia's right to self-determination, as well as fairly socialist objectives. One final symptom of change toward the Left in Catalonia was the formation of Unió Socialista de Catalunya in 1922, led by Rafael Campalans, who, together with other militants, seceded from the Spanish Socialist Party to form this new party.

The coup of Primo de Rivera in 1923 interrupted the leftist radicalization of Spanish and Catalan politics that followed the end of World War I, and represented a victory for the most conservative sectors of Spanish and Catalan society. Because the Lliga welcomed the coup, which had restored order, the only Catalan nationalist groups to oppose the dictatorship were the republicans. Foremost among these oppositional activists was Macià, whose reputation acquired mythical proportions. Catalan republicans maintained close clandestine contacts with other republican forces throughout Spain, contacts that became more frequent when the crumbling of the dictatorship became inevitable by the end of the decade. In August 1930, seven months after the resignation of Primo de Rivera and during the interim Berenguer government, various republican parties including Estat Català and Acció Catalana signed the Pact of San Sebastián. By the terms of this pact, they agreed on a series of programmatic points regarding the future organization of the Spanish state, among which was the Spanish republicans' commitment to the approval of a Statute of Autonomy for Catalonia if the Republic were to be proclaimed.

The municipal elections of April 1931 decided the political configuration of the Spanish state that would follow Primo de Rivera's dictatorship. The main competing parties in Catalonia were (1) a republican-socialist coalition, which included centrist and statewide republican parties and the Spanish Socialist Party, (2) the Lliga, (3) Esquerra Republicana in coalition with Unió Socialista de Catalunya, and (4) the Partit Català Republicà. The Unió and the Partit were participating in their first elections. Esquerra Republicana resulted from the merger of Estat Català (founded in 1923 by Macià) and the Partit Republicà Català (founded in 1917), and included affiliates of other minor republican parties. The main points of the program of Esquerra Republicana—about to become dominant in Catalan politics—were:

Self-determination for Catalonia and confederation of Catalonia with the
    other Iberian peoples.
The recognition of human rights.
The right to unionize.
The provision of insurance for workers.
Special protection for mothers and their children.
Protection for the aging.
The abolition of the death penalty.
The reform of the prison system.
The subdivision of large rural estates.
The exploitation of unused productive land.
The promotion of consumer and productive cooperatives.[10]

The Partit Català Republicà, led by Antoni Rovira i Virgili, was a slightly more progressive version of Acció Catalana and Acció Republicana, two other parties that had been founded by the restless Rovira i Virgili. This party remained more oriented toward the liberal segments of the intelligentsia, less populist, and more moderate than was Esquerra Republicana.

During the electoral campaign preceding the 1931 municipal elections, the most rancorous arguments pitted the Lliga against the Partit Català Republicà, which was perceived to be the strongest opposition party. In the end, however, and contrary to all expectations, the absolute victor of this election in Catalonia was Esquerra Republicana. In the rest of Spain—except for the Basque Country, where the conservative-nationalist coalition was victorious—socialists and republicans resoundingly defeated the dynastic parties, and the elections thus led to the proclamation of the Second Republic.

Esquerra Republicana won in Catalonia because it enjoyed the support of the anarchist CNT (the principal workers' union), and the Unió de Rabaissaires (an association for the defense of rural laborers' interests). Thanks to the support of these associations, Esquerra Republicana was able to capture the working class and rural votes that had eluded progressive Catalanism for more than 30 years (see Table 8).

Table 8. Electoral results in Catalonia, in general elections prior to the Civil War

Orientation and parties	(Percentages of votes for a given party, over total numbers of votes)[a]		
	1907	June 1931	Feb. 1936
RIGHT			
Conservative parties	17.31	0.41	12.67
Traditionalists	0.01	1.24	4.65
NATIONALISTS			
Lliga	70.02[b]	14.33	22.34
Esquerra		55.87	30.50
Other		3.42	11.57
CENTER AND LEFT			
Bloc Obrer i Camperol, Catalan Socialist Union (USC), and Unió de Rabassaires[c]		4.64	8.40
Republicans[d]	12.40	18.16	4.96
Socialists	0.25	0.73	0.75
Communists and POUM[e]		0.05	4.16
Null votes and other parties		1.15	
Abstention	39.46	31.69	28.34

Sources: Martínez Cuadrado, *Elecciones y Partidos* (1969); Tusell, *Las Elecciones* (1971).
[a]It would be preferable to compute percentages on the basis of the number of eligible voters. However, since in some of these elections voters could choose several candidates, the number of votes always exceeded the number of voters. Therefore, I have been forced to compute percentages on the basis of the number of votes. (Null votes and abstentions are excluded from totals.)
[b]This percentage corresponds to those who voted for Solidaritat Catalana (Catalan Solidarity), a coalition that included the Lliga and small progressive Catalan Republican parties.
[c]In 1931, this percentage corresponds to the Bloc Obrer i Camperol; in 1936, it corresponds to the USC and to the Unió de Rabaissaires.
[d]Under this label I have included several republican parties that competed in these elections.
[e]The POUM participated only in the 1936 election.

The main factor behind the CNT's decision to support Esquerra Republicana was the rightward shift of Lerroux's Partit Radical. This shift, the first symptoms of which can be traced back to the 1910s, resulted from Lerroux's attempt to transform the Partit Radical from a local party to a Spanish party. Because the Socialists had already captured most of the working-class votes in other urban areas of Spain, the Partit Radical was forced to appeal to segments of the middle class and to moderate its political program.[11] Once the

Partit Radical moved to the Right, the only progressive choice that the CNT could recommend to its supporters was Esquerra Republicana.

The day after the municipal elections, Macià, the president of Esquerra Republicana, proclaimed the Catalan Republic. He was soon convinced by Spanish republican leaders, however, to settle for a less ambitious plan that kept Catalonia within Spain. This compromise called for the symbolic reestablishment of the Generalitat, the medieval Catalan governing body, while negotiations took place for the approval of a Statute of Autonomy for Catalonia. This Statute was approved in 1932.

A detailing of the convoluted political dynamics that characterized Catalonia during the years preceding the Spanish Civil War is beyond our scope here. Especially after 1935, Spain and Catalonia entered a revolutionary spiral that tells us little about the hegemony of one ideology or another in Catalonia, or about the reasons for their hegemonic or nonhegemonic character. Suffice it to say that during those years Catalonia saw a trend toward the adoption of separatist and revolutionary anticapitalist solutions, over more moderate alternatives. Catalonia was, de facto, a revolutionary, independent Republic for sustained periods of time; in the end, however, when Francoist troops had gained control over most of Spain, Barcelona found itself in the paradoxical situation of being the last capital of the Spanish Republic.

It is difficult to know what the Catalans wanted during the critical period, 1935–39, or what their leaders' ultimate goals were. Did they seek a confederation of Iberian peoples? How loose a confederation? With how much self-government for Catalonia? With reference to these years, one can safely draw only a few conclusions: first, in the 1930s the Catalan bourgeoisie was firm in its support of autonomy within a united Spain; second, ample sectors within the intelligentsia, within the class of intellectuals, and within the nonmanual working class supported a progressive form of nationalism embracing as broad an autonomy as possible; and finally, the lower classes, though less concerned about the nationalist issue, sought a drastic transformation of social relations.

Two types of nationalism, then, had developed in Catalonia in reaction to the inability of successive Spanish governments either to enact the economic reforms and policies demanded by the bourgeoisie or to respond to the miserable conditions of the Catalan working class. Despite their shared grievances against the Spanish state, the two nationalisms, bourgeois and progressive, represented very different social interests. Data provided by M. Dolors Ivern i Salva summarize the social composition of the Lliga's and Esquerra's leadership during the 1931–36 period.[12] According to these data, the leadership of the Lliga included mostly lawyers (42%) and businessmen (28%), while the two major groups in Esquerra's leadership were lawyers (24%) and doctors (10%). For those leaders whose occupation is known, the greatest contrast between the leaderships of the two parties is the greater presence in the Lliga of rural and urban estate owners, businessmen, and lawyers, and the greater presence in Esquerra of doctors, nonmanual workers, and teachers. From these data one can conclude that the Lliga represented the propertied classes, while Esquerra represented the intelligentsia and the nonmanual working class.

This conclusion is reinforced by an examination of data on the corporate activities of electoral candidates of the Lliga and the nationalist republican parties during the 1916–22 period.[13] Of 35 electoral candidates presented by the Lliga during those years, 17 were members of at least one board of directors in 1922, totaling 55 directorships. In contrast, out of 20 nationalist republican candidates, only one may have belonged to a board of directors (see the note). It is interesting to note that during the same period, only 15 of 38 candidates from the major dynastic party, the Unión Monárquica Nacional, belonged to at least one board of directors, totaling 37 directorships. In Catalonia, clearly, the industrial and commercial bourgeoisie tended to side with nationalism rather than with the dynastic parties.

As we shall see next, the conditions and social interests that led to the rise of nationalism in Catalonia reappear in the ideology of some of its most influential leaders.

The Ideology of Catalan Nationalism

Both bourgeois and progressive nationalist leaders and ideologues agreed that Catalonia constituted a distinct community, one with a common culture (in which language played a pivotal role), a common history, and a common character. They differed from Basque traditionalist nationalists in their deemphasis on race as part of their national definition, in their acceptance of modernity, and in the infrequency of their calls for independence.

The bourgeois nationalist program tended to emphasize the achievement of a very broad autonomy. Authors faithful to this tradition, such as Prat de la Riba and Cambó, and even more progressive authors such as Almirall, stressed Catalan national rights, including the right to self-government, but emphasized that Catalonia was and ought to be inextricably united with Spain:

> . . . we do not aspire to independence. Regardless of how many and how serious our grievances are, regardless of the state of decline in which we find ourselves, mostly because of others, there is no one today in Catalonia who seriously favors separatism, and if some eventually do, it will be only as a last resort.[14]

Progressive nationalists, on the other hand, increasingly formulated nationalist programs that emphasized Catalonia's right to self-determination. Their ultimate goal, however, was the confederation of fully sovereign states rather than Catalan independence: "Catalonia is not separatist; it feels bound to Spain by geographic and economic ties, and its nationalism is complemented by a federalist attitude."[15]

Notwithstanding their justification of political mobilization for political autonomy, on the basis that Catalonia constituted a nation, Catalan nationalist authors and political leaders also stressed the effect that contemporary conditions in Spain had had on their decision to mobilize politically. Cambó, for instance, writes in his political *Memorias*:

> Various events have contributed to the rapid diffusion of Catalanism and to the even faster rise to political fame of its leaders:
>
> The loss of the colonies, after a series of disasters, provoked an immense loss of prestige for the state, for its representative institutions, and for the parties that ruled Spain.
>
> Catalonia's rapid enrichment, favored by the great amount of capital that was being repatriated from the lost colonies, gave Catalans that pride which is typical of new wealth, and left them prone to welcome our program, which sought to erode the Spanish state and to glorify the past, present, and future virtues and merits of Catalonia.[16]

What distinguished bourgeois and progressive nationalists more than anything else was their sociopolitical agendas. Bourgeois nationalism tended to present itself as an interclassist ideology, one that was compatible with almost any political configuration: "A free Catalonia could be uniformist, centralist, democratic, absolutist, Catholic, free-thinking, unitarist, federalist, individualist, statist, autonomist, or imperialist, without ceasing to be Catalan."[17]

In practice, however, the Lliga developed close ties with the political system of the Restoration. It was initially open to collaboration with Primo de Rivera's dictatorial government, and in the April 1931 municipal elections it sided until the last minute with the forces that opposed republicanism. Bourgeois nationalism, as exemplified by the Lliga, was a conservative, nontraditionalist ideology that welcomed capitalism. Unlike Carlism, its program did not include a strong religious component; it proclaimed itself Catholic, but was satisfied with the degree of religious freedom provided under the monarchy of Alfonso XIII. Only when the Second Republic was established did the Lliga become more actively Catholic: for example, in advocating freedom of education in opposition to the obstacles to religious education raised by the new regime's leftist governments. On economic issues, the main features of the Lliga's program were the defense of private property, industrial protectionism, and the provision of technical education to industrial workers. It originally opposed unionization, but during the Second Republic came to accept it as a means to reduce social conflict.

Progressive nationalism was always associated with democratic republicanism. On the religious issue, Esquerra Republicana advocated the laical character of the state and tried to undermine the Church's social influence by advocating the dissolution of religious orders and the prohibition of religious educational centers. Regarding social and economic policy, Esquerra Republicana vowed to collectivize industrial and agrarian private property in the long term, while enacting substantial social reforms in the short term. In practice, this meant the enactment of sweeping social reforms along social-democratic lines and the indefinite postponement of the collectivization of private property.

Throughout the nineteenth century and until the Spanish Civil War, Catalans pursued three different strategies in their efforts to create a political sphere corresponding to their culture, their level of socioeconomic development, and their particular developmental problems. These were republicanism, attempts to participate in (and even dominate) the government of Spain, and nationalism (both bourgeois and progressive).

Whereas nationalism was the only alternative for those members of the Catalan intelligentsia interested in protecting Catalan culture, the Catalan bourgeoisie relied on nationalist mobilization only as a last resort, when other autonomist strategies had failed. Consequently, two forms of nationalism emerged. One of them, bourgeois nationalism, was, as the name suggests, the vehicle used by the Catalan bourgeoisie to influence Spanish politics and to attain some form of political autonomy. The other, progressive nationalism, had as its objectives the protection of the Catalan culture and the improvement of the situation of the working class; its political goal was some form of Spanish confederation.

These two forms of nationalism reveal both the traditional identification of the Catalan elites with their culture and their lack of direct influence over state policies. The lack of a significant traditionalist nationalist movement in Catalonia demonstrates that the transition from a precapitalist to a capitalist society was smoother in Catalonia than in the Basque Country.

CHAPTER 7

Intra–Ethnic Group Conflict and the Character of Nationalism

Chapters 3 through 6 have described and analyzed the early phase of nationalism in the Basque Country and in Catalonia, focusing on those structural factors that conditioned the distinct ideological content of the two. The emergence and ideological character of the two nationalist movements in late nineteenth- and early twentieth-century Spain express dramatically the conflict between modernity and tradition in an ethnically heterogeneous state. In the early stages of Spanish industrialization, during the nineteenth century, uneven development overlapped markedly with the spatial delimitations of the two ethnically distinct communities. This overlap enhanced the ethnic identity felt by Basques and Catalans and facilitated the expression of class conflict in nationalistic terms. But the social base and the ideology of peripheral nationalism eventually reflected the different outcomes of class conflict and class alliances *within* the Basque Country and *within* Catalonia, and of conflict and alliances *between* these classes and the Spanish state.

The argument I have developed in chapters 3 through 6 can be summarized and perhaps theoretically extended, by what follows in this chapter. The breakdown of Spanish state finances, worsened by the loss of most of the American colonies, laid the groundwork for nationalist thinking by contributing to state initiatives toward economic liberalization and political centralization in early nineteenth-century Spain.

Economic liberalization drastically modified the structure of real property, of forms and relations of production, and of mechanisms for the distribution of goods. Combined with a secularization ideology, these changes antagonized broad sectors of traditional society, including the lower rural nobility, the clergy, the peasantry, and the petty bourgeoisie. Of course, the severity of the conflict between liberals and traditionalists depended on the character and intensity of these changes. In Catalonia and the Basque Country, the effects of economic and political liberalism were especially virulent, although motivated by different responses in the two cases: in the Basque Country, reaction by traditional agrarian sectors against capitalist groups and the state was related to regional structural conditions; in Catalonia, it was related to normal cyclical crisis in a period of market formation.

Although liberalism created some of the conditions for conflict between the forces of change and the forces of reaction, and between both of these and the Spanish state, *uneven development* at the Spanish level promoted conflict between the Basque and Catalan socioeconomic elites and the Spanish state. Indeed, modern industrial and commercial capitalism centered mostly on the Basque Country and Catalonia, especially in the last third of the nineteenth century, while the rest of the country remained anchored in an agrarian system with low productivity levels. Although big landowners, who largely controlled the state apparatus, and peripheral capitalist elites agreed on the need to liberalize the economy, they faced entirely different social and economic problems and had very different views about how to conduct government. Since for most of the nineteenth century the industrial and commercial bourgeoisie represented only a very small social group, it was the agrarian bourgeoisie who had the greater influence on state policy, thereby transforming class conflict between the agrarian elite and the commercial and industrial elites into conflict between the state and these commercial and industrial elites.

Centralization measures adopted by the state during the nineteenth century greatly intensified conflict between the state and the traditional and capitalist groups of Catalonia and the Basque Country. Indeed, as class conflict between traditional and capitalist social groups intensified within the two peripheries, and as conflict between the state and Basque and Catalan society heightened, the control and extension of local power mechanisms became more important for Catalan and Basque traditional and modern economic elites. These mechanisms became important both as a means to impose a particular socioeconomic structure at home and as a counterpower to the state. For the traditional elites, local autonomous institutions were seen as mechanisms for isolating their region from changes taking place in the rest of Spain, whereas for capitalist elites the local institutions were seen as a mechanism for fostering regional industrial development independently of transformations taking place in the rest of Spain. Centralization, by precluding these possibilities, exacerbated conflict in the two communities, and class differences within the Basque Country and Catalonia and between the Spanish state and each of these two communities became harder to reconcile. Because Spain was by now exposed to ideological influences originating in other European countries, the presence and memory of political autonomy, complemented by the cultural distinctiveness of Catalonia and the Basque Country, eventually facilitated the transformation of these internal and external class struggles into nationalist struggles.

The study of Catalan and Basque nationalist ideologies reveals their heterogeneous character. In the period between 1876 and the Spanish Civil War, one discovers three major types of nationalism: traditionalist, bourgeois, and progressive. In the Basque Country during this period, the most important forms were traditionalist and, to a much lesser degree, bourgeois nationalism, while in Catalonia, the dominant types were bourgeois and progressive nationalism. The content of each of these nationalist ideologies can be divided into a purely nationalist component and a political component.

The nationalist component of traditionalist Basque nationalism was characterized by a primordialist definition of the nation centered on the idea of race and religion, and by the objective of independence. Bourgeois nationalism also defined the nation in primordial terms, although race, in this variant, was less important than other elements, such as language or history; this distinction was more evident in the Catalan version of Bourgeois nationalism than in the Basque version. Bourgeois nationalism's political goal was a broad autonomy within the Spanish state: although both Basque and Catalan capitalists had their grievances against the Spanish state, they were economically dependent on a protected Spanish market. Finally, progressive nationalism defined the nation in the French democratic tradition, as a willed community. Accordingly, the objective of progressive nationalism was the achievement of self-determination as a prerequisite to deciding whether to constitute a separate state or a confederation of sovereign states.

Each of the three forms of nationalism may be matched with a primary political component: the political components of traditionalist, bourgeois, and progressive nationalisms were traditionalist, conservative, and social-democratic, respectively. Traditionalism attached primacy to religion and tradition as central principles of social organization, and to indirect representative democracy as the principle of political organization. Conservatism's principle of social organization was capitalism; and of political organization, direct representative democracy, attenuated by aristocratic or corporatist components. Finally, social democracy's principle of social organization was socialism, which attached more importance to collective property rights and equality than to private property and freedom; its principles of political organization were direct representative democracy and a republican form of government.

Each of these types of nationalism had its own distinct social base. The social base of Basque traditionalist nationalism was the petty bourgeoisie, the clergy, and the "rentier" class. The social base of bourgeois nationalism was the local bourgeoisie, defined as the segment of the bourgeoisie whose economic and social horizons were largely bounded by the community's limits.

Finally, the social base of Catalan progressive nationalism was the intelligentsia and the nonmanual working class.

Traditionalist nationalism was predominant in the Basque Country because internal class conflict far outweighed the external conflict between Basque society and the Spanish state. In the triangular relationship established between Basque capitalist society, Basque traditional society, and the Spanish state, a strong alliance formed between Basque capitalism and the state against Basque traditional society.

In the Basque Country, capitalist development was of the combined form and based on the capital-goods sector. These developmental conditions harmed large sectors of Basque society. Basque traditional society, which became the backbone of Carlism, represented a constant threat both to Basque capitalist sectors and to the Spanish liberal state. Moreover, Basque capitalism and the Spanish state developed a close economic relationship based on the pivotal role played by the Basque capital-goods sector in the state's plans to promote economic development in Spain, on the Spanish state's dependence on loans from Basque financial institutions, and on Basque capitalism's dependence on state contracts and the Spanish market. In the end, the Basque economic elite was too small to overthrow the state's power structure, but strong enough to merge with the Spanish aristocratic ruling elite.[1] Consequently, the Basque economic elite, which had become completely Castilianized, was never nationalist in its outlook. Its attitude was consistent with its economic and political interests and with its strong historical and cultural ties with the state. Instead, what developed in the Basque Country was a strong traditionalist nationalist movement that represented the symbolic modernization of Carlism. Within this movement, a small number of local capitalists and members of the intelligentsia tried to impose a bourgeois version of nationalism, one that was grounded on conflict between themselves and the state; they were generally unsuccessful, because of their small numbers and, probably, their great dependence on the Basque capitalist elite. In this sense, the failure of the Basque bourgeoisie to impose its ideology on Basque nationalism was not due to a mere tactical mistake, as a well-known historian has remarked.[2] Basque bourgeois nationalism reached its apogee only after the dictatorship of Primo de Rivera (1923–30), when a growing local bourgeoisie, which had traditionally sided with the economic elite and was frustrated with state inefficiency, transferred its support to the Basque Nationalist Party. What eventually developed in the Basque Country was thus a hybrid of traditionalist and bourgeois nationalism: autonomist, politically conservative, and fundamentalist in its religious aspects.

Catalonia, for its part, experienced an endogenous form of development based on the consumer-goods sector. This road to development reduced the severity of the transition to capitalism and facilitated the emergence of a certain commonality of interests between the agrarian and the industrial bourgeoisies. On the other hand, exchanges between the Catalan consumer-goods industry and the Spanish state were much smaller than those between the Basque capital-goods sector and the Spanish state: Catalan industry produced for the Spanish market rather than to satisfy state demand, and Catalonia's financial sector was too weak to meet the state's borrowing needs.

Thus while the Basque economic elite was able to secure a certain administrative and fiscal autonomy for the Basque Country through the Economic Agreements (Conciertos Económicos), and was well integrated into the Spanish political elite, the Catalan economic elite lacked fiscal and administrative autonomy and was excluded from the Spanish political elite. The Catalan industrial and commercial bourgeoisies had to rely on nationalist political mobilization to achieve their economic and political goals—a necessity that explains the strength of bourgeois nationalism in Catalonia compared with that of the Basque Country. Nationalism as a strategy suited both the Catalan bourgeoisie's political powerlessness and its historical attachment to Catalan culture.

The development of progressive nationalism in Catalonia and its absence in the Basque Country can be explained in the same terms. Industrialization in the two communities was followed by intense class conflict between capitalists and workers, but although the bourgeoisie's answer to working-class unrest was generally the recourse to repression, segments of the leftist intelligentsia often sided with the workers and proposed socialist reforms. In the Basque Country, historical patterns of elite cultural identification with Spain, along with intense class conflict between traditionalists and liberals during the nineteenth century, promoted the Basque leftist intellectuals' preference for a Spanish form of socialism, for the promotion of Basque traditional culture and institutional arrangements, advocated by traditionalists and central to traditionalist nationalism, came to be perceived by the majority of Basque intellectuals as an impediment to capitalist development and progress. In Catalonia, by contrast, historical patterns of elite cultural identification with Catalonia, in conjunction with relatively mild conflict between traditionalists and liberals, favored the development of nationalist socialist programs, and nationalism was not necessarily seen as a conservative ideology.

Basque and Catalan nationalism were thus the outcomes of entirely different processes. In the end, what determined the character of these two nationalist movements was not their different levels of development but their different types of development. The developmental factors just outlined helped to reproduce more long-term cultural and economic processes, which progressively defined the cultural identity of the upper classes in Catalonia and the Basque Country, as discussed in Part I. In the end, the political choices of the Basque and Catalan high bourgeoisies were determined by the combination of, basically, historically created affinities toward their region and toward a certain way of influencing Spanish politics and, secondarily, the existence of those structural factors necessary to facilitate and justify their final choices. The functioning of these historical and structural mechanisms would be displayed again in the period following the Spanish Civil War, which is the topic of Part III.

POLITICAL DIVERSITY
AND NATIONALISM
SINCE THE CIVIL WAR

Part III of this book analyzes and explains differences in the character of Basque and Catalan nationalism during the 1970s and the 1980s.
Despite strong similarities between the two nationalist movements, which
are consistent with the strong similarity between the socioeconomic structures of the two regions during this period, nationalist organizations that
were both separatist and revolutionary garnered more support in the Basque
Country than in Catalonia. The key to explaining this contrast is that within
the movement of opposition to Franco during the 1950s and 1960s the competition faced by separatist and revolutionary nationalist organizations in
their attempts to attract and retain supporters was less intense in the Basque
Country than in Catalonia.

What I propose here is a slightly amended version of Pinard's and
Nielsen's Structural Conduciveness model.[1] According to this model the
more diverse the political environment is, the narrower the political appeal of
any single organization will be and, in turn, the less heterogeneous the social
and ideological origins of its membership will be. For instance, if several
political organizations promise to promote a peripheral region's culture and
political autonomy, those people who seek this collective good will choose
one organization over another on the basis of the programmatic features on
which these organizations differ. If, on the other hand, only one organization promises this collective good, all of those who attach special value to
nationalist goals, regardless of their ideological differences on other issues,
will tend to support this organization. Other things being equal, therefore, a
particular nationalist organization is likely to gather greater popular attention and resources in a context of low political diversity (a "monopolistic" or
"oligopolistic" situation) than in a context of high political diversity (a "competitive" situation). In the former context, however, the social composition

and political aspirations of the nationalist organization's supporters is likely to be more heterogeneous than it would be in the latter.

The logic of the Structural Conduciveness model leads us to predict that the entry of a new competitor in the political game will result in a redistribution of voters along the political spectrum such that the social composition and political aspirations of each political organization's supporters become more homogeneous. The analysis presented in Part III of this book (the four chapters that follow) shows that during the late 1960s and early 1970s, separatist and anticapitalist political organizations gathered more support and resources in the Basque Country than in Catalonia in part because they mobilized in a less diverse political environment. When at the end of Francoism the Basque political environment became as diverse as the Catalan because of the active presence of pro-autonomy and procapitalist nationalist organizations, many Basque nationalists who had until then supported separatist and anticapitalist nationalist organizations transferred their support to the more moderate ones. The analysis of contemporary Basque and Catalan nationalism shows, however, that during the 1980s and early 1990s, separatist and anticapitalist political organizations continued to gather greater support in the Basque Country than in Catalonia. This persistent contrast between Basque and Catalan nationalism counters the expectations of the Structural Conduciveness model, which therefore needs to be amended.

The chapters that follow argue that the preexistence of a nondiverse political environment can retard the process of voter redistribution between political organizations when new competitors enter the political game, and can, in extreme situations, forever alter the politics of a particular state or political region. In other words, other factors being constant, including the political diversity of a given environment, political preferences are more likely to reflect the social context of a community in environments that have been politically diverse for a sustained period than they are in environments that have only recently become diverse.

To justify this hypothesis, one needs to take into account the role of secondary socialization in social movements.[2] People who are involved in political organizations tend to develop feelings of loyalty toward these organizations, and to identify with their programs, regardless of what their initial loyalty and identification may have been. Although this proposition applies more to actual militants than to sympathizers, even the latter will experience this process of secondary socialization—through having friends who are militants, through their participation in public demonstrations, and through their access to the political movement's propaganda.

Secondary socialization processes play a significant role in the explanation of the persistence of differences between the Basque Country and Catalonia in support for separatist and revolutionary organizations. Because of the low diversity of the Basque political environment compared to the Catalan, many Basques who opposed Franco gave support to or became involved in particular separatist and anticapitalist organizations even though they did not identify completely with their programs. More people, therefore, became exposed to secondary socialization processes within separatist and anticapitalist organizations in the Basque Country than in Catalonia. Had the Basque political environment been as diverse as the Catalan, many early Basque supporters of separatist and anticapitalist organizations would probably have gathered around more moderate nationalist organizations and might never have been exposed to more radical ideologies.

The Structural Conduciveness model also fails to account for the impact that the degree of diversity of the political environment can have on the political process itself and, consequently, on the development of specific political cultures. Chapter 11 demonstrates that because they did not have to compete for human and material resources with as many political organizations, Basque separatist and anticapitalist organizations had a greater impact on the political process than did similar Catalan organizations. Separatist and anticapitalist organizations were thus more visible and more effective, and their more violent actions provoked a harsher response from the Spanish government, in the Basque Country than in Catalonia. Consequently, Basques lived in a much more violent environment than did Catalans. They also developed a much more acute sense of oppression by the Spanish state and a greater attachment to the revolutionary organizations that claimed to be fighting for them. As the literature on Basque nationalism has shown, this is exactly the political climate these organizations wanted to create. They would probably not have been so successful, however, if their actions had taken place in a more diverse political environment.

In sum, during the Franco regime, Basque separatist and anticapitalist organizations faced fewer political competitors than did similar Catalan organizations. As a result, Basques were more exposed to the ideology of these organizations and to the cycle of violence they triggered.

CHAPTER 8

The Social Context of
Nationalist Mobilization

The literature on Basque nationalism since the Civil War has emphasized two major causes of Basque radicalism and violence. The first of these is the identity crisis felt by the native Basque population, a crisis brought on by rapid socioeconomic transformations and the resulting influx of immigrants from poorer Spanish regions.[1] The second factor emphasized is Francoist repression and discrimination.[2] This chapter analyzes the political and socioeconomic transformations that have taken place in the Basque Country and Catalonia since the Civil War and the ties established between these two regions and the Spanish economy and polity. The analysis seeks to determine the roles of state repression and socioeconomic structural factors in an explanation of the contrast between the Basque and Catalan nationalist movements.

The Historical Context

Following his victory in the Civil War, Franco abolished democratic rights and institutions, including the autonomy and cultural rights of Catalonia and the Basque Country. The dictatorship was initially characterized by extreme political repression, concentration of political power in the executive branch, lack of political representation, limited political and labor rights, the suppression of regional cultures, centralization of power, and official Catholicism. Although there is no clear empirical evidence from which to determine whether Franco's repression was more intense in the Basque Country or in Catalonia, there is no reason to believe that it was less intense in the latter as Horowitz suggests, at least until the late 1960s (as I will show in later chapters). In fact, his thesis is highly doubtful given that very intense

116

repression has been documented for Catalonia and in view of the greater threat that Catalonia posed to the Franco regime.[3] Before the war, Catalonia was not only staunchly nationalist but also one of the main centers of republicanism and communism in Spain.

Although the political character of the dictatorial regime prevailed until Franco's death in 1975, their most oppressive features softened over time. As Victor Pérez Díaz has noted, by the time of Franco's death a democratic culture had already developed in Spain, and this helped to ensure a smooth transition to full democracy.[4] Critical to the development of a democratic culture were reforms undertaken by the Francoist government during the 1960s, such as the democratization of labor and student representation, the loosening of controls over the press, and a greater tolerance for the expression of regional cultures. These reforms, which were implemented to increase the productivity of the Spanish economy and to enhance the legitimacy of the regime abroad, created a new climate of political competition that facilitated the subsequent transition.

One can sketch the democratic transition as follows: Franco died in the fall of 1975 and was succeeded by King Juan Carlos I as head of state. After eight months of indecision about the proper pace of reform, Adolfo Suárez was named President of the government, in July 1976, and immediately set himself the task of accelerating the transition. In December his plan for political reform was approved in a referendum, which was followed by political amnesties and the legalization of trade unions and political parties, including the Spanish Communist Party. In 1977, Suárez's party, the Unión del Centro Democrático (UCD), won the first democratic election in 41 years. The newly elected parliament drafted a constitution that addressed the political and cultural rights of nationalities such as the Catalan, the Basque, and the Galician. The approval of the new constitution was followed by intense negotiations between the Spanish government and political representatives from the Basque Country and Catalonia over the preparation of their respective Statutes of Autonomy. In 1980, these Statutes were approved by referendum.[5]

It is often noted that Spain's transition to democracy was remarkable for its speed and relatively peaceful character, yet it was not devoid of tension. Widely felt, the tension derived chiefly from the violence that characterized Basque politics, which intensified noticeably during the late 1970s while the negotiations over the Basque Statute of Autonomy were proceeding. During this period the UCD government was subject to intense pressure from the military and from Basque nationalists. The former demanded strong measures to fight separatists and an uncompromising attitude toward nationalist demands; the latter stated quite clearly that only if their political demands were met would peace be achieved in the Basque Country. This situation of political instability peaked in January 1981 when President Suárez resigned as the ruling party (UCD) unraveled amidst internal feuds. His resignation was immediately followed by Lieutenant Colonel Tejero's failed military coup. These events marked the beginning of a new phase in Spanish politics.

In October 1982 the Spanish Socialist Party won the general election. Its victory signaled the completion of the democratic transition by demonstrating that peaceful alternation of parties in power was possible. Socialist rule since has meant political continuity with the centrist policies of the UCD, as well as full membership in NATO and entry into the EEC.

Whereas the early phase of the democratic transition was characterized by democratic reform, Socialist rule has been characterized by rapid economic growth, at least until the worldwide economic recession of the early 1990s, from which Spain is just beginning to emerge. During the first twelve years of dictatorial rule (1939–51) the Spanish economy had declined to pre–Civil War levels because of the destruction produced by the Civil War and the complete political and economic isolation of the Franco regime. The lack of international legitimation of the dictatorship, along with Franco's autarchic economic policy, which radically restricted foreign trade and prevented the normal functioning of the market, contributed to the re-ruralization of Spain.

This process was reversed during the 1950s. Although for the most part Franco maintained his highly protectionist and interventionist policy, the Spanish economy grew at a respectable yearly rate of 5% from 1951 to 1957.[6] Several reasons have been mentioned for this recuperation. One of them is U.S. economic aid: following the onset of the Korean War and the Cold War, the United States' interest in using Spain as a base of operations contributed to improved relations between the two countries, and to the signing of defense and economic treaties in 1953. Other reasons that have been offered include the opening of the Spanish economy to foreign markets, the removal of government restrictions on the normal functioning of the market, and the undertaking of agrarian reform.[7]

Economic growth during this period was erratic, however, because of strong inflationary tendencies. From 1957 to 1959, the government studied possible remedies to this problem, with the assistance of international organizations such as the IMF (International Monetary Fund) and the OECD (Organization for Economic Cooperation and Development), which Spain hoped to join. In 1959, a stabilization plan was finally approved by the government. The plan consisted of draconian fiscal and monetary policies, aimed at halting inflation and reducing the budget deficit, and a broad liberalization of foreign trade. Following the initial shock of these measures, the Spanish economy grew at the spectacular yearly rate of 7% between 1961 and 1974. Over this period Spain became an urban and industrial society whose

wealth was concentrated chiefly in Madrid, the Basque Country, and Catalonia. Moreover, economic change and a dramatic increase in tourism contributed greatly to a transformation of social mores in Spain, as exemplified
by greater secularization and the diffusion of birth control.

The breakdown of the international monetary system and the two oil
crises of 1973–74 and 1980–81 slowed the modernization of the Spanish economy. From 1984 to 1990, however, Spain experienced renewed economic
growth—at the highest rate in Europe during this period—owing to the
general recovery of the world economy and strict policies implemented by
the ruling Socialist party to contain inflation and the foreign deficit. Finally,
since 1992 Spain has been experiencing the effects of the international recession.

The transformations of the Spanish economy since the Civil War, which
we turn to next, have been most dramataic in the Basque Country and Catalonia.

Post–Civil War Economic Development

In the post–Civil War period, rapid demographic and economic growth
has allowed the Basque Country and Catalonia to remain among the most
developed regions of Spain. During this period their populations grew faster
than those of other Spanish regions (Table 9), largely because of the arrival
of waves of immigrants from poorer Spanish regions (Table 10). This flow
was especially intense from 1955 to 1975, and its impact on the demographic

Table 9. Population growth rates, ratios, and proportions of total Spanish population,
Catalonia and the Basque Country, 1900–1981

Years	Growth rates (percent)			Population ratio, Catalonia/Basque	Percent of Spanish Population	
	Catalonia	Basque Country	Year		Catalonia	Basque Country
			1900	3.2	10.4	3.2
1900–10	0.7	1.1	1910	3.1	10.5	3.4
1910–20	1.2	1.3	1920	3.1	11.0	3.6
1920–30	1.7	1.5	1930	3.1	11.8	3.8
1930–40	0.4	0.7	1940	3.0	11.2	3.7
1940–50	1.1	1.0	1950	3.0	11.6	3.8
1950–60	1.9	2.6	1960	2.9	12.9	4.5
1960–70	2.6	3.2	1970	2.7	15.0	5.5
1970–81	1.5	1.3	1981	2.8	15.8	5.7

Sources: Confederación Española de Cajas de Ahorros, Estadísticas Básicas de España, Madrid
(1975). Instituto Nacional de Estadística, Censo de 1981.

Table 10. Net in-migration rates in Catalonia and the Basque Country, 1900–1981

Years	Net in-migration rates (per thousand)	
	Catalonia	Basque Country
1901–1910	30.1	22.7
1911–1920	69.4	44.5
1921–1930	128.3	31.1
1931–1940	38.8	12.2
1941–1950	83.5	25.6
1951–1960	123.3	174.0
1961–1970	157.6	159.6
1971–1981	51.3	21.0

Source: Confederación Española de Cajas de Ahorros, Estadísticas Básicas de España, for the period 1900-1970; Hernández and Mercadé, Estructuras Sociales y Cuestión Nacional en España (1986).

structure of Catalonia and the Basque Country was so dramatic that in 1981 about one-third of the inhabitants in both of these regions had been born in other parts of Spain. One cannot argue, however, that this massive influx has produced intense ethnic competition; as Table 11 shows, the immigrants have been disproportionately concentrated in blue-collar occupations, in both regions.

The magnitude of the immigration to the Basque Country and Catalonia is explained by the economic opportunities that these two regions offered the population of poorer regions during this period. Between 1960 and 1973, the GDP grew at a yearly average rate of 8% in Catalonia and 7.6% in the Basque Country (Banco de Bilbao, 1980) (Tables 12 and 13). In the same period the GDP per capita grew at a yearly average of 5.3% in Catalonia and 4.5% in the Basque Country. Catalonia's GDP represented 18.7% of Spain's total GDP in 1960, 20.1% in 1973, and 19.4% in 1985; the Basque Country's percentages in the same years were 7.5%, 7.6%, and 6.2%, respectively.

The 1973 oil crisis was felt intensely in Spain, especially between 1976 and 1986. Its impact, however, was greater in the Basque Country than in Catalonia (Tables 12 and 13), because Basque industry was much more dependent on imports of energy and because the Basque economic structure was more specialized and more industry-dependent. Indeed, though in 1955 the two economies had been equally specialized, from 1955 to 1985 the level of economic specialization proceeded inversely in the two regions, decreasing in Catalonia and increasing in the Basque Country (Table 14). In the Basque Country, the most important sectors during the post–Civil War period were metallurgy, steel, and services of various kinds. In Catalonia, the largest economic sectors in 1955 were the textile industry and commerce; but by 1985, the commercial and service sectors had become predominant.

Table 11. Occupational distribution of natives and immigrants in the Basque Country and in Catalonia

Occupation	Catalonia (percents)			Basque Country (percents)		
	Natives	Immigrants	Difference	Natives	Immigrants	Difference
Professionals	11.48	7.12	4.36	18.05	10.26	7.79
Managers	2.72	1.18	1.54	1.62	0.81	0.81
White-collar workers	18.86	10.32	8.54	17.64	9.02	8.62
Merchants and sales people	13.47	7.38	6.09	11.81	8.79	3.02
Domestic and other personal services	6.35	11.67	−5.32	9.32	12.55	−3.23
Farmers, fishermen, and related	8.47	1.80	6.67	5.05	1.26	3.79
Blue-collar workers	38.65	60.53	−21.88	36.51	57.31	−20.80
Total	100	100		100	100	
Coefficient of dissimilarity			27.20			24.03
Ratio index			0.55			0.48

Source: Censo de 1981.

Note: The ratio index (Maria Charles, "Cross-Sectional Variation in Occupational Sex Segregation," *American Sociological Review* 57, 4: 483–503) measures the degree to which immigrants in a given region are disproportionately represented in the average occupation. In a perfectly integrated labor market, the index would equal 0.

Between 1985 and 1990 the Catalan and Basque economies shared in the high growth rates experienced by the Spanish economy as a whole. The Basque economy grew at a yearly rate of 3.9%, the Catalan economy at a yearly rate of 5.4%. The Basque economic recovery resulted from a drastic

Table 12. Growth rates of the GDP and of the GDP per capita, in constant pesetas of 1980, in Catalonia and the Basque Country, 1960–89

Years	GDP growth rates (yearly percent)		GDP per capita growth Rates (yearly percent)	
	Catalonia	Basque Country	Catalonia	Basque Country
1960–73	8.0	7.6	5.3	4.5
1973–85	2.2	0.7	1.2	−0.3
1985–89	5.4	3.9		

Source: Papeles de Economía 34 and 45 (1988, 1990).

Table 13. Trends in unemployment rates in the Basque Country and Catalonia, by workers' age, 1976–86

Year	Age Group	Percent unemployment	
		Catalonia	Basque Country
1976			
	Total	3.9	4.0
	< 25	6.8	12.0
	> 24	3.1	1.5
1986			
	Total	21.0	23.5
	< 25	47.8	59.2
	> 24	13.6	13.9

Source: Giráldez and Gómez Castaño, "Empleo y Paro" (1988).

restructuring of industry based on the elimination of many large factories and specialization in steel-based products competitive in foreign markets. It is still too soon, however, to discern the long-term outcome of this restructuring.[8]

Although during the post–Civil War period the Basque Country and Catalonia were, along with Madrid, the most dynamic regions of Spain, they remained highly dependent on the Spanish market. Data on trade between the two regions and the rest of Spain illustrate their economic interdependence. In 1975, the value of Catalan imports from the rest of Spain represented 46% of the Catalan GDP, and the exports to the rest of Spain represented 49%.[9] In 1983, Basque imports from the rest of Spain represented 54% of its GDP, while exports to the rest of Spain represented 72%.[10] Similarly, imports from Spain made up 76% of total imports in Catalonia, and 86% in the Basque Country. Exports to the rest of Spain made up 86% of total exports from Catalonia and 76% of total exports from the Basque Country (Table 15).

The data presented above can be contrasted with data on trade between European countries to illustrate the high degree of economic interdependence between the Basque Country and Catalonia and the rest of Spain. In July 1992, *The Economist* reported that "for good or for ill, the technology of moving goods, services, people, and money around has ousted the European nation as the convenient unit of economic administration."[11] This assessment was based on data for trade in 1991, which showed that only the Benelux's export value exceeded 30% of their GDP; for other European countries this value was below 20%.

If these values for trade have "ousted the European nation as the convenient unit of economic administration," what can one say of the economic rationality behind independence programs for regions like Catalonia and the

Table 14. Percentage distribution of the GDP of Catalonia and of the Basque Country by activity, index of relative specialization, and percentage point change in the proportion represented by each economic sector, 1955–85

Activity component of GDP	Catalonia 1955	1969	1985	Percent change 55–85	Basque Country 1955	1969	1985	Percent change 55–85
Mining	0.8	0.5	0.7	-0.1	1.2	0.7	1.4	0.2
Construction and public works	6.0	6.2	4.3	-1.7	5.2	6.5	3.8	-1.4
Water, gas, electricity	2.1	2.2	3.1	1.0	1.6	2.5	3.0	1.4
Food, beverages, tobacco	2.5	3.8	4.2	1.7	3.2	2.6	3.0	-0.2
Textile and clothing	21.3	11.9	6.2	-15.1	3.6	2.0	1.9	-2.7
Wood	2.5	1.6	1.0	-1.5	3.0	1.6	1.2	-1.8
Paper, printing, graphic arts	1.7	1.8	2.4	0.7	3.0	2.5	2.3	-0.7
Chemical industry and related	5.2	6.8	6.2	1.0	6.1	8.0	6.0	-0.1
Pottery, glass, cement	1.7	1.7	1.6	-0.1	1.0	1.2	1.5	0.5
Metallic industries	5.3	11.8	8.7	3.4	29.1	27.8	24.6	-4.5
Agriculture	7.2	5.9	2.2	-0.5	5.8	3.9	1.3	-4.5
Fishing	0.3	0.3	0.2	-0.1	3.4	2.1	1.0	-2.4
Transport and communications	6.4	5.9	6.7	0.3	6.4	5.6	6.5	0.1
Commerce	17.1	12.8	12.8	-4.3	9.4	10.0	9.4	0.0
Savings, banking, insurance	2.7	3.9	7.5	4.8	2.3	3.4	7.0	4.7
Home ownership	4.9	5.9	5.1	0.2	4.5	5.9	4.0	-0.5
Public adm. and defense	2.1	2.4	8.4	6.3	2.3	2.7	8.9	6.6
Other services	10.4	14.7	18.8	8.4	9.0	10.8	13.8	4.8
	100.0	100.0	100.0		100.0	100.0	100.0	
Specialization index	35.1	31.9	30.8		32.5	35.7	37.3	
Index of structural change				27.8				18.3

Source: Renta Nacional de España.

Note: The specialization index is based on adding the absolute differences between the observed percentages and the expected percentages, and dividing this sum by two; the expected percentages are those that would be obtained if the GDP were evenly distributed by sector. The index of structural change is based on adding absolute percentage-point changes between 1955 and 1985 and dividing this sum by two.

Table 15. External trade for Catalonia (1967 and 1975) and the Basque Country (1983)

	Catalonia		Basque Country
Category of trade	1967	1975	1983
Imports from the rest of Spain as a percentage of the GDP	33.4	46.4	54.2
Exports to the rest of Spain as a percentage of the GDP	37.4	48.5	71.9
Imports from Spain as a percentage of total imports	68.7	76.1	85.6
Exports to the rest of Spain as a percentage of total exports	88.8	85.6	75.8

Source: Parellada, El Comerç Exterior; Censo de 1981 (País Vasco).

Basque Country, whose economic interdependence with the rest of Spain is much greater? In the future, trade interdependence will probably diminish as European economic integration proceeds. The advantages and disadvantages of independence will start to depend on other issues, such as the power of EU institutions to decide on economic and political policies, and the relative political clout of EU states of different sizes. For instance, if decision-making power and representation at the European Parliament continue to be biased toward small countries, then the costs of independence for the Basque Country and Catalonia will be lower than if, as some suggest, more populated states are able to increase their representation in EU institutions and increase their power share. In this case, the Basque Country and Catalonia could potentially benefit from continuing membership in Spain, which as of 1994 is the fifth largest European country.

Social-Structure Transformations in the Post–Civil War Era

During the post–Civil War era, demographic and economic growth, along with changes in the economic structures of the Basque Country and Catalonia, fundamentally altered the social structures of the two communities. Between 1940 and 1981, the two regions experienced the near disappearance of the agricultural sector and the growth of the industrial sector and (especially) the service sector. Thus, by 1981, the "active" population of the two regions was predominantly and evenly distributed between the industrial and service sectors (Table 16).

Table 16. Distribution by employment sector of the active population of Catalonia and the Basque Country, 1955–81

Sector	Catalonia						Basque Country					
	1955	1960	1964	1969	1975	1981	1955	1960	1964	1969	1975	1981
Farming	19.6	16.4	12.8	11.1	8.0	6.3	16.9	16.0	13.4	11.2	8.4	6.7
Industry	38.4	40.3	41.8	42.1	42.8	39.9	42.5	44.6	45.7	46.0	45.5	42.9
Construction	6.7	7.3	8.7	9.6	11.6	10.0	8.3	8.2	8.6	8.2	8.8	8.0
Service	35.4	36.0	36.8	37.2	37.6	43.7	32.3	31.2	32.3	34.7	37.2	42.4

Source: Renta Nacional de España.

Table 17. Percentage of workers earning a wage or salary in Catalonia and the Basque Country, 1955–81

Year	Percentage of workers	
	Catalonia	Basque Country
1955	62.6	66.2
1969	74.8	77.1
1975	79.7	81.8
1981	81.2	84.8

Source: Fuente: Renta Nacional de España.

An examination of the active population's distribution across occupations provides another perspective on social change in the Basque Country and Catalonia. As Table 17 reveals, by 1981 almost all of the Basque and Catalan "active" population worked for a salary or wage. Moreover, Tables 17 and 18 show that these regions developed very similar social structures. The most pertinent contrast between the two is that in 1981 the social group composed of professionals and the self-employed was proportionately larger in Catalonia than in the Basque Country. This information is consistent with the greater importance of commerce in Catalonia, as compared with the Basque Country. It suggests that the proportions of the population that belong to the petty bourgeoisie, the intelligentsia, and the bourgeoisie are, as in the early part of this century, greater in Catalonia than in the Basque Country.

Nevertheless, the proportional and numerical influence of the middle class in post–Civil War Basque society is much greater than it was in the early part

Table 18: Percentage of employed population in each professional category, in Catalonia and the Basque Country, 1981

Professional category	Percentage of employed population	
	Catalonia	Basque Country
Owners, or professionals, employing salaried workers	4.6	3.8
Owners, or professionals, not employing salaried workers	12.9	8.6
Members of production cooperatives or merchants that work in them	1.3	2.8
Full-time salaried workers	71.3	77.8
Part-time salaried workers	5.8	4.1
Unpaid family workers	3.1	1.8
Other	1.0	1.1

Source: Censo de 1981.

of the century. One would therefore expect that the middle classes played as important a role in Basque nationalist mobilization during the Franco and post-Franco periods as they had played traditionally in Catalan nationalist mobilization. Other, more subtle differences in the social structure of the two regions suggest, however, that the degree of political autonomy of the Basque bourgeoisie and intelligentsia during the Francoist period was less than that of the Catalan bourgeoisie and intelligentsia. To understand this, one needs to consider the Basque and Catalan economic structures, their impact on the relationships that the leading Basque and Catalan economic groups established with the Spanish state during the Francoist era, and their indirect effects on the potential for nationalist political mobilization of the Basque and Catalan middle classes.

Economic and Political Ties between the Upper Classes and the Franco Regime

Published studies show that Catalans were somewhat less represented within the Francoist political elite than were Basques.[12] In his study of the geographical origins of the 104 ministers named by Franco from 1938 to 1974, Amando de Miguel showed that 13.5% were born in the Basque Country, whereas only 8.6% had been born in Catalonia. In another study, Miguel Beltrán analyzed the origins of the bureaucratic elite. In a 1967 sample of 843 high bureaucratic officials, he found that 3% were born in the Catalano-Balearic region, 5% in the Basque-Navarre region. Finally, Miguel Jeréz, analyzing the geographic origin of 269 high officials sampled from the period 1938–57, found that 5.9% were born in the Basque Country, 5.2% in Catalonia. These figures suggest that underrepresentation of Catalans relative to Basques was significant only among government ministers.

The literature also shows that although leading Basque capitalists benefited from Francoist policies, so did leading Catalan capitalists in sectors such as gas production (e.g. the company Compañía Catalana de Gás, which was the largest gas-production company in Spain), metallurgy (e.g. La Maquinaria Terrestre), and shipbuilding.[13] Therefore, there is little substantive basis to the argument put forward by several Catalan authors that Franco discriminated more against the Catalan elite than against other regional elites, including the Basque elite.[14] There is also little substantive basis to the opposite argument developed by Horowitz to try to explain why the Basques have been more separatist than have the Catalans.[15]

Nevertheless, there is enough information to establish that—during the Franco era as well as during the pre–Civil War period—the Basque upper class maintained stronger economic ties with the Spanish state and market than did the Catalan upper class. The early years of the Franco regime (1939–52) were characterized by a very autarchic and interventionist economic policy that placed great emphasis on rebuilding the infrastructure that had been destroyed by the war. During this period, the market economy largely disappeared and the state became the main consumer of goods and services in Spain.[16] This situation, and the international demand for capital-goods production created by World War II, was of greatest benefit to the Basque capital-goods sector (steel production, shipbuilding, electricity, metallurgy), because of its symbiotic relationship with the state. Although there was almost no internal private demand for heavy industrial products, the state needed Basque heavy industry to rebuild the country's infrastructure and to satisfy military needs. By 1940, about two-thirds of the Spanish production of steel was located in the Basque Country, and the main consumer of this steel was the state.[17]

Catalan industry experienced the postwar years in a very different way. Although the Catalan industrial infrastructure was barely damaged during the war, Spanish standards of living were so low that there was almost no demand for consumer goods produced in Catalonia. What demand there was decreased still further thanks to the extremely low wages imposed on the workers by Franco.[18]

The volume of investment in Barcelona's and Bilbao's stock markets illustrates the relative economic conditions in Catalonia and the Basque Country in the early post–Civil War years. Between 1936 and 1942, the volume of investment experienced a tenfold increase in Bilbao, whereas it declined slightly in Barcelona.[19] Moreover, investment in Bilbao's stock market further strengthened Basque capitalism's interpendence with the Spanish state, for it was directed chiefly toward the purchase of public debt. Indeed, between 1941 and 1949,[20] public debt represented 53% of this investment. Another indication of the relative economic conditions prevailing in the Basque Country and Catalonia after the Civil War is the volume of capital investment in these regions. Data for 1941 show that 21% of the total capital invested throughout Spain was registered in Bilbao, compared with just 9% registered in Barcelona.[21]

Although the Catalan economy gradually recovered its pre–Civil War levels of economic activity and expanded at a faster rate than most other regions of Spain, its economic power and the political influence of its capitalists lagged behind the strength of Basque capitalism and the power of the Basque oligarchs.[22] As in the pre–Civil War period, Basque capitalist power was based on the strength of its banking system, which the dictatorship helped to increase.[23] In the early 1960s, seven Spanish banks controlled 70% of all deposits placed in private banks.[24] These seven banks controlled the largest Spanish corporations through stock ownership, control over credit

(60% of the total value of bank loans was provided by these seven banks), speculation in the stock market, and other indirect mechanisms.[25] None of these banks was Catalan, while four of them either were Basque (Bilbao and Vizcaya) or had very strong connections to Basque capital (Urquijo, Banesto).[26]

The monopolistic power of these seven banks over the Spanish economy increased during the dictatorship, owing to legislation which, from 1936 to 1963, prohibited the formation of new commercial banks. This legislation facilitated bank concentration and prevented the development of a Catalan banking sector; for instance, between 1940 and 1953, 21 Catalan banks were absorbed by banks in the rest of Spain.

The formation in 1946 of the "Consejo Superior Bancario" (Highest Banking Council) to advise the Ministry of Finances on banking matters institutionalized the influence of the Spanish financial sector over state policy, because representatives from the big seven played a determining role in the Council.[27] Despite its nominally consultative character, the recommendations of the Council, which often dealt with the regulation of competition between financial institutions, were usually followed by the Ministry of Finances.

During the Franco era, then, Basque capitalism solidified its leadership of the Spanish economy, while Catalan capitalism remained comparatively local in scope. The main reasons for this disparity were the type of economic specialization pursued in the two regions—capital-goods industry and banking in the Basque Country and consumer-goods industry and commerce in Catalonia—and the greater symbiosis of economic interests between Basque capitalism and the state than between Catalan capitalism and the state.

The Potential for Political Mobilization of the Middle Classes

The strength of the ties established between the regional upper classes and the Spanish economy and polity played a determining role in shaping pre–Civil War Basque and Catalan nationalism, but it was not alone in that role. The different relative sizes of the Basque and Catalan local bourgeoisies and intelligentsias also played an important role, because they determined the ability of these social groups to shape the nationalist programs in their regions. Because the middle classes in post–Civil War Catalonia and the Basque Country were almost equally large in relative terms, one might predict that the two played similar roles in nationalist mobilization in their regions. There are reasons to believe, however, that the Basque middle classes enjoyed less political autonomy than did the Catalan middle classes. Two factors can be proposed to explain this disparity: the economic structures of the Basque and Catalan regions, and the types of university that developed in these regions. Both factors bear closer attention.

The Basque economy was centered around the steel sector, which in 1955 represented 29% of the Basque GDP. This sector's main features were its extremely close connections with the two major Basque banks, the Banco de Bilbao and the Banco de Vizcaya, its high degree of monopolistic concentration, and its high degree of vertical integration.[28] For instance, in 1952, Altos Hornos de Vizcaya, the leading firm in the steel sector, owned or was the primary stockholder in eleven companies providing raw materials, and owned or was the primary stockholder in another nineteen that transformed the steel produced at Altos Hornos into more elaborate products. Altos Hornos, in turn, was controlled by the Banco de Bilbao and the Banco de Vizcaya. This example illustrates on a smaller scale, but with closer concentration, the main structural traits of Basque capitalism. At the top were two banks, the Bilbao and the Vizcaya. These banks were primary stockholders in the major companies of various monopolistic sectors of the Basque economy, such as the steel industry and the electricity sector. In turn, these companies owned or were major stockholders in a string of smaller companies. In the final analysis, a large proportion of the Basque economy was controlled by two banks and a few very large corporations. Local capitalism was largely dependent on these large corporations and on the banks that controlled them, most of which were controlled by people who held Spanish-oriented and pro-Franco attitudes.[29] In addition to constraints faced by local capitalists, members of what Smith calls the technical intelligentsia (e.g. engineers) and the humanistic intelligentsia (e.g. lawyers)[30] depended to a large measure on employment, contracts, loans, and connections controlled directly or indirectly by the owners of the big industrial and banking monopolies.

The contrast with Catalonia could not be more striking. Although there were some very large companies in Catalonia, and although numerous Catalans were present in the highest political spheres, Catalan capitalism remained largely local and fragmented, owing to its two predominant economic activities, textile production and commerce. Given the nature of its economic structure, monopolies and vertical integration were much less viable in Catalonia than in the Basque Country. Moreover, the small scale of industrial and commercial firms made them not only less dependent on loans from banks but also less attractive as an investment opportunity for banking institutions. Instead of a pyramidal noncompetitive structure such as that prevailing in the Basque Country, Catalonia was characterized by a competitive market economy where local capitalists enjoyed a good deal of autonomy, an autonomy that translated directly into the autonomy enjoyed by the sector of the intelligentsia employed by the capitalist sector. Consequently, the Catalan bourgeoisie and intelligentsia experienced fewer political and

economic constraints on their political behavior than did their Basque counterparts and were in a better position to oppose the dictatorship.

Another factor that constrained the potential for political mobilization of
the Basque bourgeoisie and intelligentsia during the Franco years was the
absence of a public university in the Basque Country. My emphasis on the
role played by the university environment is grounded in the observation
that students and academics have generally been at the forefront of political
mobilization.[31] It is likely that different university environments will differ-
entially influence the extent and character of political activism.

Differences between the Basque and Catalan university structures are quite
striking. Until 1968, the only Basque university was the Universidad de
Deusto, a private Jesuit university founded in 1886 by important members of
the Basque oligarchy (Ibarra, Vilallonga). Most of the students at the university were members of the upper classes, and until 1916 the university offered
courses only in philosophy and law. In that year, a Basque oligarch, Victor
Chávarri, and two of the few big nationalist capitalists, Pedro Chalbaud and
Ramón de la Sota y Llano, financed the foundation of a business school
within the university.[32] Until 1968, when the public University of Bilbao was
finally created, the Universidad de Deusto, an elitist private institution, was
the only university in what was one of the most developed regions in Spain.

Although the Universidad de Deusto gradually shed some of its initial elitist character by offering scholarships to competent students with little economic means, it remained too small and selective to absorb existing demand
and was unable to support the development of academic careers within the
Basque Country for university graduates.[33] Deusto did eventually become
the breeding ground for managers of the large Basque companies and the
center of recruitment to the Francoist political elite.[34] Enrolling at Deusto
was as important for an aspiring Francoist official as going to an Ivy League
school has been for the U.S. political elite.

Despite Deusto's elitist character, however, some of its students during the
late 1950s and the 1960s joined the pro-democracy opposition movement
that was developing in other Spanish universities and was particularly strong
in Madrid and Barcelona.[35] But unlike activist students in those cities, the
rebellious Basque students received no strong support from their fellow university students or, more significantly, from the faculty. Given the very strict
discipline enforced in Deusto, they had to mobilize outside the university. In
short, the Universidad de Deusto was not a place where a progressive oppositional culture could develop; it was not an environment that encouraged
the autonomous expression of dissent against the dictatorship.

The Basque Country's lack of a strong public university until very recently
has led Fusi to point out that "The Basque Country has produced great indi-
vidualities (Celaya, Blas de Otero, Zubiri, Aldecoa, Oteiza, Chillida, Caro

Baroja, among other great names from the postwar period) but has lacked a true Basque intellectual bourgeoisie—unless one considers the clergy to be the Basque intelligentsia—perhaps because of the character of the Basque language or for lack of a university tradition. . . ."[36]

The key point to be stressed here is that the lack of a university tradition was closely related to the type of development experienced by the Basque Country—sudden, spectacular, based on capital-goods production, and concentrated—and to the formidable economic and political power that the leading Basque capitalist families were able to acquire in Spain before and during Franco's dictatorship. There was no time for the development of a bourgeois culture in the Basque Country that would have encouraged the development of middle-class cultural institutions, such as public universities, imbued with the values of a local bourgeoisie. From the Spanish-oriented perspective of the Basque capitalist oligarchy, the Basque Country was merely an important locus for investment, and the Universidad de Deusto was a perfectly suitable managerial school.

In comparison with the Basque intelligentsia, the Catalan intelligentsia enjoyed greater autonomy and more opportunities for mobilization because of the existence of a large public university, the Universidad Central de Barcelona. The prestige and autonomy of the Universidad de Barcelona reflected the long history of economic and political autonomy of Catalonia, and the existence of a bourgeoisie that was much older and more self-sufficient than was the Basque bourgeoisie.

From at least the thirteenth century onwards there were numerous medieval universities in Catalonia, and the Universidad de Barcelona dates back to 1539.[37] With the advent of the Bourbon dynasty, the Universidad was closed and replaced by another university located in the small town of Cervera. But in the midst of confrontation between carlists and liberals during the 1830s, the location of the university became a source of contention: the liberals wanted it moved to Barcelona; the carlists did not. The victory of the Liberal camp in the First Carlist War finally led to the reopening of the University of Barcelona in 1842.

Although the University was an initially elitist and generally conservative institution, the fact that it was public allowed it to accommodate the growing number of students from all social strata and ideological persuasions that began crowding into it in the 1950s and 1960s, and ensured the existence of a greater ideological diversity than that prevailing at private universities such as Deusto.[38] Of course, this ideological diversity was undoubtedly related to the Catalan bourgeoisie's own ideological diversity, as well.[39] In the long run, however, the development of a university tradition facilitated the emergence of a humanistic intelligentsia that bound itself closely to the bourgeoisie while sustaining its own political vision.

An analysis of the political and economic transformations experienced in Spain since the end of the Spanish Civil War provides important clues for our understanding of political mobilization in the Basque Country and Catalonia during and after the dictatorship of General Francisco Franco.

Nationalist mobilization in the Basque Country and Catalonia was stimulated by the repressive nature of the Franco regime and by the massive influx of immigrants to these regions from elsewhere in Spain. The overdevelopment of these regions relative to the rest of Spain also encouraged nationalist mobilization, by generating conflict between the elites of the two regions and the state, concerning policies and influence. Finally, the high degree of economic interdependence between the Basque Country and Catalonia and the rest of Spain meant that there was a low potential for the development of separatist attitudes in these two peripheral regions. Therefore, the analysis presented in this chapter offers little empirical support for the identity-crisis argument or the repression-and-discrimination argument. Neither the rates of socioeconomic change in the Basque Country and Catalonia nor the intensity of repression the two regions experienced during the Francoist period justify predicting more radical nationalism in the Basque Country than in Catalonia.

The chapter has also focused on the strength of the ties that linked the Basque and Catalan upper classes with the Franco regime, and on the degree of political autonomy of the Basque and Catalan bourgeoisies and intelligentsias during the Franco regime. It has shown that the Basque capitalist elite had a greater influence over state economic-policy decisions than the Catalan capitalist elite had, and the Basque middle classes enjoyed less political autonomy than did the Catalan middle classes. These contrasts, which can be traced back to the specialization of the Basque Country in capital-goods production and of Catalonia in consumer-goods production, shaped the political behavior of the Basque and Catalan bourgeoisies and intelligentsias during the Franco period, as I show in the next two chapters.

CHAPTER 9

Basque Nationalism
since the Civil War

This chapter and the next recount the histories of the politics and anti-Francoist nationalist movements of the Basque Country and Catalonia in the years following Franco's death. The primary objective of these chapters is to reconstruct the degrees of social diversity of the leaders and participants in the two nationalist movements. The underlying logic behind this approach is that the characteristics of a nationalist movement depend as much on the goals and strategies of the particular social actors involved in the nationalist organizations as on the social composition of the movement itself. One can imagine the following scenario: In regions A and B there are two main social groups, G1 and G2, such that G1 is moderate while G2 is radical. What differentiates the two regions is that in region A, G1 does not mobilize politically, while in region B it does. Social group G2, on the other hand, mobilizes in both regions. The consequence of these regional differences in the political behavior of G1 is that politics in region A will tend to have a more radical character than will politics in region B. The critical observation to be made here is that differences between the two political movements will arise from differences in the social composition of the movements rather than from differences in such conditions as are thought to make social actors radical or moderate. This determinant role of the social composition of a movement is often ignored in comparative studies of nationalism and can lead to wrong diagnoses. What would need an explanation in the example above is the difference in the social composition of the political movements in regions A and B. It is important to know, too, whether differences in the structure of political mobilization have long-term political consequences. The next two chapters simply describe the histories and structures of nationalist political mobilization in the Basque Country and Catalonia, and Chapter 11 then focuses on the consequences of the differences between these structures.

134

This chapter examines Basque nationalist politics since the Spanish Civil War, in particular the intensity, organizational diversity, and social composition of the anti-Francoist movement in the Basque Country. Organized chronologically, the chapter distinguishes two major phases, the Francoist and the post-Francoist.

On the basis of the Basque capitalist elite's very close economic ties with the Franco regime, the Basque bourgeoisie's and intelligentsia's lack of political autonomy, and these groups' traditional cultural and political orientation toward Spain, one would expect the participation of the Basque bourgeoisie and intelligentsia in the anti-Francoist movement to be negligible. The chapter shows that this was indeed the case, and that only in the 1970s did the Basque bourgeoisie and intelligentsia mobilize in support of nationalist goals.

The Basque Nationalist Party's Opposition to Franco, 1939–59

In the Basque Country the Civil War was short-lived.[1] The Francoist army's choice of the neighboring province of Navarre, a stronghold of Carlist traditionalism, as its center of operations, and Franco's logistic need to control Basque heavy industry, meant that the Basque Country would be one of the early targets of Franco's offensive. Faced with the choice between Franco and the Republic, the Basque Nationalist Party sided with the Republic. Neither of the contending sides, however, was completely to its liking: the Francoist side embraced many of its socioeconomic and moral values but was highly centralist, while the republican side was more willing to compromise on the power-devolution issue but was increasingly leftist.[2]

In October 1936, just weeks before Madrid fell under siege, the republican government approved a Statute of Autonomy for the Basque Country. In the context of the breakdown of the central state caused by the war, the approval of the Statute greatly empowered the newly created Basque government. In its short but active life the Basque government, presided over by José María de Aguirre, enacted legislation to promote the Basque language, established law and order, and ensured food distribution to the besieged population.[3] The highly religious character of the Basque Nationalist Party ensured that there would be no religious persecution in the Basque Country, in contrast to other Spanish areas under republican control. Consequently, Franco's justification of his uprising as a crusade against communism and atheism did not have the same legitimizing effects in the Basque Country as it did in other regions of Spain.[4]

One year after war began, the Basque Country was under Franco's control and the Basque government had taken refuge in French territory. Meanwhile, the Basque Nationalist Party was divided over whether or not to continue its support of the republican army; Aguirre and his government favored continuing support, but separatist sectors within the BNP, represented by Juan Ajuriaguerra, considered the war to be already over. Views similar to those of the separatists were expressed by the "aranist" group Jagi-Jagi, which had seceded from the BNP in 1934.[5] The war had the unintended consequence of geographically separating the leadership of the BNP along ideological lines: the more pragmatic wealthy segment went into exile, while members of the more traditionalist, separatist, petty-bourgeois segment remained in the Basque Country. From 1939 to 1951, the Basque resistance in exile was organized by the Basque government in conjunction with the Spanish republican forces, while the Basque resistance within Basque territory was organized by nationalist leaders such as Ajuriaguerra and Joseba Rezola.

Optimism spread among Basque nationalists following the defeat of the Axis forces in 1945, when the Allies expressed a willingness to use diplomatic and even military pressure to support the reestablishment of the republican government.[6] This outlook led to mobilization efforts both within the Basque Country and abroad. The president of the Basque government, Aguirre, even began to organize a Basque army, trained by American advisors.[7] Aguirre's plan to invade Spain had to be shelved, however, as the Americans, worried about the threat represented by the Soviet Union, began to be more tolerant of the Franco regime.

This setback did not discourage the nationalist opposition, whose organizational capabilities had increased with the release of nationalist prisoners of war. In the Basque Country, the number of subversive actions escalated.[8] These included graffiti, the distribution of propaganda, public display of the Basque flag ("Ikurriña"), the destruction of Francoist architectural symbols, celebration of the Basque national day (Aberri Eguna), and illegal transmissions of radio messages by the president of the Basque government. In addition, an international organization for the defense and diffusion of Basque culture (Euzko Ikasle Alkartasuna) was founded in Leiden, Netherlands.[9] This group met for the first time in September 1947, in French Basque territory, and decided to illegally distribute propaganda promoting the Basque language and culture in the Spanish Basque Country.

The year 1947 saw intensified opposition to Franco in the Basque Country. The devastation caused by the Civil War, Franco's policy of economic autarchy, and his international isolationism had caused widespread misery. The socialist union (UGT), the anarchist union (CNT), and the nationalist union (STV) called for a general strike on May 1, under the auspices of the Basque government, to protest low standards of living. With roughly 20,000 workers participating, the strike posed a great challenge to the legitimacy of the Francoist regime. Franco met this act of defiance with crushing repression; many of the strikers were imprisoned or lost their jobs. Nevertheless, the workers of Vizcaya responded with another strike on May 5, and yet another on May 8, the latter extending to Guipúzcoa and involving more than 60,000 workers. The success of these strikes generated the belief that Franco's regime was about to collapse.

Most of the optimism generated by the events of 1947 evaporated quickly, however, for the Allies had begun to accept Franco's political regime, despite the efforts of republican forces and Basque nationalist forces to attract their support. These efforts included expelling the communists from the republican and Basque governments and agreeing to let the Spanish people decide on their future form of government. As the Cold War intensified, however, the Allies reached the conclusion that good relations with the Spanish government were geopolitically pivotal, and they withdrew their financial and logistical support for the republican forces in exile, including the Basque government.

In the years after 1947, Basque nationalists had to rely on the resources of the numerous organizations of Basque exiles and emigrants in Latin America to finance their opposition to Franco. Lack of international support and the violent repression exercised by the emboldened dictatorship led to a substantial reduction in levels of political mobilization in the Basque Country. The general strike of 1951, mounted in solidarity with Catalan workers, is seen by many as the Basque government's final attempt to destabilize the Franco regime through working-class mobilization.[10] For instead of weakening the dictatorship, this strike presented the government with an opportunity to dismantle the Basque resistance movement.

From 1951 until the 1970s, the Basque government in exile played only a minor role in directing the Basque nationalist movement. Having lost any hope that direct diplomatic or military pressure could be used to topple the Franco regime, José Antonio Aguirre and his successor, Jesús María Leizaola, resigned themselves to a waiting game, in the hope that Franco's desire to join the European Community would eventually force him to democratize Spain. Meanwhile, the resistance movement in the interior seized the initiative, gradually recruiting a new generation of militants.

Ajuriaguerra, who had been in exile in France since the intense repression following the 1951 general strike, returned to Spain in 1953 to reorganize the BNP in the interior.[11] He recruited new militants for Euzko Gaztedi, the youth organization of the Party, from the membership of folk-dance organizations, climbing clubs, the university, and Eusko Ikasle Alkartasuna (the cultural-diffusion arm that had itself been dismantled by the Spanish police in 1950). These new militants revitalized the Basque resistance movement.[12]

As the BNP was reorganizing, a small group of university students, organized under the name Ekin, undertook an intensive study of Basque culture and nationalist ideology. The presence in Ekin of José Luis Alvarez Emparanza (also known as "Txillardegui"), a writer and prominent member of Eusko Ikasle Alkartasuna, underscores the continuity of Basque nationalist mobilization during the Franco era. From 1952 to 1956, Ekin focused on the recruitment and cultural indoctrination of new members, and in 1956 its members joined Euzko Gaztedi, the youth group.

Given the relative passivity of the BNP's leadership, the recruitment of a new generation of nationalist militants generated tensions between the young members of Euzko Gaztedi and the old guard. These tensions came to a head in 1959 when Benito del Valle, a member of Ekin, was expelled from Euzko Gaztedi "for lack of discipline." In a show of solidarity with him (and frustrated by the reluctance of the BNP's leadership to adopt a more active stance against Franco), the other members of Ekin and a large segment of militants from Euzko Gaztedi abandoned the party and created a new organization called ETA (Euzkadi Ta Azkatasuna) in 1959.

From its beginnings and until Franco's death, this group spearheaded the Basque nationalist opposition to Franco. Although Euzko Gaztedi remained active, distributing nationalist propaganda and organizing the Aberri Eguna (the Basque national day) every year, its parent group, the BNP, ceased to lead the opposition to Franco. The splinter group ETA, always more militantly nationalist than the BNP, had taken the ascendancy, and soon evolved into a revolutionary movement that used military tactics against the Franco regime and advocated the end of capitalism.

ETA's Opposition to Franco, 1959–75

From 1959 to 1968, ETA was a small oppositional group whose patterns of political mobilization were comparable to those of other anti-Francoist organizations across Spain. During these years, the Francoist regime, in an attempt to gain acceptance in the international arena and to promote economic growth, enacted legislation making labor relations more flexible.[13] This new openness, the economic recovery that Spain had been experiencing since the mid-1950s, and the coming of age of a generation that had not experienced the Civil War, contributed to a dramatic increase in labor and political conflict.[14] Working-class mobilization over issues of labor relations was especially intense in industrial regions like the Basque Country and Catalonia, and was led mostly by unions organized at the Spanish level. In Catalonia, however, labor mobilization was complemented to a much greater extent than in the Basque Country by the activity of political groups demanding the transformation of the Spanish state's political structures. In the Basque Country only ETA led this type of political mobilization with resolve and efficacy.

Initially, ETA differed from the BNP only in its more militant attitude and its more uncompromising attitude toward the goal of independence.[15] One can say, in fact, that at this stage ETA was firmly within the radical-nationalist tradition founded by groups like Aberri or Jagi-Jagi. ETA defined the Basque nation in primordialist terms, but in its emphasis on language it had clearly departed from the racist connotations of Sabino Arana's discourse. The following quotes by Arana and Federico Krutvig, the latter a member of the Academy of Basque Language and one of the most influential early ideologues of ETA, illustrate the shift in emphasis. Arana, more than 60 years earlier, had said,

> If we had to choose between a province of Bizkaya populated by "maketos" [immigrants] that would only speak Basque language and a Bizkaya populated by Bizkaínos [people of Basque origin] that would only speak Castilian, we would certainly choose the latter, because the Basque substance, which can be purified when contaminated by foreign influence, is preferable to a foreign substance whose properties can never be changed.[16]

Krutvig, however, had this to say:

> Considering another absurd situation, I believe that a black man from the Congo, who has learnt the Basque language since he was young and who has lived among Basques, is more Basque than the son of people with Basque origins [Euskaldún], and including Basque surnames, who does not know the Basque language.[17]

Indeed, whereas for Arana the fundamental goal of nationalism had been the preservation of the Basque religious tradition, the fundamental goal of nationalism for the early leaders of ETA was to preserve Basque culture and especially the Basque language. In the early stages of the movement, this goal was considered even more important than the achievement of an independent state. Krutvig again: "It is more important to preserve, strengthen, and promote national traits, such as the language, than to obtain a state."[18]

Thus, although in its earliest stages ETA had retained a primordialist definition of the nation, it replaced race with language as the main defining trait of the Basque nation. Moreover, although immigrants were still seen as a threat to the Basques, it was not because they imperiled the purity of the Basque race, as Arana had believed, but because they contributed to the destruction of Basque culture. But the contrast was not merely semantic; Krutvig's view implied that immigrants were welcome in the Basque Country so long as they assimilated to Basque culture, whereas Arana had seen such assimilation as impossible.[19]

During this early period, ETA differed somewhat from the BNP in its more secular tone and in its more progressive socioeconomic views. ETA's membership included people with strong religious convictions, but ETA did not emphasize religion as a defining concern of the Basque nation, nor did it proclaim any programmatically religious goals.[20] Moreover, although ETA had a good opinion of the low clergy, it was highly critical of the Church's hierarchy, whom it saw as participating in the destruction of the Basque identity.[21]

ETA's social and economic views were also more progressive than were the BNP's. Though vague in the beginning, by 1962 ETA's program presented quite a clear picture of the type of society it wanted to create.[22] Its vision was critical of capitalism but not anticapitalist. In particular, ETA rejected economic liberalism, proposing instead a modification of ownership rights and an increased emphasis on society's needs, the socialization of basic economic sectors, state planning, and the promotion of cooperatives.[23] In this respect it repeated themes already present in Aberri's and Jagi-Jagi's political discourses, and introduced what many years later would become a major political theme for the Basque Nationalist Party.

In addition to advocating these social-democratic reforms, ETA was openly antagonistic toward the Basque upper class. Krutvig again: "A new class, bourgeois and oriented to Spain, has formed in the Basque Country [Euskaria], which does not have anything to do with it, regardless of how many Basque surnames its members have. This oppressing class, of Basque racial origin but of Spanish feelings, is an enemy of the Basque people, from which it differs ethnically."[24]

This expression of antagonism is reminiscent of Arana's attacks on the oligarchy of Bilbao. What differentiated ETA's early ideology most from the BNP's, however, was its commitment to a more active role in the struggles for Basque rights and against the Franco regime. This commitment called for proselytizing and for diverse forms of civil disobedience.[25] Between 1960 and 1968, ETA went well beyond its radical predecessors, moving toward socialist political positions and, for the first time, advocating the use of violence against the Spanish state. The figure who most influenced this shift was Federico Krutvig. In 1963, he fulfilled the request of a Basque friend to "publish a book that would be very nationalist, and which at the same time would be very progressive and leftist."[26] Although Krutvig did not hold the same significance for ETA that Arana still held for the Basque Nationalist Party, his book *Vasconia* dramatically shaped ETA's ideology during the 1960s.[27] *Vasconia*, like another important ETA document, "La Insurrección en Euskadi" (published in 1964), outlined a way of reasoning and a political program borrowed from Third World national-liberation movements. According to this ideology the situation of the Basque Country was one of colonialist—

later imperialist—oppression that could only be redressed through a revolutionary war.[28]

ETA's revolutionary rhetoric increasingly included among its goals the creation of a socialist society. In Krutvig's work this shift to the left was still in its preliminary stages and did not seem to have originated from his own convictions. Indeed, his justification for writing the book and his criticism of leftist ideals in the preface to the third edition (published in 1979) clearly show that for Krutvig and for many like him who advocated a nationalist revolution, social liberation was either irrelevant or secondary to the achievement of independence. For him, "Basque nationalism ought to be a leftist movement, provided one understands by 'left' the progressive movement of the discontented."[29] He held that this progressive element should pervade every single area of human life, including its scientific, economic, and political aspects.[30] Krutvig did not go much further, however, in concretizing a socialist program. His more socialist proposals, including one for reorganizing Basque society as a hierarchy of power centers whose basic unit would be the commune, were generally too detached from contemporary Basque social reality to convey a real sense of conviction. They seemed instead to build on Basque nationalist myths about the egalitarian character of Basque traditional society. His more concrete proposals—cooperativism and the socialization of banking and credit—simply repeated old themes in Basque nationalism, such as the rejection of big capitalism.

Krutvig's influence on ETA's mobilization tactics was soon evident. After 1966, ETA was dominated by followers of the anticolonialist and anti-imperialist ideology of Third World national-liberation movements; that is, by those who advocated the strategy of the "action-repression spiral."[31] The goal of this strategy was to trigger a series of political and social reactions that would eventually lead to direct confrontation between the Basque people and the state. ETA's expectation was that its acts of violence against carefully chosen military or political targets would be counteracted by indiscriminate state repression, and that the constant repetition of this action-repression cycle would progressively intensify feelings of oppression among the Basque population.[32]

ETA's actions, in conjunction with greater working-class mobilization, created exactly the political situation it had hoped for. In 1968 the Guardia Civil (a Spanish military institution charged with police-like functions) chased two members of ETA, Txabi Etxebarrieta and Iñaki Sarasqueta, as they tried to make their escape following a bank robbery. During the chase, Etxebarrieta and Sarasqueta killed a member of the Guardia Civil who was trying to arrest them. Hours later, Etxebarrieta was killed by the Guardia Civil.

Etxebarrieta's killing provoked intense reaction in the Basque Country against the police forces. ETA reacted to his death by murdering a highly unpopular character, a police inspector called Melitón Manzanas.[33] The cycle of violence continued: Franco's government ordered mass arrests, which were followed by torture, deportations, and, finally, the declaration of a State of Exception (wherein certain rights are suspended) in Guipúzcoa. In 1969, the police continued to arrest members of ETA; and finally, in 1970, sixteen members of ETA were judged by a military court. The trial was staged as a new State of Exception was declared, first in Guipúzcoa and then across Spain.

Franco's repression during 1969 and 1970 triggered an immediate public outpouring of sympathy toward ETA, which is exactly what ETA had expected. The Burgos trials, as the 1970 trials of ETA members came to be called, backfired, because they revealed just how strong the opposition to the dictatorship and its repressive forces was. Faced with a great popular outcry, which reverberated throughout Spain, and international pressure as well, Franco found himself forced to commute the nine defendants' death sentences. For the first time in decades, the Franco regime seemed vulnerable, and ETA could be said to have achieved two main objectives: to be known and admired by the population and to be able to motivate mass mobilization against the Franco regime.

Because police raids had taken a heavy toll on ETA during and after the Burgos trials, it remained relatively inactive in the two years following the trials, but in 1973 ETA made a resounding comeback, masterminding the assassination of Vice-President Carrero Blanco, Franco's heir apparent. This assassination initiated another spiral of violence, and the final years of Franco's life were thus marked by extreme violence in the Basque Country, as the number of ETA's victims increased and the government retaliated with arrests, stepped-up security measures, States of Exception, and the execution of two members of ETA just one month before Franco himself died.

The radicalization of ETA's objectives and tactics was marked by intense debate within the organization concerning the relative priority to be given to socialist and nationalist goals. In fact, one can say that ETA's shifting priorities reflected changes in its social composition.[34] For in 1966, when the first half of the 5th Assembly of ETA was held, 35% of the attendees whose social background is known (11 out of 31) had working-class origins (see Table 19). But just two years later, when the second half of the 5th Assembly convened, it "attracted all of the major figures who had been associated with ETA from its inception".[35] Their attendance reflected major changes in ETA's social composition: by now only 19% of the participants whose social background is known (6 out of 32) had working-class origins, and the veterans included Madariaga, a lawyer, Krutvig, the writer and ideologue, the two Escubi brothers, both in medical school and the sons of a doctor, and Etxebarrieta, the office worker's son who would be gunned down the following year by the Guardia Civil.

Table 19. Social background of attendees at ETA's Vth and VIth assemblies

Social background of attendees	Percentage of attendants		
	At 5th Assembly, 1st half, 12/66	At 5th Assembly, 2nd half, 3/67	At 6th Assembly, 8/70
Working class	35	19	50
Peasant/fisherman/ cattle raiser	10	22	4
Lower Nonmanual	39	31	29
Upper Nonmanual	16	28	17
	100%	100%	100%
People for whom father's occupation is known	68	61	55
Excluded from computations (see note)	23	22	17
N	40	41	29

Source: Information provided by Unzueta (Los Nietos).

Note: Social background is based on father's social class, except when this is not furnished. The percentages are based on people for whom this information is available. I have excluded from the percentage computation those students for whom Unzueta does not furnish the father's occupation and people for whom no information is available. In the upper nonmanual category, I include only owners of industrial companies and nonmanual workers whose occupation denotes the possession of a university degree or equivalent.

When ETA's 6th Assembly gathered in August 1970, many of the early leaders of ETA either had left ETA, were in exile, or had been arrested in the wave of repression that followed the first assassinations by ETA in 1968. As Clark has pointed out, the participants were "mostly young and unknown militants. . . . Most of them had been to the left of ETA at the 5th Assembly, but were also rather more inclined to seek close ties with non-Basque workers and their unions and perhaps somewhat more cautious about military initiatives."[36] The social composition of that assembly provides a clear explanation of its great concern with working-class issues: 50% of the participants whose social origins can be determined (12 out of 24) had working-class origins.

This examination of the social composition of the three ETA assemblies shows a relatively high proportion of workers and an even larger proportion of members of the lower middle class—a combination that to some extent explains the presence of both socialist and populist ideas in ETA's ideology. The analysis also suggests that a greater proportion of the first wave of ETA members, who generally emphasized the nationalist aspect of ETA's struggle, were of middle-class origins than were participants in subsequent waves; indeed, the second phase of the 5th Assembly, in which there was greater emphasis on the goal of national liberation, had a more middle-class composition than did the assemblies that preceded or followed. These dramatic changes in the social composition of ETA over time, which have also been noted by Jaúregui, Clark, and Unzueta, suggest that ETA's greater emphasis on insurrectional tactics and a socialist agenda could not have emerged without such change.[37]

On the whole, ETA maintained a delicate balance between its nationalist and socialist messages by forcing those who overemphasized one or the other to leave. Thus the founding members who were concerned solely with the cultural aspects of ETA's struggle left in the late 1960s, to form an alternative organization, Branka. Those who valued only the socialist aspects of ETA's struggle also left ETA, first in 1965 (forming ETA-Berri), then in the early 1970s (forming ETA-VI), and finally after Franco's death (forming ETA-pm).

Basque Nationalism in Democratic Spain, 1975–92

The Basque Nationalist Party

As Franco's dictatorship came to an end, the Basque Nationalist Party regained much of the initiative and support it had lost to ETA throughout the 1960s and early 1970s. Its renewed vitality reflected the growing influence of a more politically active middle class in the BNP's leadership and the increased influence deriving from the economic and political support of local business organizations.[38]

At this critical juncture in the history of Spain and the Basque Country, the BNP no longer sponsored a traditionalist program; its program had become bourgeois in both its socioeconomic and its political agendas. The "new" BNP was no longer racist or chauvinist and had become more secular. Although it still defined the Basque nation in primordialist terms, it now emphasized the cultural element, and more specifically the Basque language. As one of its publications put it, "Our duty is still to continue to promote—difficult as it may be—the survival of our national traits, of which the culture, and especially the language, is the one that best defines our individuality."[39]

The BNP's evaluation of social and economic change had also shifted. In contrast to Arana, who had staunchly opposed capitalist industrialization, the new leaders of the BNP had no quarrel with the pursuit of progress. Consequently, although references to restoring the Fueros (the old Basque laws and traditions) were still common during the 1977 elections, they soon disappeared from the BNP's campaign repertoire. Across the whole post–Civil War period, one can also detect important changes in the BNP's views of capitalism. Although a growing acceptance of capitalism was already apparent in the period preceding the Civil War, its acceptance became clearer after the war, and especially after the 1970s, when local capitalists began to support the BNP and influence its programmatic content. These business-men fully accepted capitalism but also sought autonomy for the Basque Country, so as to guide the Basque economy toward its recovery from the economic crisis of the 1970s.

Within this broad acceptance of capitalism on the part of the BNP, one can discern two slightly different positions. The first accepted industrialization and private property but was critical of unfettered capitalism and its often exploitive character, a position quite similar to that expressed before the Civil War by the political groups Aberri and Jagi-Jagi. As related by a BNP mem-ber in March 1977, it proposed

> . . . an economic democracy, where the firm's capitalist structure, characterized by the mere association of capital, will be replaced by a new structure, charac-terized by the association of producers, in which managers, workers, and cap-italists will all share the property, the management, and the profits; those firms that are unable to provide basic public services, or have become so economi-cally and politically powerful that they prevent the existence of a true democ-racy, will be nationalized.[40]

The second position was less concerned with small producers or with democracy in the workplace. Instead, its priority was making Basque indus-try more competitive in the Spanish and international markets. The main concern of those who supported this position was to mobilize political power sufficient to implement policies that would rescue Basque heavy industry from the economic crisis and loss of markets it had experienced since the early 1970s.

It appears, then, that within the socioeconomic ideology of the BNP there were, on the one hand, those who, without questioning the instituion of capitalism, decried private ownership of vast properties and sought greater worker participation, and, on the other, those who accepted capitalism in its extant form.

Despite its significant programmatic changes, the BNP continued to equivocate concerning the political role of the Basque Country within the Spanish state, and repeatedly stressed the following three claims: the right to self-determination, the attainment of broad autonomy, and the attainment of independence in an indefinite future.[41] The BNP's ambiguity on the future role of the Basque Country within the Spanish state hindered political nego-tiations between the Spanish government and the party during the transition toward democracy.

Legitimized by its historical role as the leading representative of Basque interests, the BNP was the chief negotiator with the Spanish government over the status of the Basque Country in the Spanish constitution and the content of the future Statute of Autonomy for the Basque Country. These negotiations, which took place in the context of an ever-tightening spiral of violence by ETA and repression by the Spanish security forces, were fraught with tension. Because ETA threatened the BNP's hegemony in the Basque Country, and because Spanish democrats feared an involutionist insurrection on the part of the military, violence constrained both the BNP's and the Spanish government's ability to negotiate.

In these negotiations the BNP demanded the right to self-determination for the Basque Country, a Statute of Autonomy granting as much power devolution as the state might relinquish, fiscal autonomy, and the inclusion of Navarre in the Basque Autonomous Community, the creation of which was being negotiated. It was very dissatisfied, however, with the way these issues were treated in the new Spanish constitution, and called for Basque Country voters to abstain in the December 1978 referendum on the constitution. The exclusion from the constitution of the Basques' right to self-determination led Carlos Garaicoetxea, then leader of the BNP, to declare:

> We demand that the new state respect two principles: the principle that peoples with sovereign power are the only basis for the constitution of the state, to which they belong for as long as the state upholds and respects this principle, and the principle that the state and its territorial representatives will always try to reach a consensus when delimiting their respective degrees of power and their spheres of action. . . . As Basque Nationalists we cannot accept a conception of the state according to which the state is the basis and the end of our existence.[42]

Controversy over the Basques' right to self-determination persisted during the 1979 negotiations for the approval and implementation of the Basque Statute of Autonomy. Disagreement on this issue was the underlying factor in other conflicts, such as the BNP's demand to gain absolute control over the police forces in the Basque Country, its desire for fiscal autonomy for the Basque Country, and its demand for institutional mechanisms to ensure the future entry of Navarre into the Basque Autonomous Community. Though these conflicts did not prevent the approval of the Basque Statute of Autonomy, after a referendum held in December 1979, they made the implementation of the Statute so difficult that Basque nationalist deputies actually left the Spanish Parliament for a brief period in February 1980.

During the 1980s, there was progress on the implementation of Basque autonomy. The 1979 Statute, or "Estatuto de Guernica," granted more autonomy to the Basque Country than it had ever enjoyed before. The functions it delegated to the Basque Autonomous Community included the administration of justice, of some aspects of economic policy, and of police, culture, and education. Statute provisions also authorized the creation of a Basque public-television channel, declared Basque language the official language along with Castilian, established a Basque government and democratically elected Basque parliament, and granted fiscal autonomy to the Basque Country. As for the region of Navarre, the Statute established a procedure that would enable this region to join the Basque Autonomous Community should Navarre's citizens ever so desire. Finally, both the constitution and the Basque Statute included clauses that made subsequent reform of their content possible.

Tension between the central government and the Basque authorities arose again in the 1980s, over the pace of power devolution and how to handle ETA violence. Internal disputes within the BNP, however, and between the BNP and other Basque political forces, slowly took precedence. Indeed, political discord within the BNP, a permanent feature during the period preceding the Civil War, reemerged after Franco's death.

The fact that in the post–Civil War years the lower-middle-class separatist militants in the BNP were its most active sector in opposing Franco accounts for their organizational strength when democracy was restored. These separatist elements differed from their ETA counterparts in their traditionalist social conceptions, but they shared ETA's social origins and its rejection of the Spanish state, as indicated by their success in pressuring the BNP's leadership to campaign for abstention in the 1978 referendum on the Spanish constitution. During the 1980 campaign, preceding the first postwar elections in the Basque Country, separatists and moderates again struggled for control of the party and the nomination process. This time it was the moderate faction, led by Xabier Arzállus, that achieved control of the party, echoing the results of similar struggles in the early decades of the century.

Between 1983 and 1986, internal disputes in the BNP flared up one more time. The party apparatus, controlled by moderates, as well as representatives of the BNP in the Basque government, led by the Basque president Carlos Garaicoetxea, clashed on issues of regional administration and government autonomy from party control. The party supported the idea of allocating greater control over economic resources to the municipalities, while Garaicoetxea supported the centralization of control within the Basque government. Although the underlying causes of this conflict are still unclear,[43] it became a vehicle for the expression of underlying dissatisfaction within the BNP, concerning both the rate of power devolution to the Basque Country and the limits on sovereignty imposed by the Statute of Autonomy. Eventually, the party forced Garaicoetxea to resign as head of the Basque government, whereupon he left the BNP and formed a new

party, Eusko Alkartasuna (EA). Today, EA proclaims the right of self-determination for the Basque Country, and calls for the region's eventual independence from Spain. The radicalism of EA's goals has attracted many
dissatisfied BNP members and voters.

Scholars and journalists who have analyzed BNP politics believe that the
party is still deeply divided between a group that accepts capitalist society
reluctantly and another that does so wholeheartedly. The secession of BNP
militants to form the new party, EA, corroborates that impression. As a
leader of the BNP once put it, "the BNP is, more than anything, a 'social
movement,' . . . which includes groups and personalities with diverse ideologies, from the old Christian-democrats, who are a minority today, to the
social-democrats, who constitute the majority, as well as liberals in the most
orthodox meaning of the word."[44] Or, as Zirakzadeh writes:

> . . . at the elite level, the party was never merely populist and anti-industrial. It
> was, rather, an ideologically variegated organization with two seemingly con-
> tradictory ideological traditions: (1) a theocratic and anticapitalist tradition
> that tended to be highly critical of large-scale production and of capitalists'
> exploitation of employees and (2) a more typically "Western" or "modernist"
> tradition that favored rapid industrialization and private entrepreneurship as a
> way to organize society.[45]

This last comment reflects well the ideological conflict within the BNP
throughout its history if one substitutes the word "religious" for the word
"theocratic" to describe the BNP in the contemporary period. One major
contrast between the early period of the BNP and the contemporary BNP (a
contrast that Zirakzadeh, however, does not emphasize) is that the most traditionalist faction of the party enjoyed ideological hegemony in the past,
whereas the more progressive group within the party has had much more say
in recent years.

Despite their differences, moderates and radicals within the BNP gradually
came to agree on one fundamental issue. During the transition to democracy, the BNP was often criticized by politicians and journalists for not con-
demning ETA's violence. Indeed, the BNP consistently rejected exclusive
reliance on police measures to eradicate ETA, often justified ETA's actions,
and refused to condemn the violence committed by ETA without also con-
demning the violence exerted by the police and far-right groups. This led
many Spaniards to believe that the BNP was using ETA's violence strategi-
cally to put pressure on the Spanish government during the autonomy negotiations. This attitude toward ETA, however, was not unique to the BNP, for
the democratic opposition to the Franco regime was equally mild in its condemnation of ETA in the years preceding the dictator's death.

But however one chooses to interpret the BNP's stance toward ETA in the early years of the transition to democracy, there is no doubt that as time went on expressions of condemnation became increasingly frequent, reaching their peak in the signing of the "Agreement for the Normalization and Pacification of Euskadi" in January 1988. This agreement, which unambiguously condemned all forms of violence, was signed by most of the Basque political forces, including the BNP and Eusko Alkartasuna.

ETA

Nonetheless, in the seventeen years since Franco's death, ETA's military activities have continued unabated, despite conflicts over the use of violence within the organization. The outcome of every internal dispute on the matter has been the expulsion or defection of the advocates of nonviolent means.[46] Internal disputes have been an unintended consequence of the action-repression strategy implemented by ETA since 1967.[47] Indiscriminate repression by the Francoist regime in response to ETA's actions provoked popular mobilization both within and beyond the Basque Country. It also motivated many daring young Basques to join ETA. The problem, however, was that people did not necessarily support or join ETA because of their adherence to its separatist political agenda. Many did so because ETA was overtly socialist, or because violent insurrection was seen as an effective way to challenge Franco.[48] The different motivations that led people to sympathize with ETA, and to join the organization, eroded its internal ideological homogeneity, which in turn provoked disputes, vendettas, and defections. Thus, the secession of ETA-VI in 1971 was followed by the secession of ETA's Worker's Front in 1974, the split between ETA-pm (political and military, or "pm") from ETA-m (military, or "m") in 1974, and the split within ETA-pm in 1976 between those who favored participation in conventional politics (the Pertur faction) and those who did not (the Apala faction). These splits arose as a result of disputes over the relative priority of social and nationalist goals; but after 1975, they were also based on the separate factions' acceptance or rejection of the new democratic system, of Basque autonomy, and of the government's offers of pardon for ETA militants willing to lay down their arms.

Since 1975, and as a result of these many splits, ETA has become progressively dominated by groups who spend little time debating ideological issues and see military confrontation as the only way to achieve their goal of independence for Euskadi.[49] One indication of this shift is that whereas ETA produced abundant literature during the 1960s and early 1970s (e.g. the eighteen-volume "Documentos" series), it has published very little since then.

This militaristic trend within ETA had resulted in an escalation of violence following Franco's death. The escalation came as an unpleasant surprise for those who thought ETA would cease committing acts of violence once the democratic transition and negotiations over a Statute of Autonomy for the Basque Country were under way. The number of persons killed by ETA rose from no more than three between 1968 and 1973 to 17 in 1976, 67 in 1978, and 88 in 1980.[50] Overt war between ETA and the Spanish state, complicated by anti-ETA violence exerted by far-right groups, created a climate of violence that cannot be captured simply by perusing the number of people killed by ETA. Throughout the 1980s, ETA maintained fairly high levels of violence, accounting for between 30 and 40 deaths per year. In the past few years, however, general public condemnation, more efficient police actions, and the collaboration of French police forces have led to a sustained decline in the number of killings.

ETA's concentration on military activities was complemented in the political sphere by the activities of Herri Batasuna, a political party it created in 1978, and KAS, a closely connected social movement (Patriotic Socialist Coordinating Council) that encompassed many diverse associations. Both Herri Batasuna and KAS espoused ETA's separatist and anticapitalist goals while denying formal ties with the separatist military organization. According to Ibarra, their political program, known as the "Alternativa KAS," reflected ETA's recognition that the "action-repression" strategy had failed, a failure evidenced by the lack of general popular insurrections against the Spanish state during the 1970s and 1980s.[51] The program outlined by KAS in 1976 called for a number of goals: the integration of Navarre into the Basque Country, the release of all political prisoners, self-determination for the Basque Country, the transfer of police functions to the Basque government and the removal of all Spanish police forces from the Basque Country, an improvement in people's standards of living, and the declaration of the Basque language as the sole official language in the Basque Country.

From the close of the Spanish Civil War to the present, then, two forms of nationalism have developed in the Basque Country: a bourgeois form (concentrated in the BNP) and a revolutionary form (promoted by ETA). Both of these types of nationalism have conceived the nation in largely primordialist terms with a focus on the language, a stance clearly differentiating them from early Basque nationalism, which had focused on race and religion. Both shared a strong desire for self-determination as well, though this goal was pursued far more energetically by ETA, which evolved into an unequivocally separatist organization. Both forms of nationalism also secularized their political messages, embraced progress as part of their programmatic goals, and abandoned their anti-immigrant stance. Finally, one can also detect a shared sense of despair about the state of Basque culture and socio-economic conditions, though this issue, too, was expressed more intensely in ETA's work.

But despite their strong similarities, the BNP and ETA have differed dramatically in their strategies and in their socioeconomic agendas. Whereas the BNP remained passive in the period 1952–1970, ETA was energetic, and relied on the use of physical violence. Whereas the BNP's agenda has been Christian-democratic and then social-democratic, ETA's has been revolutionary socialist.

This historical account reveals that nationalist mobilization in the Basque Country during the Francoist regime was driven for the most part by members of the lower middle class, who were militants in the BNP and ETA, and by members of the working class, who were militants in ETA. Only in the 1970s did the bourgeoisie and the intelligentsia begin to support the BNP decisively. As the next chapter will show, the passivity of the Basque bourgeoisie and intelligentsia during the Francoist regime constrasts sharply with the intense political activism of the Catalan bourgeoisie and intelligentsia during that period.

CHAPTER 10

Catalan Nationalism
since the Civil War

Though there have been numerous attempts to explain the radical nature of Basque nationalism, there have been few to explain the moderate nature of Catalan nationalism.[1] The social context of political mobilization in Catalonia during the Francoist era[2] differed significantly from that in the Basque Country, for while the Basque financial and business elite was well entrenched in the Francoist power elite, the Catalan capitalist elite stood at its margins. And whereas the economic and political autonomy of the Basque middle class was limited because of the vertical structure of the Basque capital-goods industry and the lack of a public university, that of the Catalan middle class was much greater because of the horizontal structure of the Catalan consumer-goods industry and the existence of ample mobilization opportunities at Barcelona's public university. Therefore, one would expect that the Catalan bourgeoisie and intelligentsia opposed the Franco regime with greater intensity than did the Basque bourgeoisie and intelligentsia, an expectation supported by the historical tendency of the Catalan bourgeoisie to identify more with Catalan culture than with Spanish culture.

Catalonia during the Civil War

The Spanish Civil War had more tragic consequences in Catalonia than it did in the Basque Country, for peripheral nationalism, revolutionary class mobilization, and radical anticlericalism, the three main sources of conflict leading to the war, coincided in Catalonia.

Franco's insurrection in July 1936 met resistance in Catalonia from the combined forces of a popular militia organized by the anarchist organization CNT (Confederación Nacional de Trabajadores) and by the Catalan government, which was loyal to the Spanish Republic. In the wake of the break-down of the Spanish state, the Catalan autonomous government, formed by Esquerra Republicana and other leftist political parties, was able to assume full state powers. Its task was not easy, however, for the government of Cat-alonia (the Generalitat), was confronted by both pro-Franco rebels and social revolutionaries. Organized groups within the working class—led by the most radical elements of the anarchist organization CNT-FAI and such emerging Marxist organizations as the POUM—began to collectivize indus-trial and agrarian property, burn churches, and execute priests. This revolu-tionary climate had dramatic effects on the attitudes of the Catalan political elite. As in previous periods of social unrest in Catalonia (e.g. the period of the First Republic), many Catalan political leaders looked for a quick restora-tion of order, even if it meant sacrificing democratic liberties and Catalan autonomy. Others, such as leading members of moderate and Catholic nationalist organizations like the UDC, chose to leave the country.

Unable to tame the anarchist opposition, Esquerra Republicana was soon replaced by socialists in the effective government of Catalonia. The main socialist party, the PSUC, was formed on July 23, 1936, out of the fusion of four Marxist organizations: the Catalan Communist Party (PCC), the Cata-lan Federation of the Spanish Socialist Party (PSOE), the Catalan Socialist Union (USC), and the Catalan Proletarian Party (PCP). The sudden success of the PSUC can be explained by the relative moderation of its leaders. As De Riquer has pointed out, "the PSUC, in fact, inherited the populism of Esquerra Republicana, albeit under a more radical label, and while proclaim-ing itself Marxist, it represented a moderating force in the revolutionary process".[3] Its moderation, in fact, allowed the PSUC to attract the support of the lower middle class (employees, small bureaucrats, students, progressive sectors of Esquerra Republicana), which was more radical than it had ever been, though still respectful of modest property holdings. Despite its initial moderation, however, the PSUC was increasingly influenced by the Spanish Communist Party as the war progressed, and thus alienated many socialists who would eventually abandon the party.

During the course of the war, Catalan support for the Spanish Republic was weakened by anarchism and communism, and by the increasing central-ization of power undertaken by the Spanish republican government as it retreated from Madrid to Valencia (November 1936) and then to Barcelona (November 1937). These attempts to diminish the power of Catalonia's autonomous institutions in favor of the central state alienated the leaders of Esquerra Republicana as well as Catalan separatist leaders, and with them the entire progressive element in Catalan society.

The Spanish Republic was thus deprived of the unconditional support of broad sectors of Catalan society, thereby facilitating Franco's victory. War's end was followed by the suppression of democratic rights and institutions, the dismantling of all the autonomous Catalan political institutions, and the systematic repression of the Catalan culture.[4] Thousands of Catalans either chose exile or had it forced on them. Many went first to France and then, following Hitler's invasion of France, to Latin America. Of the nationalists who stayed, many were jailed and executed, including the president of the Catalan Generalitat, Lluis Companys. Nevertheless, for almost 40 years, clandestine Catalan political and civic organizations continued their quest for democracy, autonomy, and the promotion of Catalan culture.

Their struggle can be divided into four phases: the first (1939–56) was a time of reorganization, initially abroad and then, especially after 1946, at home; the second (1956–71) saw increased mobilization centered around the workplace and the university; the third (1971–76) ushered in open mobilization by the major political forces in Catalonia; and the fourth phase, finally, is the current democratic period.

The Early Resistance Movement, 1936–56

In the early years of the Franco regime, economic-reconstruction efforts, repression, and sheer weariness prevented substantial political or military resistance inside Catalonia. Most resistance took place in exile, where former political leaders and their followers worked to reorganize their parties and institutions or volunteered to fight for the Allies in World War II. Part of this reorganization effort also involved establishing diplomatic ties with different Allied governments. Meanwhile, in Catalonia, oppositional political forces concentrated on reestablishing their party or union organizations and challenged the dictatorship only sporadically.

Immediately after the Civil War, in the midst of uncertainty about the whereabouts of Josep Irla, the Catalan government's president, some Catalan politicians formed a provisional Catalan government (the Consell Nacional de Catalunya) in London. This government, presided over by the ex-minister of culture of the Generalitat, Carles Pi i Sunyer, established diplomatic ties with Allied forces and coordinated the activities of a resistance organization, the Catalan National Front (FNC), located in the Catalan interior. (The FNC included militants from a number of radical Catalan nationalist parties, such as the old Estat Català.) But in 1945, Irla finally surfaced in France and formed the legitimate government of the Generalitat. Somewhat reluctantly, Carles Pi i Sunyer, who was more separatist than Irla, dissolved his Consell and accepted a ministerial post in the first Catalan government formed in exile.

During this period of regrouping, moderate militants defected from the major Catalan socialist parties, the PSUC and the POUM, and founded the

Movement of Catalan Socialists (MSC) in 1945. The PSUC remained strong, organized a guerrilla movement along the border between Catalonia and France, and formalized its ties to the Spanish Communist Party in 1947. Meanwhile, the anarchists of the CNT, after a promising start that placed them at the forefront of direct opposition to Franco, were weakened by internal differences between moderates and radicals, as well as by Francoist dismantling of their clandestine operations.

By the time of France's liberation in 1944, the republican political forces in the Catalan interior and abroad hoped to be able to put an end to Franco's regime with the help of the Allies. During this period there were three major Catalan parties or party coalitions.

President Irla's government in Paris coordinated efforts with an organization in the interior called the National Council of Democratic Catalonia (CNDC, 1945–52). The CNDC included representatives from various nationalist parties from the center and the left. Among them were the FNC, the newly created MSC, Esquerra Republicana, and the Democratic Union of Catalonia (UDC). Another political coalition formed during these years was the Catalan section of the National Alliance of Democratic Forces (ANFD), which was dominated by the anarchist organization CNT. Finally, there was the PSUC, which was deeply opposed to the MSC and decided to struggle on alone for the restoration of republican institutions.

The optimistic atmosphere of the time encouraged public expressions of opposition to the Franco regime in many spheres of Catalan life. The year 1946, for instance, witnessed a series of factory strikes in the industrial belt surrounding Barcelona. These were mimicked the following year, on a larger scale, in the Basque Country. Although these strikes focused on improving living conditions, they were often coordinated by leaders of the principal clandestine unions and party organizations.

Opposition to Franco was also expressed at the university. The leading organizers of this opposition were a Christian-democratic group known as the FUC (Catalan University Front) and the FNEC (the National Front of Catalan Students), which maintained close ties with the FNC.

Catalans also opposed Franco outside the factories and the university. In 1947, a religious celebration at the monastery of Montserrat, Catalonia's patron saint, turned into the first mass demonstration of Catalanism since the end of the Civil War. The original purpose of the event had been to inaugurate a throne, funded by popular donations, for a statue of the Virgin of Montserrat, but both the religious and the secular associations that organized the event seized the opportunity to create a nationalist atmosphere. They announced the event in the Catalan language and invited all kinds of popular associations with a Catalanist bent. Their campaign was highly successful: the attendance of nearly 100,000 people, the undisguised use of the

Catalan language throughout the event, and the placement of a huge Catalan flag (the "senyera"), which policemen did not dare remove, on one of the mountain peaks that surrounded the monastery, all revealed the strength of Catalan resistance to cultural homogenization during one of the most repressive periods of the Franco regime.

Republican optimism that the Allies would support the removal of Franco faded during the two years following World War II. As fear of communism increased among the Allied countries, so did accommodation to the Franco regime, in view of Franco's strong anticommunist stance and the strategic geopolitical position of the Iberian peninsula. This new stance by the Allies led to division within the republican forces in exile and to diminution of their authority over resistance organizations in the interior of Spain. Republican institutions began to exclude communists from ministerial posts, and parties such as the Spanish Socialist Party (PSOE) even played with the possibility of restoring the monarchy, hoping that these decisions would attract international support. Most organizations, however, especially those in the interior of Spain, came to understand that the international community would support the fall of the dictatorship only if it resulted from popular pressure within Spain. This realization caused widespread disillusion among the republican political forces in exile, and led, among other things, to the 1948 dissolution of the Generalitat government established in Paris. For the remainder of Franco's dictatorship, only the presidents of the Generalitat, Irla and his successor, Josep Tarradellas (1954), retained their formal authority and symbolic status.

Initially, the hands-off attitude of foreign powers strengthened the Francoist regime and weakened the democratic opposition. During the period immediately following the Civil War, some of the leading political organizations faded away (e.g. the FNC), were obliterated by the state security forces (e.g. the CNT and the POUM), or succumbed to internal divisions and Francoist repression (e.g. the PSOE, after Indalecio Prieto, its president, failed to form a monarchic coalition to bring Franco down). The National Council of Democratic Catalonia (renamed the Permanent Committee of Democratic Catalonia after being joined in 1947 by the National Alliance of Democratic Forces) survived, but remained fairly inactive.

Only the PSUC and a few Catalanist Catholic organizations kept democratic and nationalist opposition alive in the 1947–56 period. The PSUC, led by Gregorio López Raimundo, proceeded with reorganization efforts and adopted a strategy of infiltrating Francoist corporatist institutions, such as the state-sponsored labor unions and university students' unions. In 1950 this strategy bore its first fruits, with the election of communist workers to representative positions in the metallurgy and textile industries. A highly successful general strike in 1951 owed its success to the activity of these elected representatives. Following on the heels of a strike of streetcar users who opposed rising fares, the general strike, which demanded higher wages, affected some 300,000 workers in the industrial area of Barcelona.

Another important challenge to the Franco regime emerged in the form of the Catalanist activities of university students. The students' most prominent leaders were members of the Catholic, Catalanist, and democratic association called Torrás i Bages. This association undertook diverse subversive activities such as graffiti, placing Catalan flags in public places, and distributing catalanist and pro-democratic leaflets. Jordi Pujol, who would be elected President of Catalonia in 1980, was among its members, as was Joan Reventós, one of the major figures in Catalan socialism. The university students' activities were the most visible aspect of a fairly dynamic network of underground cultural institutions. Foremost among these was the Institute of Catalan Studies. The Catalan Church also played an important role in promoting cultural activities.

Thus, from 1939 to 1956, Catalan opposition to Franco proceeded uninterrupted. Though modest in comparison to mobilization in the periods that followed, it was significant, considering the severity of state repression. Although the rise of a strong, unified resistance movement was forestalled by the inheritance of a fragmented political-party system and the multiplicity of social groups participating in the opposition to Franco, there were repeated attempts to coordinate the activities of opposition groups, and a common agenda involving demands for democracy and autonomy began to emerge.

Liberalization and Catalan Mobilization, 1956–70

Throughout the late 1950s and the 1960s Catalan opposition to Francoism intensified, as democratic political organizations took advantage of greater opportunities for mobilization. As we have seen, the government enacted liberal economic policies during this period, in an attempt to integrate Spain into the world market. The need to improve productivity levels facilitated the enactment of reforms increasing the representation and bargaining power of factory workers. And in order to improve diplomatic relations with Spain's main trading partners, Franco also allowed more political freedom. Structural factors alone, however, do not completely explain either the liberalization of the Francoist regime or the rising levels of mobilization that followed. One must also consider internal political and ideological changes within the Francoist power structure—particularly the access to power of the so-called "technocrats," who espoused liberal-style economics—and the efforts of a new generation of Spaniards, born since the Civil War, who pushed for political reform through preexisting clandestine political organizations.

Three major types of political actors mobilized against Franco during this period: leftist parties, Catholic organizations, and separatist groups. All bear analysis.

The Mobilization of Political Parties of the Left

For the PSUC, the late 1950s and the 1960s were a period of intense activity focused largely in the realm of labor relations and at the university. In its first congress, held in France in 1956, the PSUC adopted a policy of national reconciliation addressed to the generation born after the Civil War, regardless of whether these young people came from families on the winning side or the losing side. The PSUC also abandoned armed struggle, choosing instead to fight for democracy through purely political means. Finally, it issued a welcome to the legions of immigrants who would soon form the majority of the Catalan working class. In adopting this policy the PSUC leaders avoided the temptation to turn class conflict into ethnic conflict (between immigrant workers and indigenous employers); rather, they promoted the cultural integration of immigrants into Catalan society, a policy that has been a continuous source of pride for the PSUC's leadership.[5]

But it was in the Catalan labor movement that the PSUC played its greatest role, by pursuing the Spanish Communist Party's strategy of infiltrating the systems of labor representation and collective bargaining created by the Francoist regime, and by supporting the spontaneous development of factory-level worker's committees that began to form in 1962. These committees eventually evolved into an organized, illegal union called the Workers' Commissions (CCOO). CCOO became the largest Catalan union during the 1960s and was the main vehicle for the PSUC's participation in labor politics, which assumed a highly conflictive character in Catalonia during this period. Only in the Basque Country, Asturias, and Madrid was working-class mobilization as intense.

The PSUC was also active at the University. Along with other groups, it lobbied for the democratization of student representation at the University of Barcelona and promoted the creation of a coordinating body made up of student delegates from the various university departments. This group, initially known as "Inter," was made a permanent, multiparty platform called the Democratic Association of Catalan Students (ADEC) and coordinated its efforts with similar organizations across Spain.

The other major party of the Catalan Left, the MSC, played a relatively minor role in the opposition to Franco during this period. For one thing, unlike the PSUC, it was not integrated into a major party at the Spanish level, which would have provided organizational and financial resources.[6] For another, again in contrast to the PSUC, it remained tentative and divided on the issue of infiltrating the quickly growing CCOO. While the MSC leaders abroad advocated either strengthening the historically weak Workers' General Union (UGT) or forming alliances with the anarchist organization CNT, MSC leaders in Catalonia favored either the creation of a new union or participation in the Workers' Commissions movement. Conflict on the labor issue was only one of many sources of disagreement between the MSC's leaders abroad (e.g. Josep Pallach) and its leaders in Catalonia (e.g. Juan Reventós, Raimón Obiols). The former, who were veering toward the more moderate political views of Germany's SPD, refused any type of coalition, whether with communists or with progressive Catholic groups. The latter, who held more Marxist political views, favored such an alliance.[7] The final outcome of this conflict, in 1966, was the breakup of the MSC, when the MSC's leadership abroad, led by Pallach, formed the Secretariat for the Orientation of Catalan Social Democracy (SODSC).

One reason the role of the MSC during this period bears scrutiny is that its membership included some of the most important Catalan political leaders of today's democratic phase of Spanish politics. These included the leaders just mentioned (Reventós, Obiols) as well as others, from a progressive political organization known as the Worker's Front of Catalonia (FOC), who joined the MSC in the late 1960s. The FOC was very active at the university and was one of the many progressive, socially committed, Catholic political organizations that developed during the 1960s. The few FOC militants included some notable current Socialist leaders, such as the current Mayor of Barcelona, Pasqual Maragall, and Eduardo Serra, who has occupied ministerial posts throughout the Spanish Socialists' tenure of power. Present-day centrist politicians, such as Roca i Junyent, President of Convergencia Democrática de Catalunya (CDC, the centrist ruling party in Catalonia since 1980), were also members of the FOC.

The Mobilization of Catholic Organizations

At the other end of the Catalan political spectrum there was a burgeoning of progressive Catholic groups that campaigned more or less openly for the preservation of Catalan identity and culture. This reflected a radical shift in the Catholic Church's attitude toward the social problems created by industrialization. In Spain, the shift meant a more receptive attitude toward Marxism, a more tolerant attitude toward political groups opposing the Franco regime, and the founding of Catholic political organizations, formed usually by priests, ex-priests, or ex-students, in progressive Catholic schools.[8] The Catholic hierarchy in Catalonia was more receptive to these changes than was the Church leadership in other Spanish regions, and some of the most

important acts of defiance against the Franco regime in Catalonia were organized under the auspices of the Church, or were at least allowed to take place
on Church property.

Among religiously motivated oppositional groups, the group known as
CC deserves special mention. It was founded in 1954 by Raimón Galí, and
Jordi Pujol was one of its leading members. The group called CC blended
Christian ideology, Catalanism, and a vaguely defined progressive message.
Some sections within this organization specialized in Catalanist activities,
others in social issues. Eventually, this division of labor created tensions, as
the contradictions between class struggle and national struggle manifested
themselves. As conflict intensified in the late 1950s, Pujol decided to distance
himself from this organization, which he saw as deviating from its original
Catalanist goal, and faulted it for not being more active.

Pujol, who has been the elected President of the Catalan autonomous government since 1980, is arguably the most important contemporary Catalan
political figure. Because of his great current stature, and because he has
played a major role in Catalan politics for the past 30 years, we will do well
to outline the content of his ideas before examining his political activities
during prior decades.

In his writings of the 1950s and 1960s (reedited during the 1970s), Pujol
expressed his belief that Catalonia constitutes a "people," which he defined
essentially in primordialist terms.[9] His view was that language and culture
are the major traits of Catalan identity. Unlike Sabino Arana, however, who
saw the uncorrupted Basque race as the essence of all virtue, Pujol believed
that the Catalan people could and should be perfected, while preserving
those core traits (e.g. the language) that make it distinctive.[10]

Pujol was heavily influenced by communitarian ideas and the thinking of
French authors like Charles Péguy and Antoine de Saint-Exupéry. These
writers had emphasized the idea that people should be involved in activities
oriented toward the achievement of collective ethical and spiritual goals.[11] It
was Pujol's conviction that individuals become persons only by living with
other people in an adequate social environment. He therefore supported
efforts to perfect the Catalan social environment, so as to create a healthy
Catalan community.

One prerequisite for the success of these efforts was, in Pujol's view, some
form of political autonomy. Although he initially favored a federal solution,
in the 1970s he expressed a stronger preference for autonomy, which he felt
was more appropriate to the special conditions of Catalonia. Pujol also
emphasized the need to develop educational institutions that would transmit
Christian values and the essence of Catalan identity. Finally, he called for
leadership in business, in the Church, and in politics. In particular, he
believed that Catalonia needed to develop a strong financial sector.

Another important aspect of Pujol's writings was his concern about the massive influx of immigrants to Catalonia. For him, immigrants represented a major threat to one of the defining traits of Catalan identity, the language, already endangered by Franco's cultural-homogenization policies. Immigrants could, Pujol feared, destroy the Catalan identity: "Destruction that will not be limited to the most genuine national traits—language, culture, even the economy, etc. . . . —but will even damage the Catalan social fabric, that is the social fabric that immigrants are already a part of."[12]

This fear repeatedly led Pujol to criticize the leaders of pre–Civil War Catalan nationalism for not having addressed the problems of the working class. But we should not misunderstand him on this point: he was not speaking in the name of the working class. As he often remarked, he was addressing the middle and lower-middle classes, which, in his opinion, were the bearers of Catalan identity and the most dynamic social sectors in Catalan society. According to Pujol, "The most lively, dynamic, and creative component of the Catalan social fabric is the petty and middle bourgeoisie."[13]

This middle class, according to Pujol, had to understand that immigrants were part of Catalonia, and that Catalonia would never form a healthy community unless immigrants were culturally and socially integrated. For him, cultural integration implied a socialization that would instill in immigrants the values that constituted Catalan identity. His nationalist ideology thus combined a desire to protect core cultural traits and a desire to shape society according to the values of the bourgeoisie.

For Pujol, however, nationalist action meant more than developing a nationalist ideology, publishing propaganda, writing graffiti, and making speeches; it also meant engaging in activities that would enhance the economic stature and political integrity of Catalonia. For this reason, he immersed himself in the financial sector and directed and coordinated many nationalist subversive acts during the late 1950s and the 1960s. Two subversive acts in particular forged a charismatic aura around him: the Galinsoga affair of 1959 and the "Palau events" of 1960. They have been recounted in detail by Crexell.[14]

The Galinsoga affair began on a Sunday in June 1959, when Luis Galinsoga, then director of the principal Catalan newspaper, *La Vanguardia*, offended churchgoers attending one of the few masses offered in Catalan by complaining about the use of Catalan during the ceremony. Despite the polite explanations offered by one of the priests, Galinsoga left the Church shouting, "All Catalans are like shit!" When news of this incident reached Pujol and his collaborators, they decided to mount a campaign to force Galinsoga's resignation, vindicating Catalans and the Catalan language in the process. The campaign involved urging advertisers, in writing, to stop promoting their products in *La Vanguardia*, publicly tearing up daily editions of *La Vanguardia*, contacting people with access to Franco (since it was he who customarily named the directors of potentially controversial newspapers), and even breaking windows in the newspaper's headquarters. Eventually, the popularity of the campaign had become so great that the state authorities were forced to remove Galinsoga from his post.

Bolstered by the success of this campaign, Pujol launched several other, more modest protests against the official repression of the Catalan language, and the Galinsoga affair, meanwhile, had boosted the confidence of other sectors of Catalan society concerned for the protection of Catalan culture. One example of the greater belligerence of the Catalan middle class was the "Manifest del Cent," a letter signed by 100 intellectuals, which demanded the teaching of Catalan in the schools and the legalization of organizations promoting Catalan culture.

The second major protest event orchestrated by Pujol was the "Fets del Palau," in 1960. That year marked the 100th birthday of one of Catalonia's major poets, Joan Maragall. To celebrate the event, a concert was planned at Barcelona's major concert hall, El Palau. Songs based on Maragall's poems were to be performed, including "El Cant de la Senyera," a work that held great symbolic importance for Catalan nationalists. Mindful of the possible consequences were the performance of this song to be permitted, the authorities demanded that it be excluded from the program. What they did not anticipate, however, was that precisely because this song was so significant, Catalan nationalists would not tolerate its exclusion from the concert's program. During the concert, a group of young people sitting in the upper levels of El Palau distributed copies of the banned song's lyrics. Suddenly, just at the point in the original concert program when "El Cant de la Senyera" was to have been performed, this group began to sing the nationalist song, and were joined quickly by the performing choir itself. Shocked and infuriated by this act of defiance, the authorities immediately ordered a search for whoever had masterminded the operation. That person turned out to be none other than Pujol, caught in possession of a virulently anti-Franco flyer he had planned to distribute while the Caudillo himself was in Barcelona. Pujol and the printer who had collaborated with him since the Galinsoga affair were judged by a military tribunal and sentenced to seven years and one year in prison, respectively (Pujol eventually spent only two years in prison). During and after the trial, a nationalist campaign was organized by both Pujol's collaborators and a number of ordinary citizens who had been galvanized by the affair itself. The campaign consisted mainly of graffiti with the names "Pujol" and "Catalonia" appearing side by side. For broad sectors of the Catalan middle class, Pujol had become a folk hero.

The Mobilization of Separatist Organizations

The role of radical nationalist organizations in Catalonia's anti-Francoist mobilization appears negligible when compared with the efforts of the PSUC and moderate Catholic organizations. These organizations are worth mentioning, however, for purposes of comparison with the Basque case. Contrary to what one might suspect, there were indeed small pockets of separatism in Catalonia. The leading separatist organization during most of the post–Civil War period was the Catalan National Front (FNC). During the 1960s, the FNC remained active in the Catalan opposition, despite many internal divisions. Most noticeable were its participation in organizing the student movement during these years, and its participation in the movement for the defense of Catalan culture.

By the late 1960s, the FNC was the main repository of the Catalan separatist tradition, though it lacked the financial support and the number of militants that would have made it a major political force. During the 1960s, the FNC experienced many of the ideological transformations typical of the Spanish opposition as a whole—basically a gradual shift toward Marxism. In 1969, a radical faction within the organization split from the FNC and formed the PSAN, which was resolutely socialist and separatist. This new party debated whether or not to follow in the footsteps of ETA in the use of a military strategy. Disagreements on this issue divided the PSAN into two factions, the PSAN and the PSAN-p, the latter advocating military insurrection (the "p" stood for provisional, in imitation of the Provisional IRA). The PSAN-p's military activities, however, unlike ETA's, were few in number and went largely unnoticed by the general public.

Another political and military group that arrived on the Catalan political scene in 1969 was the Catalan Liberation Front (FAC). This group included separatists like Batista i Roca from the old days of the Catalan National Council (1939–42), as well as militants from the youth movement of the old separatist party Estat Català, which at one point had abandoned the FNC coalition. The FAC, which was resolutely militarist, committed more than 100 acts of violence between 1969 and 1971, but because they did not lead to the loss of lives and went largely unnoticed by Catalans and other Spaniards, the FAC, like the PSAN-p, gained little following.

Political Mobilization at the University

So far, we have examined the political activities of a wide variety of political groups in Catalonia, including Marxists and non-Marxists, moderate nationalists and radical nationalists. During the 1960s, these organizations mobilized for democracy and for the defense of the Catalan culture. Despite ideological differences on many other issues, their agreement on these two issues made collaboration possible. Their willingness to set aside ideological differences in order to strengthen the anti-Francoist movement is perhaps best illustrated by mobilization at the university.

The mid-1950s signaled the beginnings of student mobilization in Spanish universities. Maravall (1978, pp. 159–61) saw four major factors accounting for student unrest: (1) attempts by the government to improve its image abroad by softening its repressive character; (2) the greater levels of dissent voiced by liberal and republican professors who had not gone into exile (Enrique Tierno Galván, José Luis Aranguren, Pedro Ridruejo); (3) the exclusion of falangists (the fascist group that formed the ideological backbone of Franco's government in the early stages of the dictatorship) from Franco's power circle and the adoption, by groups of falangist students, of increasingly leftist ideals; and (4) the efficient underground organization of the opposition parties.[15] The students' movement in Catalonia was one of the strongest in Spain, and the PSUC and many other political organizations representing a broad range of ideologies (the MSC, the FNC, the CC, and the UDC), played major roles in this movement. The goal of the students who mobilized was to replace the official student union, the SEU, with a more democratic organization, and in the 1963–64 academic year, an illegal student union, Associacío Democràtica d'Estudiants de Catalunya (ADEC), was created in Catalonia. Its activities were directly coordinated by the Democratic University Confederation of Spain (CUDE), as were many other student organizations across Spain. Later, ADEC was replaced by an assembly of student delegates who began discussing a project to create a democratic student union. A democratic student election held by these delegates in 1965 was a great success, in terms of participation.[16] Its success contrasted with the low turnout in the election of student representatives to the official student union that the regime had organized in an attempt to counteract the growing legitimacy of the student opposition.

The high point of Catalan student opposition, however, came in March 1966. This story, like the "Galinsoga affair" and the "Fets del Palau," has been told in great detail by Crexell.[17] Soon after the democratic student election, the elected delegates convened secretly in a convent near the Universidad de Barcelona and called for a general assembly in order to create a student union. (The choice of a religious site for a meeting was quite common among opposition groups, because these places lay outside the jurisdiction of civil authorities.) The assembly was attended not only by students but also by prestigious professors and intellectuals, among them the great Catalan painter Antoni Tapiés. Soon after the meeting had begun, however, the police surrounded the convent and ordered the delegates and other attendees at the clandestine meeting to surrender. The participants at the meeting refused and a standoff ensued.

Unexpectedly, the students' assembly had become a public act of disobedience against the Franco regime, with broad political repercussions. The students called a general strike, after which the university was closed by government authorities; they also arranged press conferences with foreign journalists, and public demonstrations broke out in the streets of Barcelona. The students' illegal assembly ended several days after it had begun when the police forced their way into the convent and arrested most of the participants. The event had long-lasting effects, however, on the movement of opposition to the dictatorship. Indeed, during the standoff, leaders of all the parties and civil organizations making up the Catalan opposition formed a roundtable, called the Taula Rodona, to coordinate both their responses to the situation, while it developed, and a strategy that would defend those locked in the convent. This marked the first time since the end of the Civil War that all Catalan political parties, including the PSUC, had participated in the same political coalition.

At the close of the "Caputxinada," as the events around the illegal assembly of students were called, meetings of the Taula Rodona continued, with some regularity, and facilitated the development of a common agenda. In 1969, a more specialized political club was formed. Known as the Coordinating Commission of the Political Forces of Catalonia, it included representatives from the political parties only. Along with the Roundtable (Taula Rodona), it called for the constitution of a Catalan Assembly. The Assembly was formed in 1971, and eventually became the largest organization opposing Franco in Catalonia.[18]

During the 1960s, then, a broad panoply of Catalan political forces, ranging from Catholic to Marxist organizations, undermined the Francoist regime, exposing the limitations of economic reform without political transformation. The streets, the factory, and the university were the main sites of struggle between the dictatorship and the opposition forces. Eventually, most of these organizations formed a common assembly (the Catalan Assembly), with a common agenda opposing the Francoist regime. The maturity that political groups acquired during this period, and the gradual erosion of the Francoist repressive apparatus, prepared the way for the third phase of Catalan opposition to the dictatorship. In this phase, confrontations at the university and workplace were replaced by direct mass political mobilization.

Opposition to Franco during the 1970s

The early 1970s saw the unraveling of Franco's dictatorial regime in Spain. Although it will never be known how much longer the dictatorship might have lasted had Franco not died in November 1975, it is clear that the economic, social, and political changes that had taken place during the 1960s were almost irreversible. President Arias Navarro's mild reforms, enacted soon after the assassination of President Carrero Blanco in December 1973, opened the way for the legalization of some associations, and can be seen as a clear indication that the regime itself had finally recognized that some form of democratization was inevitable.

The Catalan opposition played a crucial role during this period. The major player was the Catalan Assembly, first convened in November 1971, in a church in Barcelona. Colomer, in his study of this period, reports that the Assembly, of which the police had no knowledge, had brought together more than 300 people representing virtually every sector in Catalan society: intellectuals, workers, lawyers, peasants, fighters from both sides during the Spanish Civil War, old and young, believers and nonbelievers, ...[19] Its resolutions centered on three demands: (1) amnesty for political prisoners and exiles; (2) democratic freedoms; and (3) the reestablishment of the institutions and rights promulgated in the 1932 Statute of Autonomy. In essence, they were demanding democracy and autonomy, the same two points on which most Catalan political forces had agreed since the end of the Civil War. In the years that followed, the Assembly met with some regularity, despite police repression, to coordinate activities and to plan political campaigns. It conducted campaigns to demand amnesty and the protection of the Catalan language, and it also planned public activities, such as the celebration of its own first anniversary.

Political organizations were not alone in publicly opposing Franco. Groups of intellectuals and artists also became vocal. During the 1960s, Catalan intellectuals had already expressed their opposition to Franco with the publication of the "Manifest de Cent," a letter signed by 100 intellectuals demanding the protection of the Catalan language. At the popular level, the 1960s witnessed the development of a highly successful musical movement called the Nova Cançó, formed by singers whose musical compositions, sung in Catalan, mixed folk-musical traditions with lyrics denouncing the dictatorship.

One of the most notable expressions of nationalist and anti-Francoist sentiment was the seclusion of more than 300 intellectuals and artists in the monastery of Montserrat in December 1970, to protest the Burgos trials of several Basque separatists.[20] The list of intellectuals who gathered at Montserrat included painters such as Miró and Tapiés, film directors, singers, university professors, writers, and photographers—in other words, the Catalan intellectual elite. The document they printed and distributed stated their support for the demands of the Basque people, and demanded the abolition of the death penalty in Spain and the formation of a new state that would grant freedom as well as the right to self-determination for the peoples and nations composing the Spanish state.

The mobilization of Catalan intellectuals—the above is just one example—and of other professional associations, such as the Lawyers Association and the Association of Architects, reveals the extensive support that the Catalan middle classes offered the democratic and Catalanist cause during these years. The mobilization of these sectors in Catalan society stands in sharp contrast to the relative passivity of equivalent groups in the Basque Country.

The Democratic Phase of Catalan Nationalism, 1975–92

After Franco's death in November 1975, as the myriad political parties that formed the Catalan political landscape prepared to compete in a democratic context, much of the earlier political consensus in Catalonia broke down. Despite political disagreements, however, based primarily on different ideological conceptions of Catalonia's role in Spain, and of the way Spanish society ought to be organized, consensus generally prevailed on the issue of a Statute of Autonomy for Catalonia. Indeed, one slogan on which all could agree during the 1970s was "Llibertat, Amnistía, Estatut D' Autonomía" (Freedom, Amnesty, and Statute of Autonomy). The content of the new Spanish constitution thus provoked scarcely any conflict, and the Statute of Autonomy was approved relatively swiftly in August 1979. The Statute, like the Basque Statute of Autonomy, gave Catalonia a broad range of powers.

During the transition to democracy, the Catalan party system differed in many ways from the structure of political mobilization in the period preceding Franco's death. The only party to emerge from the period of the dictatorship with a strong organization, a well-defined program, and the prestige of having been one of the parties to oppose Franco most decisively was the PSUC. The new party system was shaped by transformations of the Catalan socialist parties and the emergence of a powerful centrist nationalist party.[21] In 1966, the Catalan socialist movement had split into two parties; the MSC, based in the interior, and the Secretariat for the Orientation of the Catalan Social Democracy (SODSC), based abroad and led by Pallach. In the years that followed, each of these factions tried to achieve hegemony within the Catalan socialist movement, and their competition was further complicated by the reemergence of the Catalan Federation of the

Spanish Socialist Party (PSOE).[22] In the 1970s, Pallach's faction, together with militants from other parties, founded various party coalitions (Reagrupament Socialista i Democràtic; Partit Socialista de Catalunya-ex-Reagrupament). The MSC, led by Joan Reventós and Raimón Obiols, followed a similar strategy (Convergencia Socialista de Catalunya; Partit Socialista de Catalunya). The confusion created in 1976 by the existence of two socialist parties with the same name, the two in competition with yet a third socialist party (the Catalan Federation of the PSOE) was eliminated in 1978. That year, soon after Pallach's death, the parties identically named Partit Socialista de Catalunya fused into a single party, which then joined the Catalan Federation of the Spanish Socialist Party to form another single party, the PSC-PSOE. Despite this merger between a purely Catalan socialist party and its Spanish counterpart, control over the party remained in the hands of the Catalan sector of the party.[23] This was especially true of the period following the party's 1980 congress.

The center of the political spectrum saw a similar regrouping and eventual crystallization into a single party.[24] In 1974, after years of political and economic activism, Pujol participated in the founding of the Democratic Convergence of Catalonia (CDC). This party favored a center-left political orientation, defining itself as nationalist, democratic, politically moderate, and socially progressive. Aimed at capturing the middle-class vote, it included followers of Pujol and a group of professionals (mostly lawyers) led by Miquel Roca i Junyent. The latter had been politically active since the 1960s, principally in the Worker's Front of Catalonia, from which several renowned socialist leaders had also been recruited. In 1978, CDC was joined by EDC (Democratic Left of Catalonia), another party created in the 1970s, led by the renowned economist Ramón Trías Fargas. This party espoused economic liberalism. Since then, the ideological scope of the CDC has been broadened even further by the electoral alliance it has maintained with the Democratic Union of Catalonia (UDC), a small party with a long tradition in Catalan politics dating back to the time of the Second Republic. Christian-democracy, liberalism, and social-democracy have thus been the main ideological currents in this nationalist party.

Less influential, but worth noting for purposes of comparison with the Basque case, are the changes in the Catalan separatist movement during these years.[25] We have seen how earnest, but how ineffectual, the two major separatist parties—the Catalan National Front (FNC) and the more violent Catalan Liberation Front (FAC) had been in the 1960s. In 1976–77, the FAC decided to combine its political and military activity, as ETA-pm had done, and renamed itself the Catalan Revolutionary Movement. Lacking support, however, from Catalan society, and exerting little influence, it finally dissolved in 1977.

The latest in this long series of militaristic separatist groups was Terra Lliure (Free Land). Its origins date to the fall of 1978, although it became Terra Lliure formally only in 1980. Throughout the 1980s, Terra Lliure tried repeatedly to organize a movement similar to ETA's, but was unsuccessful, owing to a lack of organization and visibility and a penchant for sheer ineptitude (several members died while trying to plant explosives).

Terra Lliure, like its separatist predecessors, has maintained a primordialist and democratic definition of the Catalan nation. Thus characterizing Catalonia as one single nation (sometimes called the Països Catalans, meaning all Spanish and French areas where Catalan is spoken, including the region of Valencia and the Balearic Islands), Terra Lliure has claimed the right to self-determination and advocated independence. Like ETA, Terra Lliure has juxtaposed with its nationalist message a class discourse with socialist undertones. Likewise following ETA, it has spent less time outlining the characteristics of a future independent and socialist Catalonia than denouncing the Catalan working class's poor standards of living and the progressive colonization of Catalonia by Spanish and multinational capital. This anti-imperialist message has been increasingly complemented by anti-EEC slogans, by a rejection of economic restructuring, and by environmentalist demands.

Contrary to general perceptions, then, Catalonia has a long history of violent separatist organizations, many of them sharing the revolutionary ideology of the Basque's ETA. Unlike ETA, however, they lacked the means, organization, and public support to influence their own regional politics. More recently, a new political development suggests growing support for the achievement of Catalan independence through political means. This development is the programmatic redefinition of one of the oldest Catalan political parties, Esquerra Republicana de Catalunya (ERC).

ERC, which as this book shows was one of the dominant political parties in Catalonia during the Spanish Second Republic, led a fairly somnolent existence during the Francoist era. The fact that the official President of the Generalitat in exile, Josep Tarradellas, was one of the leaders of ERC was almost the only sign of ERC's survival as an organization. The return of Tarradellas as of one of the chief negotiators for Catalan autonomy during the democratic transition helped to revitalize ERC, although it remained a minor party in Catalan politics. In the past two or three years, however, a drastic reorganization of the party, the election of a young and confident president, Àngel Colóm, and the party's resolute orientation toward the achievement of independence through peaceful and democratic means seem to have reestablished ERC as a political force to be reckoned with.

The political history of Catalonia since the end of the Civil War has been characterized by the dominance of two movements, socialism and bourgeois nationalism. In the Francoist era, both movements pressured the Franco government constantly with demands for autonomy and democracy, either separately or within multiparty oppositional coalitions. Though socialists avoided the use of nationalist rhetoric, they shared with the bourgeois nationalists a profound identification with Catalonia and Catalan culture. The strength of their attachment owes much to the fact that their leaders came from the same progressive middle class that had promoted progressive forms of nationalism in the pre–Civil War years.[26]

In other words, the nationalist political environment in Catalonia in the post–Civil War period has been as diverse as it was before, and it has been the Catalan bourgeoisie and intelligentsia, whether in socialist or bourgeois nationalist organizations, that have led the movement of opposition to the dictatorial regime of General Franco. The great intensity of socialist and bourgeois-nationalist opposition to the dictatorship has overshadowed the violent activities of separatist organizations whose programmatic discourse was much like that of ETA in the Basque Country. The implications of this history for the relative strength of separatist and anticapitalist organizations after the death of Franco are analyzed in the next chapter.

CHAPTER 11

Political Structures and Nationalism in Democratic Spain

The preceding three chapters have analyzed the social and political contexts of political mobilization in Catalonia and the Basque Country since the end of the Spanish Civil War. They have demonstrated that the two regions were almost identical in terms of level of development, social structure, and ethnic makeup. They have also shown that ETA was almost alone in opposing Franco in the Basque Country, whereas numerous political organizations opposed Franco in Catalonia.

Although extant theories of nationalism can explain both the strength of nationalism and the levels of support for independence in the Basque Country and Catalonia, they cannot account for significant differences between the Basque and Catalan nationalist political structures and cultures. To explain these differences one needs to focus on the long-term effects of the different levels of political diversity of the Basque and Catalan anti-Franco movements.

Electoral Patterns in the Basque Country and Catalonia, 1977–93

The most significant contrast between Basque and Catalan nationalism since democracy was restored in Spain is that electoral support for separatist and anticapitalist political parties has been greater in the Basque Country than in Catalonia.[1] Table 20 shows that although the moderate Basque Nationalist Party and the Spanish Socialist Party (PSOE) have been dominant in the Basque Country (sharing from 30% to 48% of the total vote), between 10% and 13% of the Basque electorate has voted for the separatist and socialist group Herri Batasuna, the political arm of ETA.

Table 20. Electoral trends in the Basque Country, 1977–93
(Percentages of votes relative to numbers of eligible voters)

GENERAL ELECTIONS

Party/parties	1977	1979	1982	1986	1989	1993
PNV (BNP)	21.3	17.7	25.1	18.5	15.1	16.9
EE[a]	4.6	5.1	6.1	12.1	5.8	
HB		9.7	11.6	11.8	11.2	10.3
EA					7.4	6.9
PSOE[a]	20.8	12.2	23.0	17.5	14.0	17.2
AP/CD/CP/PP[b]	18.1	13.0	9.2	7.9	6.2	10.3
UCD/CDS[b]			1.5	3.3	2.3	0.5
PCE/IU	3.3	3.0	1.4	0.8	1.9	4.4
Abstention	23.6	34.1	19.4	32.4	33.1	29.8

REGIONAL ELECTIONS

Party/parties	1980	1984	1986	1990
PNV (BNP)	22.0	28.4	16.8	17.2
EE	5.7	5.4	7.7	4.7
HB	9.6	9.9	12.4	11.1
EA	11.3			6.9
PSOE	8.2	15.6	15.6	12.0
AP/CD/CP/PP	7.7	6.3	3.5	5.0
UCD/CDS	2.5			0.4
PCE/IU	2.3	0.9		0.8
Abstention	41.2	31.9	28.9	38.9

Note: PNV (BNP): Basque Nationalist Party; EE: Euskadiko Esquerra; HB: Herri Batasuna;
EA: Eusko Alkartasuna; PSOE: Socialist Party; AP/CD/CP/PP: Conservative Party;
UCD/CDS: Centrists; PCE/IU: Communists.
[a]EE and the PSOE merged in the winter of 1993.
[b]In 1977 and 1979, Centrists and Conservatives participated jointly in the general elections.

No equivalent political party has achieved a similar degree of success in Catalonia. The Catalan branch of the Spanish Socialist Party (PSC/PSOE) has dominated general elections, while the moderate nationalist coalition Convergencia i Unió (CiU) has dominated regional elections (see Table 21). Meanwhile, Esquerra Republicana de Catalunya, a separatist but more pro-capitalist and more moderate party than the Basque Herri Batasuna, has had very limited electoral success, never attracting as much as 6% of the electorate.

Correlates of Nationalist Attitudes, 1977–91

Other aspects of the Basque population's political culture that distinguish it from the Catalan are a greater rejection of a Spanish identity, greater support for independence, and slightly more leftist attitudes among nationalists.

Table 21. Electoral trends in Catalonia, 1977–93
(Percentages of votes relative to numbers of eligible voters)

GENERAL ELECTIONS

Party/parties	1977[a]	1979	1982	1986	1989	1993
CiU	13.3	11.0	17.8	21.9	22.3	24.2
ERC	3.6	2.8	3.2	1.8	1.4	3.9
UCDCC	4.4					
PSC/PSOE	22.5	20.0	36.6	28.0	24.4	26.4
AP/CD/CP/PP	2.7	2.4	11.7	7.8	7.4	12.9
UCD/CDS	13.3	13.0		2.8	2.7	0.6
PSUC/PCE/IU	2.7	11.7	3.6	2.7	4.7	5.7
Abstention	22.7	31.5	21.2	31.1	32.3	24.2

REGIONAL ELECTIONS

Party/parties	1980	1984	1988	1992
CiU	17.2	29.8	27.1	25.5
ERC	5.5	2.8	2.4	4.4
PSC/PSOE	13.9	19.1	17.6	15.0
AP/CD/CP/PP		4.9	3.1	3.3
UCD/CDS	6.5		2.3	0.5
PSUC/PCE/IU	11.6	3.5	4.6	3.5
Abstention	37.9	36.1	40.6	45.0

Note: CiU: Convergencia i Unió; ERC: Esquerra Republicana de Catalunya; UCDCC: Unió del Centre i la Democracia Cristiana de Catalunya; PSC/PSOE: Socialist Party; AP/CD/CP/PP: Conservative Party; UCD/CDS: Centrists; PSUC/PCE/IU: Communists.
[a]In 1977, CiU did not exist yet, but Convergencia Democrática de Catalunya participated in a coalition called Pacte Democratic per Catalunya. UCDCC participated only in the 1977 general elections, after which its leaders went to either CiU or UCD.

The data below show, however, that this contrast between the political attitudes and behavior of the Basque and Catalan populations developed only after the Burgos trials in 1970.

In 1969, as part of a study about the Spanish social landscape, Juan Linz and a team of collaborators conducted a national survey among homemakers. The information emerging from their survey revealed that Basques identified less with their region than did Catalans.[2] Whereas 36% of the Basque respondents defined themselves as Basques, 42% of Catalan respondents defined themselves as Catalan; whereas 32% of Basque respondents defined themselves as non-Basque, 24% of Catalan respondents defined themselves as non-Catalan.

Since Linz's 1970 study, however, self-identification patterns among Basques and Catalans have undergone a dramatic reversal, although the distributions of respondents according to their ethnic identity are not strictly comparable to the 1960 distributions, because the wording of questions differed. During the 1977–91 period, the percentage of Basque respondents identifying themselves as only Basques fluctuated between a high of 37% in 1979 and a low of 31% in 1991 (see Table 22). Over the same period, the percentage of Catalan respondents identifying themselves as only Catalans fluctuated between 15% and 18%.

Trends in attitudes toward political decentralization and independence also reveal a radicalization of Basque nationalist political culture during the 1970s. Whereas in 1969, when Linz's study was conducted, more Catalans than Basques favored political decentralization over a centralized form of government (48% vs. 40%), in 1976 more Basques than Catalans supported independence (9% vs. 0%). The gap between the two regions broadened significantly until the early 1980s (25% vs. 8% in 1982) and narrowed just as significantly thereafter, as support for independence decreased in the Basque Country and increased in Catalonia. In 1991, about 15% of both Basque and Catalan respondents supported independence (see Table 23).

A third characteristic that has distinguished Basque nationalism from Catalan nationalism during the democratic transition has been the greater use of violent tactics by Basque nationalist organizations. Violent acts conducted by ETA in the Basque Country increased spectacularly during the 1970s and remained at fairly high levels throughout the 1980s. During this period, ETA enjoyed a significant degree of popular support, which contrasts sharply with the popular rejection of similarly violent nationalist organizations in Catalonia. In both 1979 and 1988, Basque respondents were asked to rate their attitudes toward ETA, while Catalan respondents were asked to rate their attitudes toward the Catalan separatist and militaristic organization Terra Lliure.[3] In both years, support for ETA in the Basque Country was greater than support for Terra Lliure in Catalonia. Although support for ETA has tended to drop in recent years, the 1988 survey results showed that whereas 11% of Basque respondents rated ETA above 5 on a scale from 0 to 10, fewer than 1% of Catalan respondents rated Terra Lliure above this level.

Clearly, sharp contrasts between the Basque and Catalan nationalist political cultures developed during the decade of the 1970s. Moreover, survey data from 1988 and 1991 demonstrate that these contrasts were to some extent matched by the development of a more leftist nationalist culture in the Basque Country. Statistical models, available from the author but not presented here, show that Basque separatists have a lower opinion of banks than do both nonseparatist Basques and Catalans in general, and that Basque nationalists condemn economic inequalities to a greater extent than do both non-nationalist Basques and Catalans in general. Differences between Basque and Catalan nationalists in their political attitudes are quite small overall. Therefore, although support for revolutionary political organizations is

Table 22. Trends in self-identification in the Basque Country and Catalonia, 1979–91

Basque Country

Self-identification	1979			1988			1991		
	Natives	Immigrants	T	Natives	Immigrants	T	Natives	Immigrants	T
Only Spanish	9.7	53.4	25.5	4.3	33.3	13.8	3.8	34.5	14.7
More Spanish than Basque	0.7	6.6	2.8	2.7	16.9	7.3	2.9	13.8	6.9
As Spanish as Basque	24.0	23.9	23.9	26.0	29.1	27.0	22.5	35.6	27.3
More Basque than Spanish	15.0	3.7	10.9	26.6	8.9	20.9	27.0	8.6	20.4
Only Basque	50.6	12.4	36.8	40.5	11.8	31.1	43.8	7.5	30.8
N	(543)	(281)	(857)	(489)	(237)	(726)	(315)	(174)	(489)

Catalonia

Self-identification	1979			1988			1991		
	Natives	Immigrants	T	Natives	Immigrants	T	Natives	Immigrants	T
Only Spanish	16.9	63.8	31.0	4.6	33.3	15.5	4.1	32.0	14.7
More Spanish than Catalan	4.2	12.1	6.5	2.1	14.9	7.0	1.9	14.7	6.8
As Spanish as Catalan	42.8	19.4	35.7	27.6	32.3	29.4	33.9	36.5	34.9
More Catalan than Spanish	15.9	2.4	11.8	36.3	12.2	27.2	36.4	8.1	25.6
Only Catalan	20.2	2.3	14.8	29.3	7.3	21.0	23.8	8.6	18.0
N	(783)	(338)	(1,201)	(474)	(288)	(762)	(319)	(197)	(516)

Source: Gunther, Sani, and Shabad, *Spain after Franco* (1986). The table for Catalonia and the Basque Country for that year is inceuded in Linz, *Conflicto en Euskadi* (1986); Análisis Sociológicos, Económicos, y Políticos (1988); Centro para la Investigación sobre la Realidad Social (1991).

Table 23. Trends in support for independence in the Basque Country and Catalonia 1976–91

| Year | Percentages (and totals) indicating support | |
	Basque Country	Catalonia
1976	9	0
	(434)	(368)
1979	25	11
	(777)	(1079)
1982	25	8
	(916)	(1176)
1988	20	12
	(722)	(674)
1991	15	16
	(428)	(458)

Sources: Jiménez Blanco et al. 1977; Gunther et al. (1986); Shabad (1986); Análisis Sociológicos, Económicos, y Políticos (1988); Centro para la Investigación sobre la Realidad Social (1991).

Note: In 1976, the published results for the Basque Country include Navarre, and the published results for Catalonia include the Balearic Islands. This should not greatly affect the results, since Navarre represented only 17 percent of the Basque sample, and the Balearic Islands represented only 12 percent of the Catalan sample. Since both Navarre and the Balearic Islands have traditionally been more divided on the nationalist issue than have the Basque Country or Catalonia, these percentages should slightly underestimate the actual percentages for the Basque and Catalan autonomous communities.

greater in the Basque Country than in Catalonia, the Basques' political attitudes are only slightly more leftist than the Catalans'.

Theories of Nationalism and Contemporary Basque and Catalan Nationalism

The findings just presented are consistent with the theories of nationalism discussed in the Introduction. High levels of support for nationalist organizations but low levels of support for independence are what these theories would predict, considering that although the Basque Country and Catalonia are overdeveloped with respect to the rest of Spain, their economies are highly interdependent with the rest of Spain's. Nevertheless, none of these theories can adequately explain why Herri Batasuna has been more successful than have similar Catalan organizations; nor can they explain the electoral and attitudinal differences between the two regions noted above and the trends observed since 1970.

From the standpoint of levels of development alone, Overdevelopment theory would predict equal or even slightly higher levels of separatism in

Catalonia than in the Basque Country, since Catalonia is somewhat wealthier than the Basque Country. However, significant support for Herri Batasuna in the Basque Country and very low support for similar political organizations in Catalonia contradict this hypothesis.

Although the Cost/Benefit approach would correctly predict a low level of support for independence in both regions, it would not predict the greater electoral success of separatist parties in the Basque Country than in Catalonia. In fact, if one relies on popular perceptions of economic interdependence with Spain, the opposite would be expected. Asked in 1991 to forecast what the economic consequences of independence would be for their region,[4] 42% of Catalan respondents and only 35% of Basque respondents thought that economic conditions would be the same or better (see Table 24).

From the standpoint of the intensity of ethnic competition, the objective differences between the two regions are so trivial that one would not expect support for separatist organizations to be greater in the Basque Country than in Catalonia. Asked in 1988 for their opinion about the statement *The best solution for unemployment would be to facilitate the return of immigrants to their region of origin,* 19% of Catalan respondents favored the statement while only 10% of Basque respondents were in favor (see Table 25).

Only Relative Deprivation theory provides a potential explanation for the fact that support for a revolutionary separatist political party is greater in the Basque Country than in Catalonia. As indicated in Chapter 8, the energy crisis of the 1970s had more harmful consequences for the more industrial Basque economy than it did for the Catalan economy. The harmful effects of that crisis

Table 24. Expectations about the economic viability of independence in Catalonia and the Basque Country, 1991

Response option	Percent of total response	
	Catalonia	Basque Country
Much better	6.9	5.5
Somewhat better	33.0	27.6
The same	2.1	1.5
Somewhat worse	20.9	17.9
Much worse	6.3	13.5
Don't know/ not available	30.8	33.5
N	(536)	(525)

Source: Centro para la Investigación sobre la Realidad Social (1991).

Note: The question asked was, "In the event that this Autonomous Community attained independence, alone or together with another Autonomous Community, do you think that in the middle run the economic conditions in the new state would be much better, somewhat better, somewhat worse, much worse, or the same as now?"

Table 25. Anti-immigrant attitudes in the Basque Country and Catalonia, 1988

| | Percent of total response | |
Response option	Catalonia	Basque Country
Strongly agree	3.9	3.4
Agree	15.2	6.9
Disagree	28.0	28.2
Strongly disagree	52.9	61.5
N	(711)	(735)

Source: Análisis Sociológicos, Económicos, y Políticos (1988).

Note: The question asked was, "The best solution to solve unemployment would be to facilitate the return of immigrants to their region of origin."

Although this table includes both natives and immigrants, the results were exactly the same when native Basques and Catalans alone were included in the analysis.

have since been compounded by the general crisis of overproduction in the steel industry worldwide. In 1988, Basque and Catalan respondents were asked to rate on a six-step scale the severity of the economic crisis. Their answers, presented in Table 26, show, unsurprisingly, that the crisis was perceived to be more serious by Basque respondents than by Catalan respondents.

This difference between the Basque Country and Catalonia does not, however, explain why Basques are more radical than Catalans. Several statistical models, available from the author but not presented here, revealed that respondents who thought that the economic crisis was very serious were not more separatist than were other respondents.

In summary, none of the theories cited above can explain the differences between Basque and Catalan nationalist politics and political cultures. To

Table 26. Perceptions about the economic crisis in the Basque Country and Catalonia, 1988

| | Percent of total response | |
Response option	Catalonia	Basque Country
Extremely serious	3.3	25.5
Very serious	26.1	45.7
Serious	35.1	21.6
Somewhat serious	28.8	5.8
Almost irrelevant	4.6	0.8
Irrelevant	2.1	0.5
N	(720)	(741)

Source: Análisis Sociológicos, Económicos, y Políticos (1988).

Note: The question asked was, "On a scale from 1 to 6 how would you rate the severity of the economic crisis in your region?"

understand these differences one has to focus on the role of political factors and, more specifically, on the role of the political diversity of the anti-Francoist movement in the Basque Country and Catalonia.

Political Diversity and Radical Politics

The characteristics of Basque and Catalan nationalism were significantly shaped by political factors. The interpretation proposed here is that Basque nationalist politics turned radical during the 1970s chiefly as a result of the political process that began to unfold when the ETA militant Txabi Etxebarrieta was killed by the state's police in 1968.

But ETA's use of violent tactics was not a sufficient cause of this radicalization. A glance at the politics of the 1960s reveals that ETA was not unique in either the Spanish or the international political contexts. The existence of Catalan separatist and revolutionary organizations, such as the Front Nacional de Catalunya, the PSAN, the FAC, and Terra Lliure, provides a clear indication that a propensity toward violence or toward revolutionary politics and rhetoric was not peculiar to the Basque Country. Two non-nationalist, non-Basque, and non-Catalan political groups in Spain, the FRAP and the GRAPO, also kidnapped and killed people during the 1970s and 1980s. In fact, a Marxist and insurrectional discourse pervaded the political propaganda of almost all groups that opposed Franco during the 1960s and early 1970s.

Generally speaking, the emergence of revolutionary Basque and Catalan nationalist organizations during the 1960s and 1970s, and their use of the rhetoric of Third World national-liberation movements, can be explained by the interaction of two factors: the combination of dictatorial rule with increased opportunities for mobilization, and the influence of the Cuban Revolution and the Algerian war of liberation on Western politics. The reemergence of the Irish Republican Army (IRA), which greatly inspired the Spanish anti-Franco movement, and the formation of many leftist revolutionary groups throughout Europe (e.g. Baader-Meinhof and the Red Brigades) bear witness to the general influence of revolutionary politics during this era.

What distinguishes ETA from other separatist or violent groups in Spain, however, is that it was able to generate a political dynamic which in the end produced a significantly more separatist and leftist political culture than any group was able to produce in Catalonia. To understand this, one needs to focus on the defining traits of Basque and Catalan political mobilization during the 1950s and 1960s.

Passivity vs. Belligerence

The major difference between the Basque and Catalan structures of oppositional politics during the Francoist period was that a multiplicity of Catalan political organizations opposed Franco while the opposition in the Basque Country lay chiefly in the hands of ETA. When one examines the social groups involved in the anti-Francoist struggle, the most noticeable difference between the two regions was the relative involvement of the bourgeoisie and the intelligentsia (both clerical and secular) — much greater in Catalonia than in the Basque Country, as noted in the literature and discussed above (Chapters 9 and 10).[5]

The contention that the bourgeoisie and intelligentsia were less active in opposing Franco in the Basque Country than in Catalonia is supported by another piece of information: official data on the penalties the state imposed on Basque and Catalan periodicals from 1964 to 1974. These data were obtained by Terrón Montero and published (in 1981) in a book on the Spanish press under the Franco regime.[6] For every periodical that was fined during the 1964–74 period, Terrón reported information on its region of publication, the title of the article that was penalized, and the justification for the fine. The goal of his study was not to compare Basque and Catalan opposition to Franco; his focus was on the limitations that Franco continued to impose on journalistic freedom during the 1960s. The raw data included in the appendix to Terrón's book, however, make it possible to measure political opposition to Franco in the Basque and Catalan written media.

An analysis of this information reveals that the Catalan media opposed Franco more often than did the Basque media. During the period Terrón studied, Catalan periodicals were fined 129 times while Basque periodicals were fined only eight times. Sometimes periodicals were fined for violating the moral values upheld by the dictatorship (e.g. the portrayal of nudity); often, however, they were fined for attacking the political system. If one restricts the analysis to this second class of fines, there remains a considerable difference between the two regions: Catalan periodicals were fined 44 times while Basque periodicals were fined the same eight times.

The most convincing empirical evidence supporting the argument that the Basque bourgeoisie was less involved than the Catalan bourgeoisie in the opposition to Franco and in defending their regional culture against Franco's homogenization policies is the population's own evaluation of this involvement. In 1988, respondents were asked to express their agreement or disagreement with the following statements: (1) *The upper classes of your region have made more efforts to defend the interests of the state than the interests of your region* and (2) *The upper classes of this Autonomous Community are responsible for the decline of your culture and for your lack of real autonomy.* In 1991, Basque and Catalan respondents were asked to express their agreement or disagreement with two other statements: (1) *During Francoism the upper classes of this Autonomous Community gave priority to the political interests of Spain instead of those of this Autonomous Community* and (2) *The upper classes of this region supported the Francoist Regime, to the detriment of this community's culture.*

Cross-tabulation results show that in 1988 50% of Catalan respondents agreed with the first statement, compared with 59% of Basque respondents (see Table 27). The percentage distribution for the second 1988 statement was very similar in the two regions: 44% agreed with the statement in Catalonia, 43% in the Basque Country. The questions in the 1991 survey, of course, refer directly to the attitudes and behavior of the regional elites during the Francoist period. Not surprisingly, the contrast between the respondents' answers was sharper in this survey: 14% and 15% of Catalan respondents agreed with the first and second statements, respectively, compared with 37% and 36% of Basque respondents (Table 27).

The consistency of the information collected from several independent sources adds credibility to the proposition that the Catalan upper classes were more involved than were the Basque upper classes in opposing the dictatorship. This finding does not mean that the Catalan bourgeoisie and intelligentsia as a whole opposed Franco; indeed, one of the reasons the Franco regime ended only with Franco's death was that the Spanish upper-middle

Table 27. Basque and Catalan perceptions of the role played by the upper class of their respective regions in defending their region's interests, 1988 and 1991

	Percent of total responses							
	1988				1991			
	(1)		(2)		(3)		(4)	
Response option	BC	CAT	BC	CAT	BC	CAT	BC	CAT
Strongly agree	18.1	15.3	11.1	11.5	36.6	14.0	35.7	15.2
Agree	40.5	34.4	32.1	32.7	44.2	60.2	40.1	55.0
Disagree	32.4	29.1	33.9	28.4	14.0	16.1	17.0	21.1
Strongly disagree	9.0	21.2	22.8	27.4	5.2	9.6	7.3	8.7
N	(469)	(581)	(504)	(581)	(344)	(322)	(342)	(322)

Sources: Análisis Sociológicos, Económicos, y Políticos (1988); Centro para la Investigacion sobre la Realidad Social (1991).

Note: (1) = The upper classes of your region have better served state interests than they have regional interests.

(2) = The upper classes of this autonomous community are responsible for the decadence of our culture and for our lack of real autonomy.

(3) = During Francoism, the upper classes of this autonomous community gave priority to the political interests of Spain instead of those of this autonomous community.

(4) = The upper classes of this region supported the Francoist regime, to the detriment of this community's culture.

classes, Basque and Catalan alike, tacitly accepted Franco's rule. Nor does this finding mean that all the members of the Basque bourgeoisie and intelligentsia remained passive during the Francoist period. Compared with Catalonia, however, the number of those who mobilized was very small.

Although one likely reason the Basque bourgeoisie and intelligentsia were less involved in nationalist politics was their greater cultural and political orientation toward Spain, Chapter 8 offered another plausible explanation—that the Basque bourgeoisie and intelligentsia had much less political autonomy than did the Catalan. Because of their economic dependence on the Spanish-oriented capitalist elite, members of the Basque bourgeoisie and intelligentsia who held nationalist ideas faced great political and economic risks when expressing these ideas or mobilizing in support of nationalist organizations. Therefore, it does not seem to be a coincidence that the Basque bourgeoisie and intelligentsia became active only when their political autonomy increased, toward the end of the Francoist period.

In the 1970s, under the impact of the energy crisis, the Basque economy began to crumble. Though the Basque capitalist elite was able to endure the crisis by shifting its investments to other Spanish regions, the local bourgeoisie was constrained to the exigencies of the Basque market; the different way in which the two social groups experienced the crisis partly explains the more active involvement of the latter in nationalist politics during this period.[7] The Basque bourgeoisie, given little choice, turned to nationalist mobilization to achieve political autonomy for the Basque Country, and thus gain greater control over the management of the Basque economy. The Basque capitalist elite's control over Basque society also declined considerably during the 1970s, thus increasing the political autonomy of the local bourgeoisie and intelligentsia. The decline in elite influence was due partly to the impact of the economic crisis, which forced many big capitalists to leave the region. More important for the decline, however, were the end of the dictatorship and the fact that the Basque capitalist elite was politically paralyzed by ETA, which forced its members to pay regular "revolutionary taxes" and threatened them with death. The paralysis of the capitalist elite not only provided the Basque bourgeoisie with a margin of political maneuvering that it had not enjoyed during the previous decades but also strongly motivated its members to become more involved in nationalist politics, so that they would not be accused of pro-Spanish attitudes by ETA and its supporters.

Political Diversity and the Success of Revolutionary Nationalist Organizations

If one takes into account the structure of political mobilization in the Basque Country and Catalonia during the Francoist period, Linz's survey findings, which show that in 1969 Catalan respondents were more nationalist than were Basque respondents, are not surprising. Whereas nationalist political mobilization had been quite intense in Catalonia since the late 1950s, it had been quite mild in the Basque Country. These different patterns of political mobilization in the two regions also explain why, when ETA initiated its armed activities in 1968 with the assassination of the chief of police of San Sebastián, Melitón Manzanas, it immediately attracted the attention of Basque anti-Francoists, of Spaniards in general, and of the international community. ETA faced little competition in becoming the symbolic center of Basque opposition to Franco, but revolutionary nationalist groups in Catalonia, such as the PSAN or the FAC, faced strong competition from other, more moderate political groups such as the PSUC and Pujol and his followers.

One particularly dramatic event illustrates the different character and social composition of political mobilization in the two regions. In December 1970, several ETA members were put on trial in what became known as the "Juicio de Burgos" (the Burgos trials).[8] In these highly publicized trials, the ETA defendants, of working-class and lower-middle-class origins, argued passionately that the Basque people and its working class were oppressed, and that ETA's goal was the formation of an independent and socialist Basque state. The trials attracted enormous interest throughout the world, and there were numerous acts of protest against the dictatorship in Spain and abroad. Perhaps the most remarkable of these demonstrations took place in Catalonia, where 300 Catalan intellectuals locked themselves inside the monastery of Montserrat to oppose the trials, demand amnesty for the defendants, and generally denounce the Francoist regime.

The contrast between the characteristics of Basque political mobilization and those of Catalan political mobilization could not be more transparent than in this particular pair of events. The Basque political activists came from the working and lower-middle classes, whereas the Catalan political activists were well-known members of the bourgeoisie and intelligentsia. The Basque militants demanded both independence and socialism for their region, while the Catalan intellectuals demanded autonomy and democracy for theirs. The former had been put on trial for killing members of the state security forces, while the latter had chosen peaceful means to achieve their goals.

The Burgos trials not only illustrate the contrast between Basque and Catalan styles of political mobilization; they are also crucial for our understanding of the development of radical nationalist politics in the Basque Country. Indeed, during the Burgos trials, ETA became enshrined as the symbol of Basque resistance, just as leftist and centrist Catalan intellectuals and members of the Catalan bourgeoisie—Jordi Pujol in particular—had come to represent Catalan resistance. The remainder of the chapter explains why this was so, and why the central role played by ETA in the Basque nationalist movement had long-lasting consequences for Basque nationalist politics.

To explain the relative success of revolutionary and separatist nationalist organizations in the Basque Country and Catalonia, one has to take into account that, other things being equal, the level of political diversity of a given environment can have significant effects on the level of popular support attained by a political organization in that environment. The greatest disadvantage to competing in a larger, more diverse, social-movement industry is that the greater the competition, the more specialized the programmatic offer by individual opposition organizations must be, and the more homogeneous the groups attracted by their message.[9] In Catalonia, democrats and nationalists opposed to Franco could identify with and support any group within a broad panoply of political organizations, depending on their own ideological preferences. If they were socialist, and sensitive to the need to preserve Catalan identity, they could identify with the PSUC; if they were centrist and nationalist, they could follow Pujol; and if they were nationalist and revolutionary, they could support organizations such as the FAC or the PSAN. In contrast, the only political organization that clearly opposed Franco in the Basque Country was ETA; thus ETA was able to appeal to a larger and ideologically more heterogeneous group of democrats and nationalists than did similar Catalan political organizations.

The literature shows that most people who entered ETA as militants, or who at least supported ETA, did so primarily because of its nationalist and anti-Francoist ideology, without necessarily identifying with its separatist and revolutionary goals.[10] Ibarra, in his detailed study of the labor movement from 1967 to 1977, arrived at the same conclusion, through his analysis of the links between ETA and the labor movement.[11] He found that although ETA became involved in the labor movement during the late 1960s, and although the labor movement itself became more sensitive to nationalist demands and participated in demonstrations of solidarity with ETA, the workers did not fully identify with ETA's goals of independence and socialist revolution. In Ibarra's view, "the bulk of the Biscayan working class was not separatist. While it adamantly opposed the trials and executions of ETA militants, this was not out of identification with ETA's strategy, but because of basic anti-Francoist solidarity."[12] In sum, in the Basque Country, as in the rest of Spain and abroad, many people identified or sympathized with ETA because it was an effective vehicle for opposition to the dictatorship.

The fact that ETA used violence to achieve its goals does not invalidate the thesis that many of its supporters were not radical. Although violence against the dictatorship was considered morally indefensible, it was somehow seen as justified by its instrumental role in the restoration of democracy. This popular reaction may, in turn, have promoted more violence on the part of ETA, since, according to Gamson, "Violence should be viewed as an instrumental act, aimed at furthering the purposes of the group that uses it when they have some reason to think it will help their cause. This is especially likely to be true when the normal condemnation which attends its use is muted or neutralized in the surrounding community, when it is tacitly condoned by large parts of the audience."[13]

It was only during the early years of the transition to democracy that Basques and Spaniards in general began to question the legitimacy of the continued murders of army personnel and policemen, and ETA itself became more divided over the use of violence to achieve its political goals. A large fraction of the organization emphasized the pursuit of class goals, another fraction emphasized nationalist goals, many opposed the use of violence (even the assassination of Carrero Blanco), and others proposed that ETA restructure itself as a normal political party after Franco's death.[14] The multiple divisions, conflicts, and private vendettas that have characterized ETA reflect the extremely diverse reasons why Basques supported ETA, as militants or otherwise. This in turn reflects the fact that ETA was one of the few political organizations to oppose Francoism in the Basque Country during the late 1960s and early 1970s.

The main reason revolutionary nationalist organizations in Catalonia, such as the PSAN or the FAC, did not have the same popular-support base and visibility as ETA had was that they were forced to compete with other organizations. It was thus more difficult for individual radical separatist organizations to present themselves as representatives of the Catalan people in general, and to attract people's support. The FAC carried out almost 100 acts of violence against the state between 1969 and 1971. Most of these involved blowing up public buildings, which on one occasion caused the death, albeit unplanned, of a member of the state security forces.[15] The dynamic created by this violence was similar to the spiral of violence in the Basque Country, although on a lesser scale: repression, arrests, military trials, shows of solidarity by lawyers' associations, mobilization of the prisoners' families, demonstrations of solidarity, etc. But who remembers the military trials of FAC's militants in September 1972? By the same token, who remembers that members of other political organizations were tried in Burgos alongside ETA's militants, or that the executions of November 1974 included not only two members of ETA but also members of other violent organizations?

It could be argued that Catalan organizations such as the FAC received less public attention than did ETA because their militants purposely avoided killing people, which reduced the public visibility of their actions and the harshness of the sentences they received.[16] Catalan separatism did indeed produce fewer victims than did Basque separatism. Nevertheless, the "Fets

del Palau," Pujol's trial in 1960 for organizing this act of opposition to
Franco, and the clandestine Assembly of Barcelona's university students and
professors in 1966, none of which involved murder or death sentences, also
served to create martyrs and charismatic leaders. What Basque and Catalan
democrats and nationalists admired was not the means involved in acts but
the acts of defiance themselves.[17]

An indirect effect of the different degrees of support and visibility that
Basque and Catalan revolutionary nationalist organizations achieved during
the early 1970s was their different abilities to recruit militants, and to recover
quickly after repression. Greater competition in the Catalan social-movement industry, compared with that in the Basque Country, limited the
recruitment potential of Catalan revolutionary nationalist organizations, as
well as their ability to recover when their militants were arrested or killed.
Although the number of militants in ETA never exceeded 600 at any given
point, it is unlikely that the FAC could ever deploy more than 50 militants.[18]
This chronic shortage of militants in Catalonia is revealed by Vera's comment
that in 1975, with 25 FAC militants in jail, very little of the organization
remained free.[19] Clark and others have noted that each wave of repression
against ETA, by contrast, brought a new wave of militant recruits. Although
the resulting ruptures of continuity in the leadership of ETA posed a constant threat of ideological shifts and internal disputes, the new waves of militants guaranteed ETA's survival.[20] This ability to recruit militants and to
recover after repression was essential for ETA's continued visibility and effec-
tiveness, two necessary conditions for the success of any social movement.[21]

The different degrees of political diversity of the Basque and Catalan environments in pre-democratic Spain therefore explain why ETA was able to
symbolize Basque opposition to Franco while similar revolutionary organizations in Catalonia failed to do so. They do not explain, however, the persistence of significant levels of support for Herri Batasuna and ETA even
during the democratic period.

The political developments that followed Franco's death are consistent
with the Structural Conduciveness model. The advent of democracy and the
arrival on the political scene of a greater number of political parties resulted
in the emergence in the Basque Country of a political-party system that was
quite similar to the one seen for so long in Catalonia. Basques voted in favor
of the Statute of Autonomy, which was negotiated on behalf of the Basque
people by the Basque Nationalist Party, and chose bourgeois nationalist parties over revolutionary nationalist parties in electoral contests. Moreover,
popular support for independence has remained low, and the legitimacy of
ETA has diminished over the years. What happened to ETA is not very different from what happened to the PSUC in Catalonia, or to the Spanish
Communist Party. Despite their having led the opposition to Franco during

the 1960s and 1970s, all of them were defeated in elections by more moderate parties. The fact that this happened reveals that the role of political capital and the logic of mobilization in shaping political structures are constrained by socioeconomic structural conditions, which in the end determine what is and what is not politically possible.

Political capital and the logic of mobilization nonetheless benefited organizations, such as ETA or the PSUC, that were active before Franco's death. Although neither the PSUC nor ETA (or its political arm, Herri Batasuna) has received as much political support as pre-transition mobilization patterns would have led one to expect, they have received a stable and substantial share of the vote since democracy was restored in Spain. To explain the persistence of support for these organizations one needs to amend the Structural Conduciveness Model by taking into account the role of secondary-socialization processes and political process.

Secondary socialization in political organizations creates bonds of loyalty that retard the redistribution of electoral support when new organizations enter the political scene. Within ETA, for instance, ideological socialization was considered the most important activity it performed.[22] It was only after 1968 and the beginnings of armed struggle that ideological indoctrination began to lose ground to military training.[23] Of course, ETA militants and supporters did not identify with its goals simply because of ideological training. Pérez-Agote's in-depth interviews with ETA militants and sympathizers have revealed that membership in the clandestine organization itself, and the experience of repression (police violence, imprisonment, etc.), also served to strengthen commitment to the movement.[24] At a more general level, the sector of the public that supported ETA was socialized into its ideology through participation in activities organized by ETA (e.g. demonstrations) and through exposure to the many publications issued by the organization during the 1960s and 1970s. In terms of publications, ETA may have been one of the most prolific revolutionary organizations in Spain's recent history. One example of this output is the eighteen-volume set of books called Documentos, which contains the most important articles and pamphlets distributed by ETA in the 1960s and 1970s.[25] Another is the abundant literature on the history of nationalism after the Spanish Civil War, which ETA members or ex-members have published, mostly in Spanish, over the years.

Another factor that can slow the redistribution of political support when a political environment becomes more diverse is the political process. The persistence of support for the party Herri Batasuna and for its parent organization, ETA, is undoubtedly related to the state repression experienced by the Basque population during the 1970s. Faced with ETA's strategy of violence, the successive Spanish governments reacted just the way ETA expected them to react, with indiscriminate repression.[26] By "indiscriminate repression" I do not mean only the use of physical violence against people the police suspected of being ETA militants, or against people attending demonstrations, though this type of repression was certainly widespread for much of the 1970s.[27] Rather, I extend the term to a broader range of police actions that disrupted the lives of the Basque population in general, such as checkpoints, identity checks, limitations on people's political rights, and even the policy of blanketing the major cities with security forces.

But the nature of these state actions was not entirely predetermined by a particular set of structural conditions. To a large extent, these state actions were strategic choices made first by the Franco governments and then by the democratic-transition governments of the late 1970s. These choices were constrained not only by structural conditions, such as the type of political regime in power, but also by the consequences of the political choices that had immediately preceded them.

The declaration of States of Exception and the Burgos trials instigated the spiral of political radicalization in the Basque Country. These measures were consistent not only with the authoritarian character of the Franco regime but also with the Spanish government's misperception of the political consequences that indiscriminate repression would bring in the Basque Country. Who could have predicted that large segments of the Basque population would mobilize in support of a separatist nationalist organization, when Linz's data themselves show that nationalist attitudes were less intense in the Basque Country than in Catalonia?

Once adopted, indiscriminate repression backfired, for although the Basque population did not necessarily support all of ETA's goals or condone its use of violence, it was emotionally loyal to the separatist organization. Many people in the Basque Country came to experience police repression as an act of occupation by a foreign army, and the daily violence reminded others of the Spanish Civil War. Memories of this period, still vivid among the Basque population, help to explain the persistence today of support for Herri Batasuna and ETA.[28]

The radicalization of the Basque population that followed in the wake of indiscriminate repression increasingly constrained the strategic choices available to the Spanish governments. These governments now faced the contradictory demands of a highly radicalized Basque population and a newly radicalized segment of the Spanish armed forces, the main target of ETA's violent actions. It is thus inappropriate to compare, as some have done, the post-Franco Spanish governments' handling of the Catalan problem with their handling of the Basque problem.[29] It is easy to forget, for instance, that every political amnesty granted to Basque political prisoners, every political concession ceded to Basque nationalists by the first transition governments, was greeted with Basque demands for more amnesty and more political con cessions, and with the disapproval of the reactionary sectors of Spanish society. The attempted military coup of February 1981 revealed great dissatisfaction among segments of the Spanish armed forces with the way the Spanish government had handled the Basque problem. In dealing with Catalan nationalists, the governments of the democratic transition were not confronted with these sorts of pressures.

In the Basque Country, as we have seen, the separatist revolutionary movement had a virtual monopoly over political opposition to Franco, while in Catalonia revolutionary separatists had to compete in a broad field of political contenders. These differences translated into the greater visibility, legitimacy, and efficacy of Basque separatists as compared with Catalan separatists. This, in turn, generated a more violent region-state confrontation in the Basque Country than in Catalonia. Specific events, finally, such as the Burgos trials in 1970 and the execution of three Basque separatists in 1975, dramatically enhanced the popular appeal of ETA's message.

In the long run, then, the continued stability in levels of support for the revolutionary nationalist organization Herri Batasuna and the sympathy that ETA continues to attract from a significant proportion of the Basque population can be largely explained by the secondary-socialization processes that ETA sympathizers were exposed to during the 1960s and 1970s and by the political capital ETA had accumulated during those years. The amended version of the Structural Conduciveness model accounts for the long-term consequences of the diversity of the political environment in any given period. The diversification of a political environment that previously failed to reflect the social context in which it took shape does not automatically translate into political outcomes that perfectly reflect the present social context. This adjustment may take a long time, or it may be precluded altogether by the political events and processes set in motion before diversification.

CONCLUSION

A Revised Explanation

"The difference between Basque and Catalan nationalists is that Basques want to leave Spain, and Catalans want to run it."[1] This comment by a Castilian analyst, though somewhat of an exaggeration, illustrates one major difference between Basque and Catalan nationalism, which is that Basque nationalism has tended to be more separatist than Catalan nationalism has. The author of the quote omits, however, one additional feature that distinguishes the two: generally speaking, Basque nationalism has consistently been more anticapitalist than Catalan nationalism has. The goal of this book has been to explain these contrasts between the Basque and Catalan nationalist movements.

The Basque Country and Catalonia have been formally included as parts of Spain for at least five centuries. Trade dependence, a long history of incorporation in Spain, and the Spanish state's failure to discriminate between Basques and Catalans undoubtedly help to explain the relatively low proportions of Basques and Catalans who support independence. There are few instances, in fact, of successful independence movements in regions that have belonged to a particular state for so long.

Throughout the book I have emphasized the crucial roles that different patterns of development have played in the two regions. These patterns determined the intensity of class conflict, the size of the regional bourgeoisies and intelligentsias and their degrees of political autonomy, and the strength of the ties between regional capitalist elites and the Spanish state. These sociostructural characteristics, in combination with the long-term political and cultural orientations of the Basque and Catalan elites, which date back to the pre-industrial period, have shaped the structure of political mobilization and, ultimately, the relative strength of separatist and anticapitalist nationalism in the regions.

In view of these findings, the traditional interpretation of Basque and Catalan nationalism reviewed in the Introduction should be revised: Basque and Catalan nationalisms emerged at the end of the nineteenth century in response to socioeconomic transformations and political- and cultural-homogenization policies undertaken by the Spanish state. Initially, those social groups most harmed by capitalist development and by state-centralization efforts mobilized in support of Spanish parties that represented their interests (e.g. the Carlist party, the Conservative party, and various republican parties with federalist agendas). Disappointed with this Spanish strategy, however, and influenced by nationalist ideas and their growing legitimacy across Europe, they eventually founded, and mobilized in support of, various nationalist political parties. The programmatic configuration of the Basque and Catalan nationalist programs was shaped by the different patterns of development characteristic of the two regions and by the traditional political and cultural orientations of the regional elites.

Basque nationalism represented the frustration of preindustrial Basque elites with the changes brought about by industrialization and centralization. The peculiar intensity of their reaction, and their success in imposing their ideological views on Basque nationalism, resulted, however, from the character of Basque capitalist development: combined and specialized in capital-goods production. The three major features of the Basque social structure that resulted from this type of development were a marginalized preindustrial elite and peasantry, a close-knit capitalist elite that became well integrated into the Spanish power elite, and a small and divided local bourgeoisie. But neither the capitalist elite nor the local bourgeosie played a major role in the development of Basque nationalism—the capitalist elite, because its economic interests and cultural orientations tied it to Spain; the local bourgeoisie, because of its small size and its strong pro-Spanish cultural and political orientations. Therefore, the social base of Basque nationalism was formed by the social groups displaced by industrialization, and included only a few members of the local bourgeoisie. Those displaced, because of their greater numerical weight, were able to impose their separatist and anticapitalist ideological discourse on the Basque Nationalist Party's program.

Catalan nationalism, by contrast, reflected the frustration of the Catalan bourgeoisie over its inability to shape Spanish policies according to its own interests. It also reflected the bourgeoisie's rejection of the cultural- and political-homogenization policies undertaken by the Spanish state during the nineteenth century. The bourgeoisie's decision to adopt a nationalist agenda, and its ability to impose its ideological program on the Catalan nationalist movement, resulted from three factors: the endogenous character of Catalan development; the specialization of Catalan industry in consumer-goods production; and the bourgeoisie's pro-Catalan cultural and political orientations. Because endogenous development and specialization in consumer-goods production facilitated the assimilation of the Catalan preindustrial elites and the peasantry into the nascent capitalist society, mobilization against social change by these social groups was much less intense than it was in the Basque Country. At the same time, although a large bourgeoisie developed during this process of industrialization, its economic and political power was much weaker than that of the Basque capitalist elite. This lack of political power commensurate with its aspirations led the Catalan bourgeoisie to adopt a nationalist strategy, after trying unsuccessfully to advance its interests through the Spanish governments and political parties.

The dictatorship of General Franco and the dramatic socioeconomic transformations experienced by the Basque Country and Catalonia after the Spanish Civil War altered the programmatic goals and the social bases of Basque and Catalan nationalism. The restoration of democracy and of national rights became significant goals in the two nationalist movements, and preindustrial social groups ceased to be a factor in either movement. Despite these changes, however, Basque nationalism remained more separatist and anticapitalist than did Catalan nationalism. The distinction between capital-goods development and consumer-goods development was again the determining factor behind this difference. Although the Basque and Catalan social structures became almost identical during the post–Civil War period, the Basque capitalist elite continued to exert greater influence over state policies than did the Catalan capitalist elite. More significantly, because of the different constraints imposed by capital-goods and consumer-goods development, the Basque local bourgeoisie and intelligentsia enjoyed less political autonomy than did the Catalan local bourgeoisie and intelligentsia. Consequently, the degree of involvement of the bourgeoisie and the intelligentsia in anti-Franco political mobilization was lower in the Basque Country than in Catalonia, and Basque radicals were in a better position to promote their separatist and revolutionary programs than were Catalan radicals. Thus, when democracy was restored after the death of Franco, separatist and revolutionary forms of nationalism were more successful in the Basque Country than in Catalonia.

Given this revised explanation of the development of Basque and Catalan nationalism and of their differences, what can be said about the future of Basque and Catalan nationalism? Two main reasons why neither Basque nor Catalan separatist parties have become dominant in their respective regions are that high proportions of the two populations identify with Spain and that similarly high proportions believe that their regions would not benefit economically from independence. These findings suggest that the political independence of either Catalonia or the Basque Country is unlikely in the near future. Although trade interdependence between these regions and

Spain will diminish as European integration proceeds, it is not the only source of interdependence with Spain, nor is European integration likely to proceed as fast at the political level as it is proceeding at the economic level. Therefore, there will be a high degree of uncertainty about the economic and political consequences of independence for Catalonia and the Basque Country for some time to come. This uncertainty should weigh heavily in the calculations of those who use economic criteria to guide their decisions. Faced with the choice between retaining their current economic prosperity in a highly decentralized Spain and risking economic and political decline in consequence of becoming independent states, Basque and Catalan nationalists may not put independence high on their political agendas.

Not everyone, however, makes political decisions on the basis of economic criteria alone. Another consideration underlying predictions about the course of nationalism in the two regions must be the degree to which Basques and Catalans identify themselves as Spaniards. Currently, only a small minority of Basques and Catalans identifies itself as only Basque or only Catalan. Given the massive presence, in their midst, of immigrants from other regions of Spain, the proportion of Basque and Catalan residents who do not identify with Spain will probably not increase dramatically in the next generation. In the short run, then, it is unlikely that the Basque Country and Catalonia could become independent by democratic means. Only a major economic crisis or the breakdown of state institutions could lead to their independence.

Although separatist tendencies are unlikely to become much stronger in the short term, support for Basque and Catalan nationalist parties is likely to become stronger. In a recent article, Lawler argues that decentralized structures, whether organizational or political, are more likely than centralized structures to enhance the emotional identification of individuals with their autonomous units than with the whole.[2] This is so because individuals come to depend more and more on the goods and services provided by the autonomous units (whether autonomous divisions within a company or regional governments in a state). The Spanish case offers ample evidence to support this prediction. Since the approval of the new Constitution in 1978, Spain has been divided into 17 autonomous communities. Although some of them, such as Catalonia, the Basque Country, and Galicia, are distinguished from the rest of Spain by language and by a history of political autonomy, others are much less culturally or historically distinctive. Nevertheless, despite the "artificial" character of most of these newly created autonomous communities, support for regional political parties and identification with these regions have steadily increased in almost all of them over the last decade. This suggests that one should expect a progressive increase in nationalist identification in the Basque Country and Catalonia over the next generation.

In the final analysis, Spain finds itself in a quandary. Regional decentralization has been necessary to alleviate nationalist conflict, but in the long run it will favor the development of even stronger nationalist sentiment. Although this strengthened nationalist sentiment may stop short of separatism, it does makes state unity far more fragile. In a situation like this, in which large proportions of the population of particular regions have developed a strong, local, nationalist sentiment, economic or political crises at the state level can more easily translate into state breakup.

It is customary to conclude investigations of this sort by commenting on the generalizability of the findings, and on their theoretical implications. This study has taken the form of a careful comparison between two very similar regions, within the same larger entity, that have experienced quite dissimilar nationalist movements. Although a study of this kind precludes definitive statements about all the conditions that will lead to the hegemony of particular forms of nationalism, it does enable one to suggest some hypotheses.

First of all, the book's findings provide mixed support for the different theories discussed in the Introduction, largely because, with the exception of the Cost/Benefit approach, these theories do not specify whether they intend to explain the intensity of nationalism or that of separatism. If one bears in mind this distinction between nationalism and separatism, the study of Basque and Catalan nationalism shows that Overdevelopment theory provides an adequate explanation for the strength of nationalism but not for the strength of separatism, since support for separatist organizations in both the Basque Country and Catalonia has been rather low. Although Laitin has subtly argued that divisions within the state-oriented and the region-oriented segments of the regional elites weaken the drive for secession in overdeveloped regions, the more decisive factor is that the Basques and Catalans have depended to a great extent on the Spanish economy. Thus, the strength of separatism in overdeveloped regions can be seen as contingent on their level of economic interdependence with the host state, as the Cost/Benefit approach would predict.

Low support for separatist organizations in the Basque Country and Catalonia is consistent with the predictions of Ethnic Competition theory, the Cost/Benefit approach, and Relative Deprivation theory. Indeed, low levels of ethnic competition, high levels of economic interdependence, and high standards of living, respectively, are conditions leading to low levels of separatism, according to these theories. These theories, however, cannot adequately explain why, despite the social characteristics just cited, support for nationalism (if not separatism) has been quite strong in the Basque Country and Catalonia. Only Overdevelopment theory can account for this finding, because of its focus on the political aspirations of the local bourgeoisies and intelligentsias of overdeveloped regions.

Finally, none of the theories cited above can explain why separatist and anticapitalist nationalist ideas have consistently received more support in the Basque Country than in Catalonia. This book's main theoretical contribution is to demonstrate that the intensity of intraregional class conflict and the diversity of the political environment are crucial to an explanation of the strength of separatism in peripheral regions.

The first factor introduces greater complexity to sociostructural explanations of nationalism. Peripheral regions are treated as "divided nations" in which the main actors are no longer simply ethnic groups located in particular regions but social groups within those ethnic groups. As the study of the early phase of Basque and Catalan nationalism has shown, the relationship between the intensity of intraregional class conflict and the strength of separatist organizations within that region's nationalist movement is positive. Although in situations of intense intraregional class conflict the least costly strategy for any class in conflict is to build class alliances at the state level, that same class will turn to separatist solutions if those alliances are impossible or fail to achieve the desired goal. Separatism is therefore an outgrowth not only of intense conflict between peripheral regions and the central state but also of intense intraregional conflict. This argument may seem to contradict Laitin's hypothesis, according to which intraregional class struggles weaken nationalist movements. In fact, however, the two hypotheses are compatible, for Laitin's applies to the explanation of the strength of *nationalist* movements while this book's applies specifically to the explanation of the strength of *separatist* movements. Therefore, one would predict a negative relationship between regional class conflict and nationalism, and a positive relationship between regional class conflict and separatism.

Part II of this book has analyzed the influence of types of development on patterns of class conflict within the Basque Country and Catalonia, and has demonstrated the significant role that class conflict played in explaining the characteristics of early Basque and Catalan nationalism. Support for nationalist parties was less prevalent in the Basque Country than in Catalonia, and support for separatist and anticapitalist goals was more prevalent within the Basque nationalist movement than within the Catalan nationalist movement. The most satisfying explanation for this contrast is that class conflict between preindustrial elites and capitalist elites was more intense in the Basque Country than in Catalonia. Conflict between these two classes was more intense in the Basque Country than in Catalonia, because Basque development was combined and centered around capital-goods production while Catalan development was endogenous and centered around consumer-goods production.

This book has also demonstrated that the strength of separatist organizations is a function of the diversity of the political environment. *Ceteris paribus*, the greater the competition faced by individual separatist organizations, the less support they will be able to garner. Moreover, I have proposed an amended version of the Structural Conduciveness model developed by Pinard and Nielsen. Their approach focuses on the current political diversity of the environment in explaining the success of a political organization, but does not consider the impact of *past* political diversity.[3] Instead, this book demonstrates that the political diversity of the environment has enduring effects on public support for specific political parties, independent of current conditions. As the comparison between Basque and Catalan nationalism shows, Basque separatist organizations have retained significant support from the population despite the diversification of the Basque political environment in the wake of Franco's death. This is so because, prior to Franco's death, Basque separatist mobilization took place in a political environment with very little diversity. Basque separatists were thus able, before Franco's death, to shape the political process and to amass political capital to a far greater extent than were Catalan separatists, who faced a more diversified environment.

More research will be needed to determine at a general level how autonomous the political diversity of the environment is with respect to the social context, and what role that diversity plays in the configuration of popular support for separatist organizations. With regard to the first question, the comparison of Basque and Catalan nationalism has suggested that the political environment does reflect the social context. For instance, one reason the local bourgeoisie played a much smaller role in the initial development of nationalism in the Basque Country than in Catalonia is that it was indeed much smaller in the former than in the latter. Nevertheless, during the Franco regime the relatively weak political mobilization of the Basque local bourgeoisie, compared to that of the Catalan local bourgeoisie, is not so easily explained by reference to the social context, which was almost identical in the two regions. A cultural and structural explanation has been proposed here. The former invokes the different cultural orientations of the Basque and Catalan bourgeoisies and intelligentsias; the latter invokes the different degrees of political autonomy of these groups. In other cases, however, one should not discount the possibility that the political sphere is largely autonomous with respect to social and cultural determinants.

As for the relative impact of the political diversity of the environment, compared with that of social factors, on the strength of separatist organizations, this book suggests that social factors are at least as important. As predicted by the sociostructural theories of nationalism the book discusses, popular support for separatist organizations in the Basque Country and Catalonia has been rather low. Yet, the political diversity of the environment can make a crucial difference, both quantitatively (e.g. in relative levels of support for separatist organizations) and qualitatively (e.g. in the political climate). Although from an international and historical perspective, support for separatist organizations in the Basque Country and Catalonia may appear to be quite similar and rather low, from a Spanish perspective Basque separatism has been perceived as intense, and significantly more intense than Catalan separatism has been. Indeed, if Basque nationalism had been as moderate as Catalan nationalism has been, the coup attempt in February 1981 would probably not have taken place. Therefore, the role of political factors, such as the degree of political diversity of the environment, should not be underestimated in studies of nationalism.

This book's final theoretical implication is that we can gain a much better understanding of nationalism by focusing on patterns instead of levels of development. The contrasts between endogenous and combined development, and between specialization in capital-goods production and consumer-goods production, have been determinant in differentiating Basque and Catalan nationalism, and may be useful in explaining the types of nationalist movements that have developed in other peripheral regions. Although the immediate explanations for the different character of Basque and Catalan nationalism have been the degrees of intraregional ethnic conflict and the political diversity of the environments in the two regions, this study has demonstrated that these two variables have been shaped by the different patterns of development experienced by the two regions. On the basis of the book's findings one can predict that in conditions of high economic interdependence between peripheral regions and the host state, economic specialization in capital-goods production by peripheral regions is more likely to lead to radical forms of nationalism than is economic specialization in consumer-goods production.

In sum, the findings of this study reveal that, except in explaining the emergence of the *idea* of nationalism, no special theory of nationalism is required. As Hechter recently pointed out,

> There is nothing about ethnic and race relations per se that warrants a special theory. Indeed the subject concerns phenomena—like group formation, solidarity, assimilation, and collective action—that also occur among many other kinds of groups, be they based on class, religion, or territory. Ethnic and race relations therefore constitute instances of more general kinds of inter-group processes.[4]

The spirit of this quote has been the guiding thread of this study.

Sources

This book uses both historical and contemporary data on Catalonia and the Basque Country. One major source of information for the period preceding the Spanish Civil War is the literature on nationalism and socioeconomic development in the two regions. Much of the literature on socioeconomic development that I have used has been published in the last five to ten years, and so far has not, to my knowledge, been incorporated into analyses of Basque and Catalan nationalism. That it has not lies perhaps in the fact that the study of Basque and Catalan nationalism has generally been conducted by Spanish social historians, who have not been very concerned with the systematic study of the effect of developmental patterns on nationalism. One major exception, an early contribution to the study of the influence of economic development on nationalism, is Fernández de Pinedo's *Crecimiento Económico y Transformaciones Sociales del País Vasco, 1100–1850* (Madrid: Siglo XXI, 1974).

I have made a special effort to determine whether explanations offered for nationalism in the Basque Country were applicable also in Catalonia, and vice versa, by compiling comparable quantitative information. One important source of information has been the *Anuario Financiero y de Sociedades Anónimas* [Directory of Corporations and Financial Institutions] of 1922. This Directory was published annually from 1914 to at least the late 1950s by a private publishing house, based in the Basque industrial city of Bilbao. The first year for which extensive information was provided for both financial and nonfinancial corporations was 1922, which explains why I did not choose an earlier date. The stated goal of this publication was to inform businessmen. Although the information compiled in this publication was provided voluntarily by the companies themselves, the compilers of the Directory provide comparative figures to demonstrate the completeness of its coverage. Manuel

González Portilla, in *La Formación de la Sociedad Capitalista en el País Vasco, 1876–1913* (San Sebastián: Haranburu, 1981), and other scholars have used the information contained in the Directory, but to date no one had transferred this information to a computer database. I owe to González Portilla the idea to use the data for my research, and I would like to thank Santiago de la Hoz, María Teresa Delgado, and Sarolta Petro for their assistance in creating this dataset, which includes more than 11,000 records of information. Each record represents a member of the Board of Directors of a particular company, and includes the names of the person and the company, the economic sector in which the company operated, the company's assets, and the province where the company was located.

My main sources of information for the post–Civil War period are, again, the literature on nationalism and socioeconomic development in the two regions. Two representative surveys that I designed, which were conducted in the Basque Country and Catalonia in 1988 and 1991 have also been important sources of information. These surveys were conducted by ASEP (Análisis Sociológicos, Económicos, y Políticos) and CIRES (Centro para la Investigación sobre la Realidad Social). Although I cannot test my macrostructural argument at the individual level of analysis, these databases are useful for testing alternative hypotheses and specific components of my argument.

Finally, I have relied on many additional primary sources. In particular, I have collected all the information on Basque and Catalan nationalism published by the Spanish weekly *Cambio 16*, from 1971 to 1980, to analyze the political dynamics of the two regions during this critical decade.

Notes

Introduction: An Analytical Approach

1. Francesc Cambó, *Memorias* (1987), p. 74.
2. Ibid., p. 41.
3. Cited by Cambó, p. 78.
4. What follows is a sample of well-known studies: Jaume Vicens Vives, *Industrials i Polítics (Segle XIX)* (1961); Jordi Solé Tura, *Catalanisme i Revolució Burgesa* (1967); Juan J. Linz, "Early State-Building and Late Peripheral National-ism Against the State: The Case of Spain" (1973), Vol. II, pp. 32–116; Stanley Payne, *El Nacionalismo Vasco* (1974); José A. González Casanova, *Federalisme i Autonomía a Catalunya* (1974); Javier Corcuera Atienza, *Orígenes, Ideología y Organización del Nacionalismo Vasco, 1876–1904* (1979); Juan J. Linz, "Some Com-parative Thoughts on the Transition to Democracy in Portugal and Spain" (1981); Marianne Heiberg, "Urban Politics and Rural Culture: Basque Nationalism" (1982), pp. 355–387; Francesc Hernández, *La Identidad Nacional en Cataluña* (1983); Juan P. Fusi, *Pluralismo y Nacionalidad* (1984); Ander Gurrutxaga, *El Código Nacionalista durante el Franquismo* (1985); Xabier Arbós, "Central Versus Peripheral Nationalism in Building Democracy: The Case of Spain" (1987), pp. 143–159; Cyrus E. Zirakzadeh, *A Rebellious People* (1991); Hank Johnston, *Tales of Nationalism* (1991).
5. Payne, *El Nacionalismo Vasco* (1974); Fusi, *Pluralismo y Nacionalidad* (1984).
6. Fusi, *Pluralismo y Nacionalidad* (1984); Gurrutxaga, *El Código Nacionalista* (1985); Donald Horowitz, *Ethnic Groups in Conflict* (1985).
7. Linz, "Early State-Building" (1973); Payne, *El Nacionalismo Vasco* (1974); Johnston, *Tales of Nationalism* (1991).
8. Charles Tilly, *Coercion, Capital, and European States* (1990); John Breuilly, *Nationalism and the State* (1993); Michael Mann, *The Sources of Social Power II* (1993).
9. Ernest Gellner, *Nations and Nationalism* (1983); Benedict Anderson, *Imag-ined Communities* (1983).

10. The Internal Colonialist variant of the Relative Deprivation argument has been presented by Michael Hechter (*Internal Colonialism: The Celtic Fringe in British National Development, 1536–1966* (1975). Its Modernization theory variant is implicit in the work of Gellner, *Nations and Nationalism* (1983), Horowitz, *Ethnic Groups* (1985), and, to some extent, Anderson, *Imagined Communities* (1983).

11. Tom Nairn, *The Break-up of Britain* (1977); Peter A. Gourevitch, "The Reemergence of 'Peripheral Nationalisms': Some Comparative Speculations on the Spatial Distribution of Political Leadership and Economic Growth" (1979); David Laitin, "The National Uprisings in the Soviet Union" (1991).

12. Fredrik Barth, *Ethnic Groups in Conflict* (1969); Michael Hannan, "The Dynamics of Ethnic Boundaries in Modern States" in *Development and the World System: Educational, Economic, and Political Change, 1950–1970* (1979); François Nielsen, "Ethnic Solidarity in Modern Societies: A Dynamic Analysis" (1985); Susan Olzak, *The Dynamics of Ethnic Competition and Conflict* (1992).

13. Horowitz, *Ethnic Groups* (1985); Hudson Meadwell, "Ethnic Nationalism and Collective Choice Theory" (1989); Hudson Meadwell, "Cultural and Instrumental Approaches to Ethnic Nationalism" (1989); Michael Hechter, "The Dynamics of Secessionism" (1992).

14. Liah Greenfeld, *Nationalism: Five Roads to Modernity* (1992); Rogers Brubaker, *Citizenship and Nationhood in France and Germany* (1992). For the distinction between state-led and state-seeking nationalism, see Charles Tilly, "States and Nationalism in Europe, 1492–1992" (1994).

15. Miroslav Hroch, *Social Preconditions of National Revival in Europe* (1983); Kathryn Verdery, *Transylvanian Villagers* (1983); Daniel Segal, "Nationalism, Comparatively Speaking" (1986); Hobsbawm, *Nations and Nationalism* (1990); John Comaroff, "Humanity, Ethnicity, Nationality: Conceptual and Comparative Perspectives on the USSR" (1991); Breuilly, *Nationalism and the State* (1993).

16. Breuilly.

17. Michael Hechter, *Principles of Group Solidarity* (1987); Michael Hechter, "Nationalism as Group Solidarity" (1987); Charles Furtado and Michael Hechter, "The Emergence of Nationalist Politics in the USSR: A Comparison of Estonia and the Ukraine" (1992).

18. Meadwell, "Cultural and Instrumental Approaches" (1989).

19. Maurice Pinard, *The Rise of a Third Party: A Study in Crisis Politics* (1975); J. D. McCarthy and M. N. Zald, "Resource Mobilization and Social Movements: A Partial Theory" (1977); François Nielsen, "Structural Conduciveness and Ethnic Mobilization" (1986).

20. Jeffery Paige, *Agrarian Revolutions* (1978).

21. William Sewell Jr., "Three Temporalities: Toward an Eventful Sociology" (forthcoming).

22. Alexander Gerschenkron, *Economic Backwardness in Historical Perspective* (1962).

23. Sewell.

24. Tilly, *Coercion, Capital* (1990); Breuilly, *Nationalism and the State* (1993); Mann, *The Sources of Social Power* (1993); Gellner, *Nations and Nationalism* (1983); Anderson, *Imagined Communities* (1983).

25. Elie Kedourie, *Nationalism* (1993); Anderson, *Imagined Communities* (1983).

Chapter 1. State-building in the Iberian Peninsula

1. The main sources for this chapter are: Pierre Bonassie, *Cataluña Mil Años Atrás* (1987); Roger Collins, *The Basques* (1986); Joseph O'Callaghan, *A History of Medieval Spain* (1975); Luis Suárez Fernández, *Historia de España* (1970), "La Expansión Marítima de los Vascos a Fines de la Edad Media," in *Páginas de la Historia del País Vasco*, ed. Universidad de Navarra (Pamplona: Ediciones Universidad de Navarra, 1980), pp. 49–58, and "Las Raíces Históricas de la Pluralidad" (1981); Pierre Vilar, *La Catalogne dans l'Espagne Moderne: Recherches sur les Fondements des Structures Nationales* (1962); Luis G. de Valdeavellano, *Curso de Historia de las Instituciones Medievales* (1952); Marc Bloch, *Feudal Society* (1961); Perry Anderson, *Passages from Antiquity to Feudalism* (1974); Pierre Chaunu, *La España de Carlos V* (1976); Janine Fayard, *Les Membres du Conseil de Castille à l'Epoque Moderne, 1621–1746* (1979); Antonio Domínguez Ortíz, *La Sociedad Española en el Siglo XVII* (1963), and *El Antiguo Régimen: Los Reyes Católicos y los Austrias* (1973); Fernand Braudel, *The Mediterranean and the Mediterranean World in the Age of Phillip II* (1975), *The Perspective of the World* (1984); Valentín Vázquez de Prada, "La Epoca Moderna: Los Siglos XVI a XIX" (1981); Gregorio Monreal, "Annotations Regarding Basque Traditional Political Thought in the Sixteenth Century" (1985); John Lynch, *Spain under the Habsburgs* (1964); Emiliano Fernández de Pinedo, *Crecimiento Económico y Transformaciones Sociales del País Vasco, 1100–1850* (1974); Gianfranco Poggi, *The Development of the Modern State: A Sociological Interpretation* (1978).

2. Vilar, *La Catalogne* (1962).

3. Ibid.; Braudel, *The Perspective of the World* (1984).

Chapter 2. Fiscal Crisis, Centralization, and Rebellion

1. The main sources for this chapter are John H. Elliott, *The Revolt of the Catalans* (1963); Fernández de Pinedo, *Crecimiento Económico* (1974); Vilar, *La Catalogne* (1962); Lynch, *Spain Under* (1964); Vázquez de Prada, "La Epoca Moderna" (1981); Monreal, "Annotations" (1985); Domínguez Ortíz, *La Sociedad Española*, *El Antiguo Régimen* (1963); David Laitin, "Language and the Construction of States: The Case of Catalonia in Spain" (1994).

2. Elliot, *The Revolt* (1963); Vilar, *La Catalogne* (1962).

3. Elliot.

4. Fernández de Pinedo, *Crecimiento Económico* (1974), pp. 61–77.

5. Ibid., p. 70.

6. The different types of economic ties linking the two regional elites with the state are also reflected perfectly in the cultural realm. Throughout history, the Catalan elite has spoken Catalan. This reflects a certain cultural affinity with the region and also a particular pattern of social and economic exchanges; after all, the language has a basic communicative function. In contrast, elites in the Basque Country have tended to speak in Castilian. For instance, amidst the conflicts described above, the Junta General of Vizcaya decreed in 1613 that, from then on, only those reading and writing in Romance language (Castilian) would be eligible for the Junta. As Fernández de Pinedo has pointed out, the significance of this measure can

be better understood if one takes into account that in this period the proportion of the population that could read Romance, even in Castile, was very small. Moreover, the impact of the Basque upper class's choice of Castilian over the Basque language was dramatically reflected in the literary production in the Basque Country. Prior to the second half of the eighteenth century, only 21 books in Basque had ever been published (Ibon Sarasola, *Historia Social de la Literatura Vasca* [1976], p. 183).

7. There is good evidence, however, indicating that Castilian had become the hegemonic official language in Catalonia since the end of the 1640 revolt; see Laitin, "Language and the Construction" (1994).

8. Jesús Cruz, "Hidalguía, Bourgeoisie, and Revolution: Change and Persistence in the Formation of the Spanish Middle Class: Madrid 1750–1850" (1992).

PART II: Patterns of Development and Nationalism
before the Civil War

1. Anderson, *Imagined Communities* (1983); Hobsbawm, *Nations and Nationalism* (1990).

2. Clifford Geertz, *The Interpretation of Cultures* (1963); Neil Smelser, "Mechanisms of Change and Adjustment to Change" (1969); Gellner, *Nations and Nationalism* (1983); Hechter, *Internal Colonialism* (1975) and "Group Formation and the Cultural Division of Labor" (1978); Comaroff, "Humanity, Ethnicity, Nationality" (1991); Horowitz, *Ethnic Groups* (1985).

3. Nairn, *The Break-up* (1977). Other explanations, such as Charles Tilly's ("States and Nationalism"; 1994) and Eric J. Hobsbawm's (*Nations and Nationalism*; 1990) provide alternative but complementary arguments for the development of popular nationalism during the nineteenth century. I emphasize Nairn's argument because his discussion of nationalism facilitates the transition to my own explanation of programmatic differences between Basque and Catalan nationalism.

4. The greater ethnic-mobilization potential that exists in these situations of overlap has also been emphasized by Hechter (*Internal Colonialism*; 1975) and Horowitz (*Ethnic Groups;* 1985), among others.

5. Linz, "Early State-Building" (1973); William A. Douglass, "Introduction," (1985).

6. Donald Horowitz (*Ethnic Groups;* 1985) provides a very similar distinction between the type of nationalism that emerges in underdeveloped areas and that which emerges in overdeveloped areas.

7. Gourevitch, "The Reemergence" (1979); Laitin, "The National Uprisings" (1991).

8. Baruch Knei-Paz, *The Social and Political Thought of Leon Trotski* (1978).

9. Gerschenkron, *Economic Backwardness* (1962); Eric Hobsbawm, *The Age of Revolution* (1962); James Kurth, "The Political Consequences of the Product Cycle: Industrial History and Political Outcomes" (1979).

10. John Scott, "Intercorporate Structures in Western Europe: A Comparative Historical Analysis" (1987).

11. Gerschenkron, *Economic Backwardness* (1962), p. 15.

12. Scott, p. 217.

Chapter 3. Capitalist Industrialization

1. I use the word "fully" because there is growing evidence that integration was proceeding quite fast in the years preceding the War of Succession, at both the economic and cultural levels; see Carlos Martínez Shaw, *Cataluña en la Carrera de Indias* (1981); Laitin, "Language and the Construction" (1994).

2. Vilar, *La Catalogne* (1962); Vicens Vives, *Manual de Historia Económica de España* (1959); Jordi Maluquer de Motes, "La Historia Económica de Cataluña" (1984).

3. Vilar.

4. Ibid.; Pere Pascual, *Agricultura i Industrialització a la Catalunya del Segle XIX* (1990).

5. Vilar, *La Catalogne* (1962); Vives, *Manual de Historia* (1959); Maluquer de Motes, "La Historia Económica" (1984); Albert Carreras, "Fuentes y Datos para el Análisis Regional de la Industrialización Española (siglos XIX y XX)" (1990); Pascual, *Agricultura i Industrialització* (1990).

6. J. K. J. Thomson, *A Distinctive Industrialization: Cotton in Barcelona, 1728–1832* (1992).

7. Jordi Nadal, *El Fracaso de la Revolución Industrial en España, 1814–1913* (1975).

8. Pascual, *Agricultura i Industrialització* (1990).

9. Ibid.

10. Carreras, "Fuentes y Datos" (1990).

11. Ibid.

12. F. Simón, *La Desamortización Española en el Siglo XIX* (1973); Fernández de Pinedo, *Crecimiento Económico* (1974) and "Etapas del Crecimiento Económico de la Economía Vasca (1700–1850)" (1984); R. Uriarte Ayo, "Capacidad Productiva y Producción Habitual en la Siderurgia Tradicional Vizcaína: Factores Determinantes y Aproximación Cuantitativa" (1985).

13. Fernández de Pinedo, *Crecimiento Económico* (1974).

14. Manuel González Portilla, *La Formación de la Sociedad Capitalista en el País Vasco, 1876–1913* (1981); Manu Montero, *Mineros, Banqueros, y Navieros* (1990).

15. Nadal, *El Fracaso* (1975).

16. The lower figure is provided by Montero, *Mineros, Banqueros, y Navieros* (1990); the higher figure is provided by Antonio Escudero, "Capital Minero y Formación de Capital en Vizcaya (1876–1913)" (1990).

17. Joseph Harrison, "La Industria Pesada, el Estado, y el Desarrollo Económico en el País Vasco (1876–1936)" (1983); J. M. Valdaliso, "Grupos Empresariales e Inversión de Capital en Vizcaya" (1988).

18. Actually, the corporation was more extended in the Basque Country than in Catalonia, where small family firms were relatively more common.

19. Manuel Tuñón de Lara, *Estudios sobre el Siglo XIX Español* (1972); Carlos Moya, *El Poder Económico en España* (1975).

20. Jordi Maluquer de Motes, "Cataluña y el País Vasco en la Industria Eléctrica Española, 1901–1935" (1985).

21. Harrison, "La Industria Pesada" (1983); González Portilla, *La Formación* (1981); Montero, *Mineros, Banqueros, y Navieros* (1990).

22. Harrison, "La Industria Pesada" (1983).

23. Tuñón de Lara, *Estudios* (1972); Moya, *El Poder Económico* (1975); Jaume Vicens Vives, *Los Catalanes en el Siglo XIX* (1986).
24. In Moya, *El Poder Económico* (1975).
25. Maurice Zeitlin, *Landlords and Capitalists* (1989); González Portilla, *La Formación* (1981).
26. Ybarra y Bergé, *Política Nacional en Vizcaya* (1947); Antoni Jutglar, *Historia Crítica de la Burguesía a Catalunya* (1984).

Chapter 4. Patterns of Development, and Traditionalist Reaction

1. John F. Coverdale, *The Basque Phase of Spain's First Carlist War* (1984).
2. Pere Pascual, "Carlisme i Societat Rural: La Guerra dels Set Anys en la Conca d' Odena," (1980).
3. Vicens Vives, *Los Catalanes* (1986).
4. Corcuera, *Orígenes, Ideología y Organización* (1979); Coverdale, *The Basque Phase* (1984).
5. Pablo Fernández Albadalejo, *La Crisis del Antiguo Régimen en Guipúzcoa* (Madrid: Akal, 1975); Fernández de Pinedo, *Crecimiento Económico* (1974).
6. For instance, Jaume Torres Elías, *Liberalismo y Rebeldía Campesina* (1973); Josep M. Mundet i Gifré, *La Primera Guerra Carlina a Catalunya* (1990); Vilar, *La Catalogne* (1962).
7. Pascual, *Agricultura i Industrialització* (1990).
8. Ibid.
9. Ibid.
10. Pascual, "Carlisme i Societat Rural" (1980).
11. Fernández Albadalejo, *La Crisis* (1975); Fernández de Pinedo, *Crecimiento Económico* (1974).
12. Fernández Albadalejo, *La Crisis* (1975); Pascual, "Carlisme i Societat Rural" (1980).
13. Coverdale, *The Basque Phase* (1984).
14. Ibid.
15. Vicente Garmendia, *La Ideología Carlista (1868–1876)* (1984).
16. Vicens Vives, *Los Catalanes* (1986); Pascual, "Carlisme i Societat Rural" (1980).
17. Fernández de Pinedo, "Etapas" (1984).
18. José Extramiana, *Historia de las Guerras Carlistas* (1980); Vicente Garmendia, *La Ideología Carlista* (1984).
19. Pascual, *Agricultura i Industrialització* (1990); Vicens Vives, *Los Catalanes* (1986).
20. Nadal, *El Fracaso* (1975).
21. Manuel González Portilla, "La Industria Siderúrgica en el País Vasco: del Verlaggsystem al Capitalismo Industrial" (1977).
22. Garmendia, *La Ideología Carlista* (1984).
23. Coverdale, *The Basque Phase* (1984).

Chapter 5. Basque Nationalism, 1876–1936

1. Jon Juaristi, *El Linaje de Aitor* (1987).
2. Javier Cuesta, *El Carlismo Vasco: 1876–1900* (1985).
3. Ibid.
4. Juan J. Solozabal, *El Primer Nacionalismo Vasco* (1975); Antonio Elorza, *Ideologías del Nacionalismo Vasco* (1978); Corcuera, *Orígenes, Ideología, y Organización* (1979).
5. Cuesta, *El Carlismo Vasco* (1985). It should be noted that the Liberal and Conservative parties did not participate in this election. Basque liberals presented either independent candidates or candidates sponsored by the Unión Vasco-Navarra. Once the Liberal and Conservative parties started to compete in Basque elections, support for the Unión Vasco-Navarra dwindled rapidly.
6. Corcuera, *Orígenes, Ideología, y Organización* (1979); Sabino Arana y Goiri, *Obras Escogidas* (1965).
7. Corcuera, *Orígenes, Ideología, y Organización* (1979). He calls this group the "nonmonopolistic" bourgeoisie, in contrast to the "monopolistic" sector represented by the industrial and financial elites.
8. Ibid.; Elorza, *Ideologías* (1978).
9. Corcuera, *Orígenes, Ideología, y Organización* (1979); González Portilla, *La Formación* (1981).
10. Emiliano Fernández de Pinedo, "Las Dudosas Bases Económicas del Primer Nacionalismo Vasco en el Ultimo Cuarto de Siglo XIX" (1985).
11. Arana, *Obras Escogidas* (1965), p. 178.
12. Ybarra y Bergé, *Política Nacional* (1947).
13. Corcuera, *Orígenes, Ideología, y Organización* (1979); Elorza, *Ideologías* (1978); José Luis de La Granja, *Nacionalismo y II República en el País Vasco* (1986). These people were Ramón de la Sota y Llano, Ramón de la Sota Aburto, Rafael Picavea, Tomás Domingo Epalza, José Eizaguirre, Antonio Maguregui Ozamiz, Gorgonio Rentería Leniz, Carlos Solano y Adán de Yarza, Mariano de la Torre Carricarte, Ignacio Rotaeche Velasco, Antonio Arroyo, Anacleto Ortueta Azkuenaga, Mario Arana, Isaac López Mendizabal, Miguel Urreta, Ramón Bikuña Epalza, Avelino Barriola Azpirúa, Santiago Alda Jubera, Eduardo Landeta Aburto, Pedro Chalbaud Errazquín, José Horn Areilza, and Federico Zabala.
14. Anthony Smith, *The Ethnic Revival* (1981).
15. Corcuera, *Orígenes, Ideología, y Organización* (1979); Cuesta, *El Carlismo Vasco* (1985); Miguel Martínez Cuadrado, *Elecciones y Partidos en España (1868–1931)* (1969).
16. Corcuera, *Orígenes, Ideología, y Organización* (1979); Cuesta, *El Carlismo Vasco* (1985); Martínez Cuadrado, *Elecciones y Partidos* (1969).
17. In Corcuera, *Orígenes, Ideología, y Organización* (1979), p. 129.
18. Ibid., p. 189.
19. Solozabal, *El Primer* (1975); Corcuera, *Orígenes, Ideología, y Organización* (1979).
20. Ibid.
21. Ibid.

22. The list of members is as follows: Juan de Eguileor, José Larrea, Juan de Luzurraga, Cosme Elguezabal, Angel Gandariasabeitia, Juan Urresti, Manuel Sota Aburto, Juan de Aramburri, Luis Uresti, Salvador Echeita, José de los Heros, Cristobal Cenitagoya, Domingo de Orueta, José Maria Errazti, Uribe-Echevarría, Luis de Vitorica, Luciano Pastor, José Zinkunegui, Jenaro Piker, Jenaro Boneta.

23. The members on this list are Luis Arana Goiri, Angel Zabala, Baltasar Amezola, Manuel Eguileor Orueta, Ceferino de Jemeín y Lamburri, Santiago Meabe Bilbao, Eli Gallástegui.

24. Arana, *Obras Escogidas* (1965), pp. 73–75.

25. Ibid., [1894], p. 207; ibid., [1897], p. 207.

26. Engracio de Arantzadi, *Ereintza: Siembra de Nacionalismo Vasco (1894–1912)* (1980 [1935]), p. 320.

27. Arana, *Obras Escogidas* (1965), p. 192.

28. Ibid., p. 113.

29. Solozabal, *El Primer* (1975); Corcuera, *Orígenes, Ideología, y Organización* (1979).

30. Arana, p. 217.

31. Initially, Sabino Arana developed a program that was focused only on Vizcaya; it was only later that he started to outline a project involving all the Basque provinces, including Navarre. Even then, however, he envisioned the Basque Country as a loose confederation of Basque states, each maintaining its own sovereignty. The idea of a big Basque Country was indeed a bourgeois invention, one that could be traced to the liberal conception of the nation-state as an economically viable state: Hobsbawm, *Nations and Nationalism* (1990).

32. Arana, p. 158.

33. In Corcuera, *Orígenes, Ideología, y Organización* (1979), p. 445.

34. Elorza, *Ideologías* (1978), pp. 396–403.

35. Ibid.

36. Ibid.; La Granja, *El Nacionalismo Vasco* (1986), p. 51.

37. Ibid.

38. Ibid.

39. This election had a two-round format. My comments refer to the first round, which is more directly comparable; see Javier Tusell, *Las Elecciones del Frente Popular* (1971).

40. La Granja, *El Nacionalismo Vasco* (1986), p. 566.

41. Marianne Heiberg, "Inside the Moral Community: Politics in a Basque Village" (1985), pp. 265–285.

42. In this referendum 42% of the electorate abstained. Of those who did vote, 79% approved the project.

Chapter 6. Catalan Nationalism, 1876–1936

1. Vicens Vives, *Los Catalanes* (1986).

2. Miquel Izard and Borja de Riquer, *Coneixer la Historia de Catalunya* (1983), vol. 4.

3. Ibid., p. 145.

4. Ibid., p. 170.

5. Santiago Albertí, *El Republicanisme Català i la Restauració Monárquica* (1972), p. 29.

6. Angel Duarte, *El Republicanisme Català a la Fí del Segle XIX* (1987).

7. "Anti-Catalanism" is to be distinguished from anti-decentralization or anti-autonomy positions. To attack Catalanism was to attack the Lliga, as Culla i Clará has demonstrated in *El Republicanisme Lerrouxista a Catalunya (1901–1923)* (1986); see also José Alvarez Junco, *El Emperador del Paralelo: Lerroux y la Demagogia Populista* (1990).

8. Manuel Lladonosa i Vall-Llebrera, *Catalanisme i Moviment Obrer: El CADCI entre 1903 i 1923* (1988).

9. Ibid., p. 51.

10. Anna Salles, *Quan Catalunya Era d'Esquerra* (1988).

11. Culla i Clará, *El Republicanisme* (1986); Alvarez Junco, *El Emperador* (1990).

12. M. Dolors Ivern i Salva, *Esquerra Republicana de Catalunya (1931–1936)* (1988).

13. The list of candidates for the Lliga is as follows: Morera i Galicia, Rusiñol i Prats, Cambó i Batlle, Beltrán i Musitu, Ventosa i Calvell, Rahola i Molinas, Albafull i Vidal, Miracle Mercader, Bertrand i Serra, Trías de Bes, Aunos Pérez, Camps i Olzinelles, Roses i Arus, Claret i Asols, Masó i Valentí, Llige i Pages, Fortuny Miralles, Llonch Canameras, Vehils i Grau, Rodes i Baldrich, Creixell i Iglesias, Puig de la Bellacasa, Martínez Domingo, Vidal i Tarrago, Albo i Martí, Rafols i Martí, Ventós i Mir, Plà i Carreras, Matheu i Ferrer, Estapé i Pages, Recasens i Mercadé, Maristany i Benito, Pou de Foxa, Mallol i Bosch.

The list of nationalist republican candidates includes the following: Rovira i Virgili, Pascual i Salichs, Figueroa i María, Robert i Rabada, Domingo i Sanjuán, Maciá i Llussa, Quintana i de León, Albert i Pey, Ventosa i Roig, Casanovas i Maristany, Palet i Barba, Serra Canameras, Marfa Serra, Layret i Foix, Pinilla i Fornell, Santalo Parvorell, Pi i Sunyer, Riu Puig, Moles i Ormella, Companys i Jover.

The list of UMN candidates includes the following: Girona i Vidal, Bosch i Alsina, Marfa Clivillés, Menacho Peirón, Ríus, Olano Loyzaga, Turull Comadran, Sala Argemí, Ballbe Pomar, Garriga, Pons i Tusquets, Fournier i Cuadrós, Moxo Sentmenat, Gabín Bages, Serradell i Farras, Ríu i Periquet, Nicolau i Sabater, Kindelán de la Torre, Colom i Cardany, Arquer i Vives, Cussó i Maurell, Ragúll Alabau, Martínez Vargas, Sáenz Bares, Mita i Camps, Salellas i Ferrer, Torras i Villa, Sostres i Llobet, Goicoechea y Cosculluela, Prida i Jorro, Canals i Vilaró, Morenes i García, Maristany, Marcet i Palet, Segura Solsona, Puig i Ravenga, Romeu i Freixa. Sometimes, the absence of the second last name in the list of members of the corporations' Boards of Directors has created some ambiguities in the matching of names. In these few cases, I have generally looked at the location of these companies to ascertain that a given person lived in Catalonia.

14. Valentí Almirall, *Lo Catalanisme* (1978; first published in 1886), p. 93.

15. Antonio Rovira i Virgili, *Catalunya i Espanya* (1988; first published in 1915), p. 6.

16. Cambó, *Memorias* (1987), p. 41.

17. Enric Prat de la Riba, *La Nacionalitat Catalana* (1978; first published in 1906), p. 45.

Chapter 7. Intra–Ethnic Group Conflict and the Character of Nationalism

1. Moya, *El Poder Económico* (1975).
2. Corcuera, *Orígenes, Ideología, y Organización* (1979), p. 590.

PART III: Political Diversity and Nationalism since the Civil War

1. Maurice Pinard, *The Rise of a Third Party* (1975); J. D. McCarthy and M. N. Zald, "Resource Mobilization" (1977); Nielsen, "Structural Conduciveness" (1986).
2. McCarthy and Zald, "Resource Mobilization" (1977); Doug McAdam, "Recruitment to High-Risk Activism: The Case of Freedom Summer" (1986).

Chapter 8. The Social Context of Nationalist Mobilization

1. Payne, *El Nacionalismo Vasco* (1974), p. 325; Fusi, *Pluralismo y Nacionalidad* (1984), p. 208; Horowitz, *Ethnic Groups* (1985), p. 252; Hobsbawm, *Nations and Nationalism* (1990), p. 140.
2. Fusi, *Pluralismo y Nacionalidad* (1984); Gurrutxaga, *El Código* (1985); p. 435; Horowitz, *Ethnic Groups* (1985), pp. 231–252.
3. Josep Benet, *Catalunya Sota el Regim Franquista* (1978).
4. Víctor Pérez Díaz, *The Return of Civil Society* (1993).
5. José María Maravall, *La Política de la Transición* (1981); Richard Gunther, Giacomo Sani, and Goldie Shabad, *Spain after Franco: The Making of a Competitive Party System* (1986); Pérez Díaz, *The Return* (1993).
6. José María Delgado i Ribas, "La Industrialización y el Desarrollo Económico de España durante el Franquismo" (1987).
7. Ibid., pp. 173–174.
8. Julio Alcaide Inchausti et al., "El Desarrollo Económico Español y la España Desigual de las Autonomías" (1990).
9. M. Parellada, *El Comerç Exterior de Catalunya* (1982).
10. Dirección de Estadística del Gobierno Vasco, *Census of 1981*.
11. *The Economist*, vol. 324, 7767 (1992): 9.
12. Amando de Miguel, *Sociología del Franquismo* (1975); Miguel Beltrán, *La Elite Burocrática Española* (1977); Miguel Jeréz, *Elites Políticas y Centros de Extracción en España (1938–1957)* (1982).
13. Ramón Tamámes, *Los Monopolios en España* (1967); Manuel González Portilla and José María Garmendia, *La Posguerra en el País Vasco* (1988); José María Lorenzo Espinosa, *Dictadura y Dividendo* (1989).
14. Among others, Faustino Miguélez Lobo and Carlota Solé, *Classes Socials i Poder Polític en Catalunya* (1987).
15. Horowitz, *Ethnic Groups* (1985).
16. Lorenzo Espinosa, *Dictadura* (1989), p. 29.
17. González Portilla and Garmendia, *La Posguerra* (1988), p. 46.
18. Ros Hombravella, *Catalunya: ¿Una Economía Decadent?* (1991), pp. 39–40.

19. González Portilla and Garmendia, *La Posguerra* (1988), p. 22.

20. Ibid.

21. Ibid., p. 20.

22. Ros Hombravella, *Catalunya* (1991), p. 41.

23. Moya, *El Poder Económico* (1975).

24. Tamámes, *Los Monopolios* (1967).

25. Ibid., p. 15.

26. Ibid., pp. 24–27.

27. Ibid., pp. 28–33.

28. Ibid.; M. García Crespo, R. Velasco, and A. Mendizabal, *La Economía Vasca durante el Franquismo* (1981); Lorenzo Espinosa, *Dictadura* (1989).

29. Tamámes, *Los Monopolios* (1967).

30. Smith, *The Ethnic Revival* (1981).

31. Seymour Martin Lipset, *Student Politics* (1967); José María Maravall, *Dictadura y Disentimiento Político* (1978).

32. Carmelo Sáenz de Santamaría, *Historia de la Universidad de Deusto* (1978).

33. In Spain, unlike the United States, the idea of a competitive university system did not exist until very recently. Spain was divided into university districts, each district including several provinces. Students attending a public university were expected to go to the university in their district, which in the case of Basque students was the university of the Castilian city of Valladolid.

34. Alfonso Pérez-Agote, *La Reproducción del Nacionalismo: El Caso Vasco* (1984), p. 64.

35. Maravall, *Dictadura* (1978).

36. Fusi, *Pluralismo y Nacionalidad* (1984), p. 209.

37. Ricardo García Carcel, *Historia de Cataluña: Siglos XVI–XVIII* (1985).

38. Josep Arqués, *Cinc Estudis Historics sobre la Universitat de Barcelona (1875–1895)* (1985).

39. Ibid., pp. 25–66.

Chapter 9. Basque Nationalism since the Civil War

1. This chapter is based on primary and secondary sources. For the period preceding Franco's death, my analysis is based entirely on information from secondary sources. I have found Beltza's, Clark's, Garmendia's, and Zirakzadeh's work particularly informative: Beltza, *Nacionalismo Vasco y Clases Sociales* (1976) and *El Nacionalismo Vasco en el Exilio* (1977); Robert Clark, *The Basques: The Franco Years and Beyond* (1980) and *The Basque Insurgents* (1984); José Mari Garmendia, *Historia de ETA* (1980); Cyrus E. Zirakzadeh, *A Rebellious People* (1991). But I should point out that much less is known about the BNP than about ETA, and that the literature on ETA often suffers from interpretive biases, owing to the fact that its authors are typically ex–ETA militants (e.g. Beltza) or very sympathetic toward this organization.

For the democratic phase of Basque nationalism, I have relied on secondary sources and on an exhaustive analysis of articles about Basque nationalism published in the Spanish weekly *Cambio 16* from 1971 to 1980. The description of the electoral process in the Basque Country since 1975 is based on my own analysis of electoral data.

For the study of nationalist ideology, I have relied on secondary sources and on my own analysis of books, propaganda pamphlets written by different parties, and newspaper interviews with nationalists. More specifically, for the analysis of ETA's ideology I have relied mostly on Jaúregui's and Ibarra's excellent analyses and on my reading of Krutvig's book *Vasconia*, which presents ETA's ideology better and more coherently than any other published work. These works are Gurutz Jaúregui Bereciarty, *Ideología y Estrategia Política de ETA* (1981); Pedro Ibarra Güell, *La Evolución Estratégica de ETA: 1963-1987* (1987); Federico Krutvig, *Vasconia: Estudio Dialéctico de una Nacionalidad* (1979; first published in 1963). To compare changes in the social composition of ETA with changes in its dominant ideology, I have analyzed quantitatively the information about the social origins of ETA members included in a book by Patxo Unzueta, *Los Nietos de la Ira* (1988). The analysis of the BNP's ideology has been far more difficult, because the BNP has thus far maintained its documents in very strict secrecy. Therefore, I have had to rely on original texts included in some of the histories of contemporary Basque nationalism, on interviews published in the weekly *Cambio 16*, and, in the analysis of Eusko Alkartasuna's ideology, on original declarations included in Justo De la Cueva's study of the BNP's breakup: de la Cueva, *La Escisión del PNV* (1988).

2. De la Granja, *El Nacionalismo Vasco* (1987), p. 63.

3. Juan Pablo Fusi, "La Guerra Civil en el País Vasco: Una Perspectiva General" (1987), p. 46.

4. Gurrutxaga, *El Código Nacionalista* (1985).

5. Beltza, *El Nacionalismo Vasco* (1976).

6. Ibid.

7. Ibid., p. 32.

8. José Mari Garmendia and Alberto Elordi, *La Resistencia Vasca* (1982), p. 181.

9. Clark, *The Basque Insurgents* (1984).

10. Beltza, *El Nacionalismo Vasco* (1976); Clark, *The Basque Insurgents* (1984); Garmendia and Elordi, *La Resistencia* (1982).

11. For some time, Ajuriaguerra's relations with the BNP's leadership were strained because he advocated a more active role for the resistance movement, and had previously been criticized by the BNP's leadership for dealing with British Intelligence through information channels established and funded by the Americans. See Garmendia and Elordi, *La Resistencia* (1982), pp. 23-257).

12. Koldo San Sebastián, *Historia del Partido Nacionalista Vasco* (1984), p. 89.

13. Maravall, *Dictadura y Disentimiento* (1978).

14. Ibid.

15. Jaúregui, *Ideología y Estrategia* (1981).

16. Arana, *Obras Escogidas*, p. 188.

17. Krutvig, *Vasconia* (1979 [1963]), p. 27.

18. Ibid., p. 297.

19. Jaúregui, p. 101.

20. Ibid., p. 131.

21. Krutvig, p. 258.

22. Jaúregui, pp. 98-99.

23. This program was presented in 1962. See Beltza, *El Nacionalismo Vasco* (1976), p. 96.

24. Krutvig, p. 66.

25. Jaúregui; Clark, *The Basque Years* (1980) and *The Basque Insurgents* (1984); John Sullivan, *ETA and Basque Nationalism: The Fight for Euskadi (1890–1986)* (1988).

26. Krutvig, p. VI.

27. Jaúregui.

28. Beltza, *Nacionalismo y Clases Sociales* (1976).

29. Krutvig, p. 266.

30. Ibid., p. 311.

31. Ibarra, *La Evolución Estrategia* (1987).

32. Ibid.

33. Clark, *The Basque Insurgents* (1984).

34. This quantitative analysis is based on raw information provided in Unzueta, *Los Nietos* (1988).

35. Clark, p. 45.

36. Ibid., p. 52.

37. Ibid.; Jaúregui, *Ideología y Estrategia* (1981); Unzueta, *Los Nietos* (1988).

38. Zirakzadeh, *A Rebellious People* (1991), pp. 101–111.

39. Euzkadi Buru Batzar in 1960, cited in Beltza, *El Nacionalismo Vasco* (1976), p. 102.

40. Told by a BNP member to *Cambio 16* (March 1977).

41. Euskadi Buru Batzar (1947), in Beltza, *El Nacionalismo Vasco* (1976), p. 131; Euzkadi Buru Batzar (1966), in San Sebastián, *Historia del Partido* (1984), p. 99; Xabier Arzállus, in *Cambio 16* (August 1976).

42. Garaicoetxea to *Cambio 16* (December 11, 1978).

43. Zirakzadeh, *A Rebellious People* (1991); De la Cueva, *La Escisión* (1988); Fernando Reinares, "The Basque Autonomous Elections of 1986," (1987).

44. In *Cambio 16* (July 16, 1978).

45. Zirakzadeh, p. 111.

46. Jaúregui, *Ideología y Estrategia* (1981).

47. Ibarra, *La Evolución* (1987).

48. Pedro Ibarra Güell, *El Movimiento Obrero en Vizcaya (1967–1977)*, (1987).

49. Ibarra.

50. Clark, *The Basque Insurgents* (1984), p. 133.

51. Ibarra.

Chapter 10. Catalan Nationalism since the Civil War

1. Very recently, however, in his book *Tales of Nationalism* (1991), Johnston suggests an explanation for this contrast that is a variant of the social-composition thesis that I have advanced in the Introduction to this book. Catalan nationalists were more moderate than Basque nationalists because they had been less cut off from the earlier nationalist generation. While older Basque nationalists were pas-

sive during the Francoist regime, older Catalan nationalists were very active. According to Johnston, a more active older generation would have imbued the Basque nationalist movement with the same pragmatism that characterized the Catalan. This is a plausible argument, which has the merit of focusing on the characteristics of the Basque and Catalan nationalist movements rather than on traditional socioeconomic explanations. It is an incomplete argument, however, because it conceptualizes the Basque and Catalan nationalist movements as if each of them were represented by a single organization. It thus overlooks the competition between different nationalist organizations representing different political agendas and the factors that may have led a particular organization to be more or less successful.

2. This chapter, like the previous one, is based on primary and secondary sources. For the period preceding the early 1970s, my analysis is based entirely on secondary sources. Of these publications I have found Colomer's (1976), Crexell's (1982, 1987), Johnston's (1991), Miguélez and Solé's (1987), and Vera's (1981) work particularly helpful: Josep M. Colomer, *Assamblea de Catalunya* (1976); Joan Crexell, *El Consell de Guerra a Jordi Pujol* (1982) and *La Caputxinada* (1987); Johnston, *Tales of Nationalism* (1991); Faustino Miguélez Lobo and Carlota Solé, *Classes Socials* (1987); Jordi Vera, *La Lluita Armada als Països Catalans: Historia del FAC* (1985). I would like to point out, however, that the counterpart to the tendency in the study of Basque nationalism to focus excessively on ETA is the tendency in the study of Catalonia to focus excessively on bourgeois mobilization.

For the post–Franco period, I have relied on secondary sources and on extensive analysis of the information published in the weekly magazine *Cambio 16* from 1971 to 1980.

For the study of the electoral process in Catalonia, I have relied on my own analysis of electoral data. Finally, for the analysis of Catalan nationalist ideology, I have relied on secondary sources, including the splendid work by Colomer (*Espanyolisme y Catalanisme* [1984]), and on my own analysis of newspaper interviews and of books published by Jordi Pujol, Trías Fargas, and Roca i Junyent.

3. Borja De Riquer Permanyer, "Aproximació al Paper de les Forces Polítiques i Sindicals" (1988), pp. 83–99; see also Jordi Sabater, *Anarquisme i Catalanisme* (1986), p. 71.

4. Benet, *Catalunya Sota* (1978).

5. Gregori López Raimundo, "Momentos Destacados de la Trayectoria del PSUC," in *Nuestra Utopía: PSUC, Cincuenta Años de Historia de Cataluña* (1986), pp. 218–231.

6. It must be said that the MSC's situation would not have been much better had it been integrated into the Spanish Socialist Party (PSOE), like the minuscule Catalan Federation of the PSOE. Indeed, the PSOE itself was undergoing a major crisis that lasted until the early 1970s, owing to internal divisions and to Francoist repression inside Spain.

7. Gabriel Colomé, *El Partit dels Socialistes de Catalunya* (1989).

8. The experiences of religiously oriented people who underwent this shift toward Marxism have been very well illustrated by Johnston, *Tales of Nationalism* (1991).

9. Jordi Pujol, *Una Política per Catalunya* (1976), *La Immigració, Problema i Esperança de Catalunya* (1976), *Entre L'Acció i L'Esperança/1: Des dels Turons a l'Al-*

tra Banda del Ríu (1978), and *Entre L'Acció y L'Esperança/2: Construir Catalunya* (1979).

10. Pujol, *Una Política* (1976), p. 41.
11. Joan Marcet, *Convergencia Democrática de Catalunya* (1987).
12. Pujol, *La Immigració* (1976), p. 32.
13. Pujol, *Construir* (1979), p. 266.
14. Crexell, *El Consell* (1982).
15. Maravall, *Dictadura y Disentimiento* (1978), pp. 159–161.
16. Crexell, *La Caputxinada* (1987).
17. Ibid.
18. Colomer, *Assamblea* (1976).
19. Ibid., p. 41.
20. Kepa Salaberri, *El Proceso de Euskadi en Burgos* (1971).
21. Marcet, *Convergencia* (1987); Colomé, *El Partit* (1989).
22. The PSOE, deeply divided and weakened by Francoist repression, had played a negligible role in the opposition to Franco during the 1939–72 period. However, following the Congresses of Toulouse (1972) and Suresnes (1974), the PSOE became more active in Spanish politics. In these two Congresses, Felipe González, who represented the socialist opposition in the interior, defeated Llopis, who represented the socialist opposition abroad. This change in leadership radically transformed the PSOE's ideological and generational composition.
23. Colomé, *El Partit* (1989).
24. Marcet, *Convergencia* (1987).
25. Vera, *La Lluita* (1985); Jaume Fernández Calvet, *Terra Lliure: 1979–1985* (1986); Terra Lliure, *Catalunya Terra Lliure* (1988).
26. This middle-class social composition of the Catalan socialists is evidenced in Marcet, *Convergencia* (1987), and Colomé, *El Partit* (1989), in the organizational history of the PSC, and in the biographies of the major leaders of the PSC-PSOE.

Chapter 11. Political Structures and Nationalism in Democratic Spain

1. The most significant studies on Basque and Catalan electoral politics include Francisco Llera Ramos, *Postfranquismo y Fuerzas Políticas en Euskadi* (1984) and "El Sistema de Partidos Vascos: Distancia Ideológica y Legitimación Política" (1984); Juan J. Linz, *Conflicto en Euskadi* (1986); Richard Gunther, Giacomo Sani, and Goldie Shabad, *Spain after Franco: The Making of a Competitive Party System* (1986); Colomé, *El Partit* (1989).
2. The report in question was the Informe Foessa 1970; see Linz, "Early-State Building" (1973).
3. Gunther, Sani, and Shabad, *Spain after Franco* (1986), p. 362.
4. The question read: "In the event that this Autonomous Community attained independence, alone or together with another Autonomous Community, do you think that in the middle run the economic conditions in the new state would be much better, somewhat better, somewhat worse, much worse, or the same as now?"

5. Salaberri, *El Proceso* (1971); Pérez-Agote, *La Reproducción* (1984); Miguélez and Solé, *Classes Socials* (1987); Johnston, *Tales of Nationalism* (1991).

6. Terrón Montero, *La Prensa en España Durante el Régimen de Franco* (1981).

7. Zirakzadeh, *A Rebellious People* (1991).

8. Salaberri, *El Proceso* (1971).

9. McCarthy and Zald, "Resource Mobilization" (1977), p. 1234.

10. Pérez-Agote, *La Reproducción* (1984).

11. Ibarra, *El Movimiento* (1987).

12. Ibid., p. 546.

13. William Gamson, *The Strategy of Social Protest* (1975), p. 81.

14. Angel Amigo, *Pertúr. ETA 71–76* (1978).

15. Vera, *La Lluita* (1985).

16. Ibid., p. 26.

17. This is an issue that is missing from people's discussions of ethnic conflict in places such as Yugoslavia. Ethnic rivalries may indeed exist, but to explain why they evolve into warfare one needs to invoke additional factors. Without these additional factors, one can imagine other ways in which these ethnic rivalries could have been expressed. In other words, the fact that there are differences in the way a problem (e.g. ethnic conflict) is expressed does not necessarily mean that the problem itself is different, either in its character or in its intensity.

18. Clark, *The Basque Insurgents* (1984), pp. 220–221; Vera, *La Lluita* (1985).

19. Vera, *La Lluita* (1985), p. 125.

20. Amigo, *Pertúr* (1978).

21. M. Lipsky, "Protest as a Political Resource" (1968); S. Alinsky, *Rules for Radicals* (1971).

22. Beltza, *El Nacionalismo Vasco* (1977); Jaúregui, *Ideología y Estrategia* (1981).

23. Clark, *The Basque Insurgents* (1984), p. 224.

24. Alfonso Pérez-Agote, *La Reproducción* (1984); also Pérez-Agote, *El Nacionalismo Vasco a la Salida del Franquismo* (1987).

25. *Documentos "Y"* (1979), vols. 1–18.

26. Ibarra, *La Evolución* (1987).

27. Clark, *The Basque Insurgents* (1984); Gurrutxaga, *El Código* (1985).

28. Pérez-Agote, *El Nacionalismo Vasco* (1987).

29. Fusi, *Pluralismo y Nacionalidad* (1984).

Conclusion

1. *The Economist*, vol. 310, 7593 (1989), 21.

2. Edward Lawler, "Affective Attachments to Nested Groups: A Choice-Process Theory" (1992).

3. Pinard, *The Rise of a Third Party* (1975); Nielsen, "Structural Conduciveness" (1986).

4. Michael Hechter, "Rational Choice Theory and the Study of Race and Ethnic Relations," (1986), p. 265.

References Cited

Agirre, Julen. *Operación Ogro*. Paris: Ruedo Ibérico, 1974.
Albertí, Santiago. *El republicanisme Català i la restauració monárquica*. Barcelona: Albertí, 1972.
Alcaide Inchausti, Julio, et al. "El desarrollo económico español y la España desigual de las autonomías," *Papeles de Economía* 45 (1990): 2–61.
Alinsky, Saul. *Rules for Radicals*. New York: Random House, 1971.
Almirall, Valentí. *Lo Catalanisme*. Barcelona: Edicións 62, 1978 [1886].
Alvarez Junco, José. *El emperador del Paralelo: Lerroux y la demagogia populista*. Madrid: Alianza, 1990.
Amigo, Angel. *Pertúr: ETA 71–76*. San Sebastián: Hordago, 1978.
Anasagasti, Iñaki, and Koldo San Sebastián. *Los años oscuros*. San Sebastián: Txertoa, 1985.
Anderson, Benedict. *Imagined Communities*. London: Verso, 1983.
Anderson, Perry. *Lineages of the Absolutist State*. London: New Left Books, 1974.
——. *Passages from Antiquity to Feudalism*. London: New Left Books, 1974.
Anes, Gonzalo. *El antiguo régimen: Los Borbones*. Madrid: Alfaguara, 1975.
Arana Goiri, Sabino de. *Obras escogidas*. San Sebastián: Haranburu, 1965 [1897].
Arana Pérez, Ignacio. *La Liga Vizcaína de productores y la política económica de la Restauración: 1894–1914*. Bilbao: Caja de Ahorros de Vizcaya, 1988.
Arbós, Xabier. "Central versus Peripheral Nationalism in Building Democracy: The Case of Spain," *Canadian Review of Studies in Nationalism* 14 (1987): 143–159.
Arqués, Josep. *Cinc estudis historics sobre la Universitat de Barcelona (1875–1895)*. Barcelona: Columna, 1985.
Azaola, José M. "Aproximación a las capitales vascas," in [University of Navarra], *Páginas de historia del País Vasco*. Pamplona: Ediciones de la Universidad de Navarra, 1980.
Balcells, Albert. *Rafael Campalans, socialisme Català*. Montserrat [Barcelona]: Publicacions de l'Abadía de Montserrat, 1985.
Banco de Bilbao. *Renta Nacional de España*. Madrid: Banco de Bilbao, 1980, 1987, and 1989.

Barahona, Renato. *Vizcaya on the Eve of the First Carlist War*. Reno: University of Nevada Press, 1989.

Barbagallo, Francesco, et al. *Franquisme: Sobre resistencia i consens a Catalunya (1939–1959)*. Barcelona: Crítica, 1990.

Barrera, Andrés. *La dialéctica de la identidad en Cataluña: Un estudio de antropología social*. Madrid: CIS, 1985.

Barth, Frederick. *Ethnic Groups and Boundaries*. Boston: Little, Brown, 1969.

Bécarud, Jean. "La nobleza española desde Alfonso XII hasta 1931: Presentación en conjunto y comparación con otras aristocracias europeas," in *Les élites espagnoles a l'époque contemporaine*, Actes du colloque d'histoire sociale d'Espagne. Pau: Université de Pau, 1982, pp. 59–82.

Beltrán, Miguel. *La elite burocrática española*. Barcelona: Ariel, 1977.

[Beltza]. *Nacionalismo vasco y clases sociales*. San Sebastián: Txertoa, 1976.

——. *El nacionalismo vasco en el exilio*. San Sebastián: Txertoa, 1977.

——. *Meditación y alienación. Del carlismo al nacionalismo burgués*. San Sebastián: Txertoa, 1978.

Benet, Josep. *Catalunya sota el regim franquista*. Barcelona: Blume, 1978.

Bilbao Bilbao, Luis M. "Renovación tecnológica y estructura del sector siderúrgico en el País Vasco durante la primera etapa de la industrialización (1849–1880): Aproximación comparativa con la industria algodonera de Cataluña," in Manuel González Portilla, Jordi Maluquer de Motes, and Borja de Riquer Permanyer, eds., *Industrialización y nacionalismo*. Bellaterra [Barcelona]: Universitat Autònoma de Barcelona, 1985, pp. 211–228.

Bloch, Marc. *Feudal Society*. Chicago: University of Chicago Press, 1961.

Bonassie, Pierre. *Cataluña mil años atrás*. Barcelona: Península, 1975.

Braudel, Fernand. *The Mediterranean and the Mediterranean World in the Age of Phillip II*. New York: Harper & Row, 1983.

——. *The Perspective of the World*. New York: Harper & Row, 1983.

Braungart, Richard, and David L. Westby. "Class and Politics in the Family Backgrounds of Student Political Activists," *American Sociological Review* 31 (1966).

Breuilly, John. *Nationalism and the State*. Chicago: University of Chicago Press, 1993.

Brubaker, Rogers. *Citizenship and Nationhood in France and Germany*. Cambridge: Harvard University Press, 1992.

Cambio 16 (1971–1980).

Cambó, Francesc. *Por la concordia*. Barcelona: Biblioteca de Cultura Catalana, 1986 [1923].

——. *Memorias*. Madrid: Alianza editorial, 1987.

Carballo, Roberto, Antonio García Temprano, and José A. Morán Santín. *Crecimiento económico y crisis estructural en España (1959–1980)*. Madrid: Akal, 1981.

Caro Baroja, Julio. *Los vascos*. Madrid: Istmo, 1971.

——. *Introducción a la historia social y económica del pueblo vasco*. San Sebastián: Txertoa, 1974.

Carr, Raymond, and Juan Pablo Fusi. *Spain: From Dictatorship to Democracy*. London: George Allen & Unwin, 1979.

Carreras, Albert. "La producción industrial catalana y vasca, 1844–1935: Elementos para una comparación," in Manuel González Portilla, Jordi Maluquer de Motes, and Borja de Riquer Permanyer, eds., *Industrialización y nacionalismo*. Bellaterra: Universitat Autònoma de Barcelona, 1985, pp. 197–210.

——. "Fuentes y datos para el análisis regional de la industrialización española," in Jordi Nadal and Albert Carreras, eds., *Pautas regionales de la industrialización española (siglos XIX y XX)*. Barcelona: Ariel, 1990, pp. 3–22.

Charles, Maria. "Cross-National Variation in Occupational Sex Segregation," *American Sociological Review* 57, 4 (1992): 483–503.

Chaunu, Pierre. *La España de Carlos V*. Barcelona: Península, 1976.

Clark, Robert. *The Basques: The Franco Years and Beyond*. Reno: University of Nevada Press, 1980.

——. *The Basque Insurgents*. Madison: University of Wisconsin Press, 1984.

Claveras, Joan, et al. *Capitalismo español: De la autarquía a la estabilización (1939–1959)*. Madrid: Cuadernos para el Diálogo, 1974.

Collins, Roger. *The Basques*. New York: Blackwell, 1986.

Colomé, Gabriel. *El partit dels socialistes de Catalunya*. Barcelona: Ediciòns 62, 1989.

Colomer, Josep M. *Assemblea de Catalunya*. Barcelona: l' Avenç, 1976.

——. *Espanyolisme i Catalanisme*. Barcelona: L'Avenç, 1984.

Comaroff, John. "Humanity, Ethnicity, Nationality: Conceptual and Comparative Perspectives on the USSR," *Theory and Society* 20 (1991): 661–688.

Confederación Española de Cajas de Ahorros. *Estadísticas básicas de España*. Madrid: Confederación Española de Cajas de Ahorros, 1975.

Converse, Philip, and Georges Dupeux. "Politicization of the Electorate in France and the United States," *Public Opinion Quarterly* 26 (1962).

Corcuera Atienza, Javier. *Orígenes, ideología y organización del nacionalismo vasco (1876–1904)*. Madrid: Siglo XXI, 1979.

Coverdale, John F. *The Basque Phase of Spain's First Carlist War*. Princeton, N.J.: Princeton University Press, 1984.

Crexell, Joan. *El consell de guerra a Jordi Pujol*. Barcelona: Edicions de la Magrana, 1982.

——. *La Caputxinada*. Barcelona: Edicions 62, 1987.

Cruz, Jesús. "Hidalguía, Bourgeoisie, and Revolution: Change and Persistence in the Formation of the Spanish Middle Class: Madrid 1750–1850," unpublished Ph.D. dissertation, Department of History, University of California, San Diego, 1992.

Cuadrat, Xavier. *Socialismo y anarquismo en Cataluña (1899–1911)*. Madrid: Ediciones de la Revista del Trabajo, 1976.

Cucurull, Felix. *Panorámica del nacionalismo catalán*. Madrid: Editora Nacional, 1975.

Cuesta, Javier. *El carlismo vasco: 1876–1900*. Madrid: Siglo XXI, 1985.

Culla i Clarà, Joan. *El republicanisme Lerrouxista a Catalunya (1901–1923)*. Barcelona: Curial, 1986.

de Arantzadi, Engracio. *Ereintza: Siembra de nacionalismo vasco (1894–1912)*. San Sebastián: Aunamendi, 1980 [1935].

de Fuente, Lucas. *Diego López de Haro V, magnate de Castilla, señor de Vizcaya y fundador de Bilbao*. Bilbao: Caja de Ahorros de Vizcaya, 1987.

de la Cueva, Justo. *La Escisión del PNV*. Bilbao: Txalaparta Argitaldaría, 1988.

de la Granja, José L. *Nacionalismo y II República en el País Vasco*. Madrid: CIS, 1986.

——. "El nacionalismo Vasco ante la Guerra Civil," in Carmelo Garitaonandia and José Luis de la Granja, eds., *La Guerra Civil en el País Vasco*. Bilbao: Servicio editorial de la Universidad del País Vasco, 1987, pp. 53–89.

del Castillo, Pilar. *La financiación de partidos y candidatos en las democracias occidentales*. Madrid: CIS, 1985.

Delgado i Ribas, José María. "El impacto de las crisis coloniales en la economía catalana (1787–1807)," in Josep Fontana, ed., *La economía española al final del antiguo régimen*. Madrid: Alianza, 1982, pp. 97–171.

——. "La industria naviera en Cataluña y en el País Vasco: Un estudio comparativo (1750–1850)," in Manuel González Portilla, Jordi Maluquer de Motes, and Borja de Riquer Permanyer, eds., *Industrialización y nacionalismo*, Ballaterra: Universitat Autònoma de Barcelona, 1985, pp. 89–109.

de Miguel, Amando. *Sociología del franquismo*. Barcelona: Euros, 1975.

de Riquer Permanyer, Borja. "Aproximació al paper de les forces politiques i sindicals," in *Catalunya i la guerra civil (1936–1939)*. Barcelona: Publicacions de l'Abadía de Montserrat, 1988, pp. 83–99.

Deutsch, Karl. *Nationalism and Social Communication*. New York: Wiley, 1966.

Dirección de Estadística del Gobierno Vasco, *Censo de 1981*. Bilbao: Gobierno Vasco.

Documentos "Y" [various authors]. San Sebastián: Hordago, 1979, Vols. 1–18.

Domínguez Ortiz, Antonio. *La sociedad española en el siglo XVII*. Madrid: Consejo Superior de Investigaciones Científicas, 1963.

——. *El antiguo régimen: Los reyes Católicos y los Austrias*. Madrid: Alfaguara, 1973.

Douglass, William A. 1985. "Introduction," in William A. Douglass, ed., *Basque Politics: A Case Study in Ethnic Nationalism*. Reno: University of Nevada Press, 1985, pp. 1–18.

Duarte, Angel. *El republicanisme Català a la fí del segle XIX*. Vic [Barcelona]: Eumo, 1987.

Economist, The (1989), vol. 310, 7593:21.

——. (1992), vol. 324, 7767:9.

Eisinger, Peter K. "The Conditions of Protest Behavior in American Cities," *American Political Science Review* 67: 2 (1973): 11–28.

Elliott, John H. *The Revolt of the Catalans*. Cambridge: Cambridge University Press, 1963.

Elorza, Antonio. *Ideologías del nacionalismo vasco*. San Sebastián: Haranburu, 1978.

Escudero, Antonio. "Capital minero y formación de capital en Vizcaya (1876–1913)," in Jordi Nadal and Albert Carreras, eds., *Pautas regionales de la industrialización española*. Barcelona: Ariel, 1990, pp. 106–123.

Extramiana, José. *Historia de las guerras Carlistas*. San Sebastián: Haranburu, 1980.

——. "Elites vascas en busca de una nación: Segunda mitad del siglo XIX," in *Les élites espagnoles a l'époque contemporaine*, Actes du Colloque d'Histoire Sociale d'Espagne. Pau: Université de Pau, 1982, pp. 17–26.

Fanon, Frantz. *Los condenados de la tierra*. México: FCE, 1963.

Fayard, Janine. *Les membres du conseil de Castille a l'époque moderne (1621–1746)*. Genève: Société de l'Ecole de Chartes, 1979.

Fernández Albadalejo, Pablo. *La crisis del antiguo régimen en Guipúzcoa*. Madrid: Akal, 1975.

Fernández Calvet, Jaume. *Terra Lliure: 1979–1985*. Barcelona: El Llamp, 1986.

Fernández de Pinedo, Emiliano. *Crecimiento económico y transformaciones sociales del País Vasco: 1100–1850*. Madrid: Siglo XXI, 1974.

——. "Etapas del crecimiento económico de la economía vasca (1700–1850)," *Papeles de Economía Española* 20 (1984): 309–318.

——. "Las dudosas bases económicas del primer nacionalismo vasco en el último cuarto de siglo XIX," *Cuadernos de Alzate*, Spring (1985).

Fernández de Pinedo, Emiliano, and José Luis Hernández Marco. *La industrialización en el norte de España*. Barcelona: Crítica, 1988.

Fernández Pardo, Francisco. *La independencia vasca: La disputa sobre los fueros*. Madrid: Nerea, 1990.

Furtado, Charles, and Michael Hechter. "The Emergence of Nationalist Politics in the USSR: A Comparison of Estonia and the Ukraine," in Alexander Motyl, ed., *Thinking Theoretically about Soviet Nationalities*. New York: Columbia University Press, 1992, pp. 169–204.

Fusi, Juan Pablo. *Política obrera en el País Vasco*. Madrid: Turner, 1975.

——. *Pluralismo y nacionalidad*. Madrid: Alianza Editorial, 1984.

——. "La guerra civil en el País Vasco. Una perspectiva general," in Carmelo Garitaonandia and José Luis de la Granja, ed., *La guerra civil en el País Vasco*. Bilbao: Universidad del País Vasco, 1987, pp. 43–53.

Gamson, William. *The Strategy of Social Protest*. Homewood, Ill.: The Dorsey Press, 1975.

Gárate Ojanguren, María. "El comercio colonial guipuzcoano durante el siglo XVIII: Diferencias respecto del caso catalán," in Manuel González Portilla, Jordi Maluquer de Motes, and Borja de Riquer Permanyer, eds., *Industrialización y nacionalismo*. Bellaterra: Universitat Autònoma de Barcelona, 1985, pp. 125–137.

Garayalde, Iñigo, and Juan Luis Llorens. "Reestructuración industrial del País Vasco," *Información Comercial Española* 598 (1983): 49–61.

García Carcel, Ricardo. *Historia de Cataluña: Siglos XVI–XVII*. Barcelona: Ariel, 1985.

García Crespo, Milagros, Roberto Velasco, and Arantxa Mendizabal. *La economía vasca durante el Franquismo*. Bilbao: La Gran Enciclopedia Vasca, 1981.

García Delgado, José María. "La industrialización y el desarrollo económico de España durante el Franquismo," in Jordi Nadal, Albert Carreras, and Carles Sudrià, eds., *La economía Española en el siglo XX*. Barcelona: Ariel, 1987, pp. 164–190.

García Venero, Maximiliano. *Historia del nacionalismo catalán*. Madrid: Editora Nacional, 1942.

Garmendia, José Mari. *Historia de ETA*. San Sebastián: Haranburu, 1980.

Garmendia, José Mari, and Alberto Elordi. *La resistencia vasca*. San Sebastián: Haranburu, 1982.

Garmendia, Vicente. *La ideología carlista (1868–1876)*. Zarautz [Guipúzcoa]: Diputación Foral de Guipúzcoa, 1984.

——. "Carlism and Basque Nationalism," in William A. Douglass, ed., *Basque Politics: A Case Study in Ethnic Nationalism*. Reno: University of Nevada Press, 1985, pp. 137–154.

Geertz, Clifford. *The Interpretation of Cultures*. New York: Pantheon Books, 1963.

Gellner, Ernest. *Nations and Nationalism*. Ithaca: Cornell University Press, 1983.

Gerschenkron, Alexander. *Economic Backwardness in Historical Perspective*. Cambridge: Harvard University Press, Belknap Press, 1962.

Giráldez, María Teresa, and Teresa Gómez Castaño. "Empleo y paro a nivel regional: 1976–1986," *Papeles de Economía Española* 34 (1988): 267–299.

Gispert, Carles, and Josep M. Prats. *España: Un estado plurinacional*. Barcelona: Blume, 1978.

González Casanova, José A. *Federalisme i autonomia a Catalunya*. Barcelona: Dopesa, 1974.

González Portilla, Manuel. "La industria siderúrgica en el País Vasco: Del verlangssystem al capitalismo industrial," in Manuel Tuñón de Lara, ed., *Crisis del antiguo régimen e industrialización en la España del Siglo XIX*. Madrid: Cuadernos para el Diálogo, 1977, pp. 117–181.

——. *La formación de la sociedad capitalista en el País Vasco (1876–1913)*. San Sebastián: Haranburu, 1981.

——. *Estado, capitalismo y desequilibrios regionales (1845–1900): Andalucía, País Vasco*. San Sebastián: Haranburu, 1985.

——. "Las nuevas siderurgias vascas y los primeros sindicatos," in José L. García Delgado, *La España de la Restauración: Política, economía, legislación, y cultura*. Miguel Artola et al. Madrid: Siglo XXI, 1985, pp. 153–171.

——. *La siderurgia vasca (1880–1901)*. Bilbao: Servicio editorial de la Universidad del País Vasco, 1985.

González Portilla, Manuel, and José María Garmendia. *La posguerra en el País Vasco*. San Sebastián: Kriselu, 1988.

Gourevitch, Peter A. "The Reemergence of 'Peripheral Nationalisms': Some Comparative Speculations on the Spatial Distribution of Political Leadership and Economic Growth," *Comparative Studies in Society and History* 21: 3 (1979): 303–322.

Grabolosa, Ramón. *Carlins i liberals: La darrera guerra Carlina a Catalunya*. Barcelona: Aedos, 1972.

Greenfeld, Liah. *Nationalism: Five Roads to Modernity*. Cambridge: Harvard University Press, 1992.

Gunther, Richard, Giacomo Sani, and Goldie Shabad. *Spain after Franco: The Making of a Competitive Party System*. Berkeley: University of California Press, 1986.

Gurrutxaga, Ander. *El código nacionalista vasco durante el Franquismo*. Madrid: Anthropos, 1985.

Hannan, Michael T. "The Dynamics of Ethnic Boundaries in Modern States," in Michael T. Hannan and John Meyer, eds., *National Development and the World System: Educational, Economic, and Political Change, 1950–1970*. Chicago: University of Chicago Press, 1979, pp. 253–275.

Harrison, Joseph. "La industria pesada, el estado, y el desarrollo económico en el País Vasco (1876–1936)," *Información Comercial Española* 598 (1983): 21–32.

Hechter, Michael. *Internal Colonialism: The Celtic Fringe in British National Development, 1536–1966*. London: Routledge and Kegan Paul, 1975.

——. "Group Formation and the Cultural Division of Labor," *American Journal of Sociology* 84 (1978): 293–318.

——. "Internal Colonialism Revisited," in Edward Tiryakian and Ronald Rogowski, eds., *New Nationalisms in the Developed West*. Winchester, Mass.: Allen & Unwin, 1985, pp. 17–27.

——. "Rational Choice Theory and the Study of Race and Ethnic Relations," in John Rex and David Mason, eds., *Theories of Race and Ethnic Relations*. New York: Cambridge University Press, 1986, pp. 264–280.

——. "Nationalism as Group Solidarity," *Ethnic and Racial Studies* 10: 4 (1987): 415–426.

——. *Principles of Group Solidarity*. Berkeley: University of California Press, 1987.

——. "The Dynamics of Secession," *Acta Sociologica* 35 (1992): 1–17.

Hechter, Michael, and Margaret Levi. "The Comparative Analysis of Ethnoregional Movements," *Ethnic and Racial Studies* 2 (1979): 260–274.

Heiberg, Marianne. "Urban Politics and Rural Culture: Basque Nationalism," in Stein Rokkan and Derek W. Urwin, eds., *The Politics of Territorial Identity*. London: Sage Publications, 1982, pp. 355–387.

——. "Inside the Moral Community: Politics in a Basque Village," in William A. Douglass, ed., *Basque Politics: A Case Study in Ethnic Nationalism*. Reno: University of Nevada Press, 1985, pp. 265–285.

Heine, Hartmut. *La oposición política al Franquismo: De 1939 a 1952*. Barcelona: Crítica, 1983.

Hernández, Francesc. *La identidad nacional en Cataluña*. Barcelona: Vicens Vives, 1983.

Hernández, Francesc, and Francesc Mercadé. *Estructuras sociales y cuestión nacional en España*. Barcelona: Ariel, 1986.

Hobsbawm, Eric J. *The Age of Revolution*. New York: Penguin Books, 1962.

——. *Nations and Nationalism since 1780*. New York: Cambridge University Press, 1990.

Hobsbawm, Eric J., and Terence Ranger. *The Invention of Tradition*. New York: Cambridge University Press, 1983.

Horowitz, Donald. *Ethnic Groups in Conflict*. Berkeley: University of California Press, 1985.

——. "How to Begin Thinking Comparatively about Soviet Ethnic Problems," in Alexander Motyl, ed., *Thinking Theoretically about Soviet Nationalities: History and Comparison in the Study of the USSR*. New York: Columbia University Press, 1992, pp. 9–23.

Hroch, Miroslav. *Social Preconditions of National Revival in Europe*. Cambridge: Cambridge University Press, 1983.

Ibáñez (first name not given), and Marco Gardóqui. *Anuario Financiero y de Sociedades Anónimas*. Bilbao: Ibáñez and Marco Gardóqui, 1922.

Ibarra Güell, Pedro. *La evolución estratégica de ETA (1963–1987)*. Donostia: [San Sebastián]: Kriselu, 1987.

——. *El movimiento obrero en Vizcaya: 1967–1977*. Bilbao: Universidad del País Vasco, 1987.

Instituto Nacional de Estadística. *Censo de 1887*. Madrid: Instituto Nacional de Estadística.

——. *Censo de 1981*. Madrid: Instituto Nacional de Estadística.

Ivern i Salva, M. Dolors. *Esquerra Republicana de Catalunya (1931–1936)*. Montserrat: Publicacions de l'Abadía de Montserrat, 1988.

Izard, Miquel. "El rechazo a la modernización capitalista, Cataluña y Euskadi, similitudes y diferencias," in Manuel González Portilla, Jordi Maluquer de Motes, and Borja de Riquer Permanyer, eds., *Industrialización y nacionalismo*. Bellaterra: Universitat Autònoma de Barcelona, 1985, pp. 375–387.

Izard, Miquel, and Borja de Riquer Permanyer. *Coneixer la historia de Catalunya*. Barcelona: Vicens Vives, Vol. IV, 1983.

Jaúregui Bereciarty, Gurutz. *Ideología y estrategia política de ETA*. Madrid: Siglo XXI, 1981.

Jeréz, Miguel. *Elites políticas y centros de extracción en España (1938–1957)*. Madrid: CIS, 1982.

Jiménez Blanco, José, Manuel García Ferrando, Eduardo López–Aranguren, and Miguel Beltrán. *La conciencia regional en España*. Madrid: CIS, 1977.

Johnston, Hank. *Tales of Nationalism*. New Brunswick, N.J.: Rutgers University Press, 1991.

Juaristi, Jon. *El linaje de aitor*. Madrid: Taurus, 1987.

Jutglar, Antoni. *Historia crítica de la burguesía a Catalunya*. Barcelona: Anthropos ed. del Hombre, 1984.

Kedourie, Elie. *Nationalism*. London: Blackwell, 1993.

Knei-Paz, Baruch. *The Social and Political Thought of Leon Trotsky*. Oxford: Clarendon Press, 1978.

Krutvig, Federico. *Vasconia: Estudio dialéctico de una nacionalidad*. Bilbao: Ediciones Vascas, 1979 [1963].

Kurth, James. "The Political Consequences of the Product Cycle: Industrial History and Political Outcomes," *International Organization* 33: 1 (1979): 1–34.

La Granja, José L. "The Basque Nationalist Community during the Second Spanish Republic (1931–1936)," in William A. Douglass, ed., *Basque Politics: A Case Study in Ethnic Nationalism*. Reno: University of Nevada Press, 1985, pp. 155–174.

——. *Nacionalismo y II República en el País Vasco*. Madrid: Centro de Investigaciones Sociológicas, 1986.

——. "El nacionalismo vasco ante la guerra civil," in *La guerra civil en el País Vasco*. Bilbao: Universidad del País Vasco, 1987, pp. 53–89.

Laitin, David. "Hegemony and Religious Conflict: British Imperial Control and Political Cleavages in Yorubaland," in Peter Evans, Dietrich Rueschemeyer, and Theda Skocpol, eds., *Bringing the State Back In*. New York: Cambridge University Press, 1985, pp. 285–317.

——. "The National Uprisings in the Soviet Union," *World Politics* (1991): 139–177.

——. "Language and the Construction of States: The Case of Catalonia in Spain," *Politics and Society* 22 (1994): 5–29.

Lane, Robert E. "Fathers and Sons: the Foundations of Political Belief," *American Sociological Review* 24 (1959).

Lawler, Edward J. "Affective Attachments to Nested Groups: A Choice-Process Theory," *American Sociological Review* 57: 3 (1992): 327–340.

Levi, Margaret, and Michael Hechter. "A Rational Choice Approach to the Rise and Decline of Ethnoregional Political Parties," in Edward Tiryakian and Ronald

Rogowski, eds., *New Nationalisms in the Developed West*. Winchester, Mass.: Allen & Unwin, 1985, pp. 128–147.

Linz, Juan J. "Early State-Building and Late Peripheral Nationalism Against the State: The Case of Spain," in S. N. Eisenstadt and Stein Rokkan, eds., *Building States and Nations*. Beverly Hills, Calif.: Sage, 1973, Vol. II, pp. 32–116.

——. "Some Comparative Thoughts on the Transition to Democracy in Portugal and Spain," in Jorge Braga de Macedo and Simón Serfaty, eds., *Portugal Since the Revolution: Economic and Political Perspectives*. Boulder, Colo.: Westview, 1981, pp. 25–47.

——. "From Primordialism to Nationalism," in Edward Tiryakian and Ronald Rogowski, eds., *New Nationalisms in the Developed West*. Winchester, Mass.: Allen & Urwin, 1985, pp. 203–254.

——. *Conflicto en Euskadi*. Madrid: Espasa-Calpe, 1986.

Lipset, Seymour Martin. *Student Politics*. New York: Basic Books, 1967.

Lipset, Seymour Martin, and Stein Rokkan. *Party Systems and Voter Alignments*. New York: Free Press, 1967.

Lipsky, Michael. "Protest as a Political Resource," *American Political Science Review* 62 (December 1968): 1144–1158.

Lladonosa i Vall-Llebrera, Manuel. *Catalanisme i moviment obrer: El CADCI entre 1903 i 1923*. Montserrat: Publicacions de l'Abadía de Montserrat, 1988.

Llera Ramos, Francisco J. *Postfranquismo y fuerzas políticas en Euskadi*. Bilbao: Servicio editorial de la Universidad del País Vasco, 1984.

——. "El sistema de partidos vascos: Distancia ideológica y legitimación política," *Revista del Centro de Investigaciones Sociológicas* 28 (October–December 1984), pp. 171–206.

López-Aranguren, Eduardo. *La conciencia regional en el proceso autonómico español*. Madrid: CIS, 1983.

López Raimundo, Gregori. "Momentos destacados de la trayectoria del PSUC," in [Planeta], *Nuestra utopía: PSUC, cincuenta años de historia de Cataluña*. Barcelona: Planeta, 1986, pp. 218–231.

Lorenzo Espinosa, José María. *Dictadura y dividendo*. Bilbao: Universidad de Deusto, 1989.

Lynch, John. *Spain under the Habsburgs*. New York: Oxford University Press, 1964.

Maluquer de Motes, Jordi. "La historia económica de Cataluña," *Papeles de Economía Española* 20 (1984): 268–281.

——. "Cataluña y el País Vasco en la industria eléctrica española 1901–1935," in Manuel González Portilla, Jordi Maluquer de Motes, and Borja de Riquer Permanyer, eds., *Industrialización y nacionalismo*. Bellaterra: Universitat Autònoma de Barcelona, 1985, pp. 239–252.

Mann, Michael. *The Sources of Social Power*. Cambridge: Cambridge University Press, 1993, Vol. II.

Maravall, José María. *Dictadura y disentimiento político*. Madrid: Alfaguara, 1978.

——. *La política de la transición (1975–1980)*. Madrid: Taurus, 1981.

Marcet, Joan. *Convergencia Democrática de Cataluña*. Madrid: CIS, 1987.

Marsal, Juan F., Francesc Mercadé, Francesc Hernández, and Benjamín Oltra. *La nació com a problema: Tesis sobre el cas Català*. Barcelona: Edicions 62, 1979.

Martí i Julià, Domènec. *Per Catalunya i altres textos*. Barcelona: Edicions de la Magrana, 1984.

Martín de Retana, José María, ed. *La gran enciclopedia vasca*. Bilbao: La Gran Enciclopedia Vasca, 1966.

Martínez Cuadrado, Miguel. *Elecciones y partidos de España (1868–1931)*. Madrid: Taurus, 1969.

———. *La burguesía conservadora (1874–1931)*. Madrid: Alfaguara, 1973.

Martínez Shaw, Carlos. *Cataluña en la carrera de Indias*. Barcelona: Crítica, 1981.

Marx, Karl. *The Eighteenth Brumaire of Louis Bonaparte*. New York: International Publishing, 1926 [1852].

McAdam, Doug. *Political Process and the Development of Black Insurgency, 1930–1970*. Chicago: University of Chicago Press, 1982.

———. "Recruitment to High-Risk Activism: The Case of Freedom Summer," *American Journal of Sociology* 92: 1 (1986): 64–90.

———. "Tactical Innovation and the Pace of Insurgency," *American Sociological Review* 48 (December 1986): 735–753.

McCarthy, John D., and Mayer N. Zald. "Resource Mobilization and Social Movements: A Partial Theory," *American Journal of Sociology* 82 (May 1977): 1212–1241.

Meadwell, Hudson. "Forms of Cultural Mobilization in Québec and Brittany, 1870–1914," *Comparative Politics* (1983): 401–415.

———. "Cultural and Instrumental Approaches to Ethnic Nationalism," *Ethnic and Racial Studies* 12 (1989): 309–328.

———. "Ethnic Nationalism and Collective Choice Theory," *Comparative Political Studies* 22: 2 (1989): 139–154.

Mercadé, Francesc, Francesc Hernández, and Benjamín Oltra. *Once tesis sobre la cuestión nacional en España*. Barcelona: Anthropos ed. del Hombre, 1983.

Miguélez Lobo, Faustino, and Carlota Solé. *Classes socials i poder polític en Catalunya*. Barcelona: PPU, 1987.

Molas, Isidre. *Lliga Catalana*. Barcelona: Edicions 62, 2 vols., 1971.

Monreal, Gregorio. "Annotations Regarding Basque Traditional Political Thought in the Sixteenth Century," in William A. Douglass, ed., *Basque Politics: A Case Study in Ethnic Nationalism*. Reno: University of Nevada Press, 1985, pp. 19–50.

Montero, Manu. *Mineros, banqueros y navieros*. Leioa [Vizcaya]: Departamento de Historia Contemporánea de la Universidad del País Vasco, 1990.

Moore, Barrington. *The Social Origins of Dictatorship and Democracy*. Boston: Beacon Press, 1966.

Moya, Carlos. *El poder económico en España*. Madrid: Túcar, 1975.

Mundet i Gifré, Josep M. *La primera guerra carlina a Catalunya*. Barcelona: Publicacions de l'Abadía de Montserrat, 1990.

Nadal, Jordi. *El fracaso de la revolución industrial en España, 1814–1913*. Barcelona: Ariel, 1975.

———. "El fracaso de la revolución industrial en España: Un balance historiográfico," *Papeles de Economía Española* 20 (1984): 108–125.

Nagel, Joan. "The Ethnic Revolution: The Emergence of Ethnic Nationalism in Modern States," *Sociology and Social Research* 68 (1984): 417–434.

Nagel, Joan, and Susan Olzak. "Ethnic Mobilization in New and Old States: An Extension of the Competition Model," *Social Problems* 30 (1982): 127–139.

Nairn, Tom. *The Break-up of Britain*. London: New Left Books, 1977.

Nielsen, François. "The Flemish Movement in Belgium after World War II: A Dynamic Analysis," *American Sociological Review* 45 (1980): 76–94.

——. "Ethnic Solidarity in Modern Societies," *American Sociological Review* 50 (1985): 133–149.

——. "Structural Conduciveness and Ethnic Mobilization," in Susan Olzak and Joan Nagel, eds., *Competitive Ethnic Relations*. New York: Academic Press (1986), pp. 173–198.

O'Callaghan, Joseph F. *A History of Medieval Spain*. Ithaca: Cornell University Press, 1975.

Oltra, Benjamín, Francesc Hernández, and Francesc Mercadé. *La ideología nacional catalana*. Barcelona: Anagrama, 1981.

Olzak, Susan. "Ethnic Ties and Political Mobilization: Comment on Leifer," *American Journal of Sociology* 89 (1983): 189–191.

——. "Ethnicity and Theories of Ethnic Collective Behavior," *Research in Social Movements, Conflicts, and Change* 8 (1985): 65–85.

——. *The Dynamics of Ethnic Competition and Conflict*. Stanford, Calif.: Stanford University Press, 1992.

[Ortzi]. *Historia de Euskadi: El nacionalismo vasco y ETA*. Paris: Ruedo Ibérico, 1975.

Paige, Jeffery. *Agrarian Revolutions*. New York: The Free Press, 1978.

Parellada, Martí. *El comerç exterior de Catalunya*. Barcelona: Edicions 62, 1982.

Pascual, Pere. "Carlisme i societat rural: La guerra dels set anys en la conca d'Odena," *Recerques* 10 (1980): 51–91.

——. *Agricultura i industrialització a la Catalunya del segle XIX*. Barcelona: Crítica, 1990.

Payne, Stanley G. *El nacionalismo vasco*. Barcelona: Dopesa, 1974.

Peled, Yoav, and Gershon Shafir. "Split Labor Market and the State: The Effect of Modernization on Jewish Industrial Workers in Tsarist Russia," *American Journal of Sociology* 92: 6 (1987): 1435–1460.

Pérez-Agote, Alfonso. *La reproducción del nacionalismo: El caso vasco*. Madrid: CIS, 1984.

——. *El nacionalismo vasco a la salida del franquismo*. Madrid: CIS, 1987.

Pérez Díaz, Víctor. *The Return of Civil Society*. Cambridge: Cambridge University Press, 1993.

Pinard, Maurice. *The Rise of a Third Party: A Study in Crisis Politics*. Montreal: McGill-Queen's University Press, 1975.

Pinard, Maurice, and Richard Hamilton. "Motivational Dimensions in the Québec Independence Movement: A Test of a New Model," *Research in Social Movements, Conflict, and Change* 9 (1986): 225–280.

Pinilla de las Heras, Esteban. *Estudios sobre cambio social y estructuras sociales en Cataluña*. Madrid: CIS, 1979.

Poggi, Gianfranco. *The Development of the Modern State: A Sociological Introduction*. Stanford, Calif.: Stanford University Press, 1978.

Prat de la Riba, Enric. *La nacionalitat catalana*. Barcelona: Edicions 62, 1978 [1906].

Pujol, Jordi. *Una política per Catalunya*. Barcelona: Portic, 1976.

——. *La immigració, problema i esperança de Catalunya*. Barcelona: Portic, 1976 [1958].

——. *Entre l'acció i l'esperança/1: Des dels turons a l'altra banda del ríu*. Barcelona: Portic, 1978 [1960].

——. *Entre l'acció i l'esperança/2: Construir Catalunya*. Barcelona: Portic, 1979 [1958].

Reinares, Fernando. "The Basque Autonomous Elections of 1986," *Electoral Studies* 6: 2 (1987): 169–173.

Ribas i Massana, Albert. *L'economía catalana sota el franquisme (1939–1953)*. Barcelona: Edicions 62, 1978.

Roca i Farreras, J. Narcís. *El Catalanisme progressiu*. Barcelona: Edicions de la Magrana, 1983 [1886].

Roca i Junyent, Miquel. "Una visión política desde Cataluña (catalanizar España)," Lecture given at Club Siglo XXI in November 1977 [publisher not named].

Rogowski, Ronald. "Causes and Varieties of Nationalism: A Rational Account," in Edward Tiryakian and Ronald Rogowski, eds., *New Nationalisms in the Developed West*. Winchester, Mass.: Allen & Unwin, 1985, pp. 87–109.

Ros Hombravella, Jacint. *Catalunya: Una economía decadent?* Barcelona: Barcanova, 1991.

Rovira i Virgili, Antonio. *Catalunya i Espanya*. Barcelona: Edicions de la Magrana, 1988 [1915].

Sabater, Jordi. *Anarquisme i Catalanisme*. Barcelona: Edicions 62, 1986.

Sáenz de Santamaría, Carmelo. *Historia de la Universidad de Deusto*. Bilbao: La Gran Enciclopedia Vasca, 1978.

Salaberri, Kepa. *El proceso de Euskadi en Burgos*. Paris: Ruedo Ibérico, 1971.

Salles, Anna. *Quan Catalunya era d'esquerra*. Barcelona: Edicions 62, 1988.

San Sebastián, Koldo. *Historia del partido nacionalista vasco*. San Sebastián: Txertoa, 1984.

Sarasola, Ibon. *Historia social de la literatura vasca*. Madrid: Akal, 1976.

Scott, John. "Intercorporate Structures in Western Europe: A Comparative Historical Analysis," in Mark S. Mizruchi and Michael Schwartz, eds., *Intercorporate Relations*. New York: Cambridge University Press, 1987, pp. 208–233.

Segal, Daniel A. "Nationalism, Comparatively Speaking," *Journal of Historical Sociology* 1 (1986): 301–321.

Sewell, William H., Jr. "Three Temporalities: Toward an Eventful History," in Terrence J. McDonald, ed., *The Historical Turn in the Human Sciences*. Ann Arbor: University of Michigan Press, in press.

Shabad, Goldie. "Las elecciones de 1982 y las autonomías," in Juan J. Linz and José R. Montero, eds., *Crisis y cambio: Electores y partidos en la España de los años ochenta*. Madrid: Centro de Estudios Constitucionales, 1986, pp. 525–587.

Simón, F. *La desamortización española en el siglo XIX*. Madrid: Instituto de Estudios Fiscales, 1973.

Sirvent, Gabriel. "Algunes notes sobre la implantació sindical de socialistes i anarquistes a Catalunya, abans dels anys de la primera guerra mundial," in Manuel González Portilla, Jordi Maluquer de Motes, and Borja de Riquer Permanyer, eds., *Industrialización y nacionalismo*. Bellaterra: Universitat Autònoma de Barcelona, 1985, pp. 555–568.

Smelser, Neil J. "Mechanisms of Change and Adjustment to Change," in William Faunce and William Form, eds., *Comparative Perspectives on Industrial Society*. Boston: Little, Brown, 1969, pp. 33–54.

Smith, Anthony D. *The Ethnic Revival*. New York: Cambridge University Press, 1981.

Solé Tura, Jordi. *Catalanisme i revolució burgesa*. Barcelona: Edicions 62, 1967.

Solozabal, Juan J. *El primer nacionalismo vasco*. Madrid: Túcar, 1975.

Suárez Fernández, Luis. *Historia de España*. Madrid: Gredos, 1970.

——. "La expansión marítima de los vascos a fines de la Edad Media," in *Páginas de historia del País Vasco*. Pamplona: Ediciones de la Universidad de Navarra, 1980, pp. 49–58.

——. "Las raíces históricas de la pluralidad," in *La España de las autonomías*. Madrid: Espasa Calpe, 1981, Vol. I, pp. 23–73.

Sudrià, Carlos. "Formas de industrialización y desarrollo bancario en Cataluña y Euskadi (1840–1936)," in Manuel González Portilla, Jordi Maluquer de Motes, and Borja de Riquer Permanyer, eds., *Industrialización y nacionalismo*. Bellaterra: Universitat Autònoma de Barcelona, 1985, pp. 253–266.

Sullivan, John. *ETA and Basque Nationalism: The Fight for Euskadi, 1890–1986*. London: Routledge, 1988.

Tamames, Ramón. *Los monopolios en España*. Madrid: ZYX, 1967.

——. *La república: La era de Franco*. Madrid: Alianza Universidad, 1976.

——. *La oligarquía financiera en España*. Barcelona: Planeta, 1977.

Tavera García, Susana. "Notes sobre l'anarco-sindicalisme basc i català, 1917–1920," in Manuel González Portilla, Jordi Maluquer de Motes, and Borja de Riquer Permanyer, eds., *Industrialización y nacionalismo*. Bellaterra: Universitat Autònoma de Barcelona, 1985, pp. 569–578.

Tedde, Pedro. "Banca privada y crecimiento económico en España, 1874–1913," *Papeles de Economía Española* 20 (1984): 169–184.

Terra Lliure. *Catalunya Terra Lliure*. Sant Boi de Llobregat [Barcelona]: Lluita, 1988.

Terrón Montero, Javier. *La prensa en España durante el régimen de Franco*. Madrid: CIS, 1981.

Thomson, J. K. J. *A Distinctive Industrialization: Cotton in Barcelona, 1728–1832*. Cambridge: Cambridge University Press, 1992.

Tilly, Charles. *The Vendée*. Cambridge: Harvard University Press, 1964.

——. *From Mobilization to Revolution*. Boston: Addison-Wesley, 1978.

——. *Coercion, Capital, and European States*. Oxford: Blackwell, 1990.

——. "Ethnic Conflict in the Soviet Union," *Theory and Society* 20 (1991): 569–581.

——. "States and Nationalism in Europe 1492–1992," *Theory and Society* 23 (1994): 131–146.

Torres Elías, Jaume. *Liberalismo y rebeldía campesina*. Barcelona: Ariel, 1973.

Tortella Casares, Gabriel. *Los orígenes del capitalismo en España*. Madrid: Tecnos, 1973.

Trías Fargas, Ramón. *Catalunya i el modern concepte de regió económica*. Barcelona: Dalmau, 1966.

——. *Introducció a l'economía de Catalunya: Un anàlisi regional*. Barcelona: Edicions 62, 1972.

——. *Nacionalisme i llibertat*. Barcelona: Destino, 1979.

Tuñón de Lara, Manuel. *Historia y realidad del poder*. Madrid: Edicusa, 1967.

——. *Estudios sobre el siglo XIX español*. Madrid: Siglo XXI, 1972.

Tusell, Javier. *Las elecciones del Frente Popular*. Madrid: Cuadernos para el Diálogo, 1971.

Unzueta, Patxo. *Los nietos de la ira*. Madrid: El País, 1988.

Uriarte Ayo, R. "Capacidad productiva y producción habitual en la siderurgia tradicional vizcaína. Factores determinantes y aproximación cuantitativa," in Manuel González Portilla, Jordi Maluquer de Motes, and Borja de Riquer Permanyer, eds., *Industrialización y nacionalismo*. Bellaterra: Universitat Autònoma de Barcelona, 1985, pp. 73–88.

——. "La minería vizcaína del hierro en las primeras etapas de la industrialización," in Emiliano Fernández de Pinedo and José Luis Hernández Marco, eds., *La industrialización en el norte de España*. Barcelona: Crítica, 1988, pp. 154–178.

Valdaliso, José M. "Grupos empresariales e inversión de capital en Vizcaya, 1886–1913," *Revista de Historia Económica* 6: 1 (1988): 11–40.

Valdeavellano, Luis G. *Curso de historia de las instituciones españolas*. Madrid: Revista de Occidente, 1952.

Vázquez de Prada, Valentín. "La época moderna: Los siglos XVI a XIX," in R. Acosta, ed., *La España de las autonomías*. Madrid: Espasa Calpe, 1981, Vol. I, pp. 77–110.

Vera, Jordi. *La lluita armada als Països Catalans: Historia del FAC*. Sant Boi de Llobregat: Lluita, 1985.

Verdery, Kathryn. *Transylvanian Villagers*. Berkeley: University of California Press, 1983.

Vicens Vives, Jaume. *Manual de historia económica de España*. Barcelona: Vicens Vives, 1959.

——. *Industrials i polítics (Segle XIX)*. Barcelona: Vicens Vives, 1961.

——. *Historia de España y América*. Barcelona: Vicens Vives, 1982, Vol. 5.

——. *Los Catalanes en el siglo XIX*. Barcelona: Alianza Editorial, 1986.

Vilar, Pierre. *La Catalogne dans l'Espagne moderne: Recherche sur les fondements des structures nationales*. Paris: SEVPEN, 1962.

Ybarra y Bergé, Javier de. *Política nacional en Vizcaya*. Madrid: Instituto de Estudios Políticos, 1947.

Zeitlin, Maurice. *Landlords and Capitalists*. Princeton: Princeton University Press, 1989.

Zirakzadeh, Cyrus E. *A Rebellious People*. Reno: University of Nevada Press, 1991.

Index